Lesbians in Academia

Contents

**Lesbian Studies, Queer Studies:
Theorizing the Lesbian Experience**

Acknowledgments

As we are lesbians in academia, this book has both personal and professional meaning for us. We dedicate this book to the lesbian faculty at the University of Vermont who were part of our regular social dinners in 1982–1983 and who made us aware of issues facing lesbians in academia. We would like to thank our departments for their continuing enthusiasm for our work, and our students for continuing to question our assumptions. We would also like to thank Penelope Dugan for the book's subtitle, "Degrees of Freedom," which she so graciously allowed us to borrow. This book was completed while Esther was a Visiting Scholar at the Institute for research on Women and Gender at Stanford University and then a Visiting Fellow at Clare Hall, Cambridge University.

We owe a special debt to the authors in this book who were willing to share their life experiences as lesbians in academia, as well as to those authors who willingly read a large number of narratives in order to provide the theoretical analysis of the book's themes. Finally, we thank Philip Rappaport, formerly at Routledge, for his enthusiasm and support, and William Germano at Routledge for continuing to support this book project.

Introduction

Beth Mintz and Esther Rothblum

This book has been many years in the making. We, the editors, have known each other since 1982 when Esther joined the faculty of the University of Vermont as a young assistant professor. Beth had recently gotten tenure and it was a time when women faculty were few, lesbians fewer, and out lesbians visibly absent.

We were close friends and racquetball partners, and our locker room conversation consistently turned to attempts to make sense of our situation. Unlike women who entered academia after traditional roles as wives and mothers, we, as many academic lesbians of our generation, had never been married; and we did not have children. In those days universities rarely made allowances for maternity leave or stopped the tenure clock for women with family responsibilities, and in this way we were "one of the boys." Our lives in our town (as opposed to the gown) lesbian community allowed for fluidity and integration of our social and professional lives; our nontraditional family status allowed us the flexibility to pursue our careers.

But we were not totally out. While everyone "knew," it remained unspoken and the topic had not yet informed our teaching or research activities. The few older lesbians on our faculty were quite closeted and when we heard their stories we understood why. As part of the generation described so well by Kennedy and Davis (1993), being out had serious costs for them and the lesson they had learned was passed on to us. Yet it was an exciting time for women in general in the academy and for lesbians, too. Women, white women at least, were entering academia in much larger numbers; research on lesbians and gay men was increasing in visibility; and women were beginning to write about their experiences in the ivory tower.

In understanding women's presence in academia, though, a tension remained between our impressions of women's progress and of concrete evidence to support these claims. Women's studies programs were developing; curriculum transformation in terms of gender, at least, was taking place; and women students had broken the gender barrier—so much so that today many U.S. colleges have a majority of female students. At the same time, however, female faculty continued to remain in the minority. Even today, it is a rare department that has more women than men on its faculty, even in many traditionally female professions such as social work, education, and library science. And the more elite the institution, the smaller the percentage of women. At Yale, for example, only 17 percent of all associate and full professors are female; here at the University of Vermont, 12 percent of our full professors are women (Academe, 1996). At Harvard, female full professors as a group earn about $15,000 less than their male counterparts, while at our institution the gap is "only" about $5,500 (Academe, 1996).

Indeed the numbers remain troubling to this day, but our understanding of the experiences of women have become more complete. Beginning with an analysis of women as a general category in the academic world (American Association of University Women, 1989; Bronstein et al, 1986; Chamberlain, 1988; Rothblum, 1988; Sandler and Hall, 1986), subsequent work has emphasized difference among women focusing upon the experiences of working-class women (Dews et al. 1995; Tokarczyk and Fay, 1993) and women of color in the academy (Bronstein et al., 1993; hooks, 1989, 1993; Williams, 1994; Winthorn, 1989).

But what of the specifically lesbian experience as part of women's presence? We watched the rise of women's studies as a legitimate area of scholarly inquiry; we experienced the expansion of publishing outlets for research on lesbians; and we came further and further out ourselves. In these ways it was clear that change was indeed upon us but we were unsure of the pace, magnitude, and implications of the change. We felt the same tension between the impression of rapid institutional change and concrete evidence needed to support that impression that we found when trying to evaluate the general role of women in the academy. Moreover, this tension was highlighted by our interactions with younger lesbian faculty who were more assured, more open, and more out than some of us had ever dreamt of being. And in this tension between our own experience of the system and the openness of younger women around us lies the origin of this volume. Earlier in our careers, we tried to understand our relative ease in getting tenure by considering the freedom that lesbianism afforded, yet recognizing the risk of our difference. When we look at many younger women today, we wonder if that risk has disappeared. We undertook this research because available literature does not address this question or other questions about the academic lesbian experience, about its variability, about its complexity, and about the way that it is changing. We are interested in these issues because they are important to our understanding of academia, about the role of women in academia, and about the lesbian experience in that context. We are also interested because they help us make sense of our world and help us to understand our place in that world.

In planning this anthology, then, we wanted to provide a variety of accounts of academic life, lesbian style. We were interested in what it means to be a lesbian in a college or university setting. How being closeted or out affected the personal and professional lives of academic lesbians. These were the specific questions that we asked when we searched for narratives for this volume. What we really wanted was something less specific: A collection of articles that would describe lesbian experiences and, when taken together, would capture the variety and complexity that we believe comprises life for lesbians as academics.

We also had other goals. We wondered about the impact of identity politics on prospects for change in the university. We wondered about the barriers between women that the rise of women's studies has in some ways exacerbated. And we wondered about the prospects of women working together for progressive change. With these thoughts in mind, we solicited a series of theoretical articles discussing the experiences of working-class women, women of color, and older women in academia. We specifically asked how the experiences of lesbians in academia compared with those of each of these groups and we very quickly learned that this would not further our understanding of how women could work together. Because, as Tokarczyk and Sowinska point out in their "Lesbians, Class, and Academia," such a question underscores the artificiality of our categories, suggesting that our identities do not overlap. Here we rephrase our question: How can women who experience the academy quite differently work together toward achieving common goals?

As a first step in soliciting manuscripts for this book, we distributed flyers at professional conferences and sent announcements to a large number of newsletters and email bulletin boards. The response was overwhelming; we were only able to accept 40 percent of the proposed narratives. In considering submitted abstracts, we emphasized variety accepting those that would complement each other best by presenting diverse factors including: degree of outness, length of time being out, geographical distribution, type of academic setting, and age. Not surprisingly, we received a number of abstracts by lesbians who were similar in these respects, and had to decide which to accept to increase the diversity of experiences. We decided to limit narratives primarily to those by full-time faculty in the United States, and thus did not include many narratives by graduate students or lesbians in the academic job market.

The resulting articles are diverse in both content and style, and vary remarkably in tracing the professional paths of academic lesbians. We would like to touch on a few themes.

First, we found that the particular academic setting did not predict the women's experiences. There was as much variation in levels of acceptance of lesbians in small Catholic colleges or Mormon institutions as in liberal colleges in what we think to be progressive states. This was particularly striking in the case of two authors from different disciplines writing about the same university. Similarly, the authors themselves were often unable to predict the reactions of colleagues, students, administrators, and friends, and were sometimes shocked at either level of acceptance or the level of heterosexism. Occasionally individual acceptance and perceptions of institutional environment collided, as in the case of a job interview that Christy Ponticelli describes, where she is outed by a sympathetic faculty member who later warned her not to talk about "it" too much. Of course, there was a qualitative difference between institutional settings that welcomed the women because they were lesbian and those institutions that were trying to purge lesbians from the system. In other words, some lesbians were being fired, and others hired, because of their sexual orientation.

What was often most consistent in predicting the women's experiences was the particular academic cohort they represented. We have thought about these cohorts as representing "distinct generations," each accompanied by vastly different experiences. The first generation are the first women faculty in a particular department. Often shunned by male colleagues and male and female graduate students, these first women (even today) receive little support and often significant antagonism in their departments. If they survive, many are justifiably bitter; few receive recognition for breaking the gender barrier in their disciplines.

The second generation may be just the second or third woman hired in a department and following the initial adjustment to the presence of women, may well be taken for granted. This second generation (we consider ourselves part of this group) in turn takes much of its acceptance for granted. We do not credit the women who came before us and made our entrance possible and even relatively painless. Our training was as orthodox as possible—we went to appropriate schools and programs and did so at a young age, without husbands and children. When first generation women see how much easier things are for us compared to their experiences, they can feel further denigrated.

The third generation of women is profoundly different. They come from undergraduate majors or graduate programs in which women were clearly visible (though they may still perceive male colleagues as having more opportunities). Often, they worked with female professors or mentors. Some of them were strongly mentored by mothers who were professionals; some of their mothers are committed feminists. They often came out as lesbians very early in their academic career, and were out while on the job market.

As one might expect, these three generations vary with disciplines. Fields that are still predominantly male may be struggling through the first generation of women, while areas in which women are more numerous may already be in the third generation. This explains why women in the same institution (even those with offices next to one another) can feel they are living in two different worlds, and why to these stories can often seem so contradictory.

But on the whole, the accounts that follow are quite positive. Only one author elected to write anonymously. Of course, those who are most closeted would not choose to submit a chapter for this book so our sample is far from representative: We did not hear from lesbians at military or fundamentalist Christian colleges, for example. Interestingly, two lesbian colleagues to whom we sent the accepted proposals, one from Britain and the other from Australia, expressed surprise at the number and diversity of authors who were out and having a relatively easy time of it. Was this typical of the U.S. lesbian academic experience, they asked. It is possible that being a lesbian in academia is easier for U.S. women who have assumed academic positions in higher proportions than women in many other nations. Consequently, a greater percentage of women in academia also means more lesbians and perhaps more support for lesbians.

Once we had received the narrative chapters, we asked Mary Stuck, a sociologist, and Penelope Dugan, a professor of writing, to analyze the lesbians' themes through their respective lenses. In our attempt to understand some of the ways in which women who experience academic life differently can work together effectively, we asked two faculty of color, Maria Gonzalez and Roxanne Lin to compare the narratives to those of women of color in the academy. Michelle Tokarcyk and Suzanne Sowinska, who have written previously about working-class women, examined the lesbians' narratives in relation to the writings of working-class academic women and

Phyllis Bronstein, who has written about older women, compared the lesbians' concerns to those of older women, in general. Our sample varies in age, class background, and ethnicity, and our interest was in exploring the details of each group's experience in the academy.

This book goes to press as queer theory is establishing itself as a major force in lesbian studies, and so we asked a scholar of queer theory, Lynda Goldstein, to examine the narratives from this point of view. Sheila Jeffries, who has critiqued queer theory as making lesbians invisible, provides a lesbian feminist perspective on the queer experience.

In the lesbian tradition, we want briefly to include our own "stories" of becoming lesbians in academia. We note that the larger variability in the lesbian experience that the book explores is illustrated in our stories, as well. Since Beth is from a slightly earlier cohort, we begin with her account.

I, Beth, arrived at the University of Vermont as an assistant professor in 1977, "straight" out of graduate school on Long Island. During my graduate training, for reasons that are understandable in retrospect—the suburban (read isolated) setting of the university, the absence of women's studies as a legitimate area of inquiry at a major research institution, the small number of women on the faculty—the women's movement seemed to have passed us by. When as a faculty member I was asked to teach a course on women and society (because I was one), I began reading the literature and struggling through the ideas and implications of the field. Consistent with the times, it was the students who were the most radical, the ones who pushed me to go beyond the material, to understand the relationship between theory and life, to see the personal as political (to use the terms of the day).

And, indeed, I did as they asked: I became a strong feminist, something that was more popular among students then. I went through the usual stages of consciousness raising: I began to see the world differently, I began to get angry. Eventually that anger resolved but not before I found myself screaming at our associate dean in public when he suggested that he had a nice single man for me to meet. By the end of the first semester teaching "my" women's course, I came away thinking that if the students learned a fraction of what I had, it was a great success. And one of the things that I learned was that there was something called a lesbian. Sure, I always knew about such things but now I actually knew some. These were the students who pushed me the hardest, who were most committed to my feminist education and development (and I would like to take this opportunity to thank them for their efforts). And as I became more interested (read intrigued), I began meeting some women in the community.

Those were heady times. Many lesbians were feminists and radical feminism was at its peak; women were exploring their lives and their possibilities. Nonmonogamy was under investigation, but the political was broader than the lesbian experience: An important part of activism centered around providing shelter to battered women and building a viable antirape movement. This was the climate in which I came out, at least the climate of the community where I lived. Campus was quite another matter. There were a few lesbians around and our energy was focused on starting a women's studies program. We were quite visible and articulate on women's issues in general but in terms of lesbian identity, the university culture was one of silence and that was the model I followed. I found it particularly awkward not to do so because everyone at work knew me as straight and to change this perception would take what I thought to be a dramatic act. An announcement or something: "Excuse me but. . . ."

By the time Esther Rothblum joined us, we were a handful of lesbian faculty trying to find our way. Gradually we came out, but not without apprehension and hesitation, our fear rooted in the experience of women who came before us. In retrospect, the negative consequences of coming out are not apparent. The advantages are the same as those repeated time after time in the narratives to follow: Chatting about weekend plans using we instead of I; an openness that was previously missing; political activity on gay/lesbian/bisexual issues that had been precluded. Note, however, that on our campus, even though we are more out than ever before with few consequences, lesbians are not a strong force. We do not have a strong presence in our women's studies program, we do not have a lesbian or gay/lesbian/bisexual faculty group. The reason for this, I believe is because we are so few. When we first came to the university, new female hires were disproportionately lesbian because, we believe, the flexibility that lesbianism afforded allowed us to pursue our careers in ways not available to women with family responsibilities. The irony, I suppose, is that when barriers to women in academia became more penetrable, the proportion of lesbians decreased and, thus, even though lesbian faculty on our campus are more out than ever before, we remain relatively invisible.

Moreover, here at least, the generational shift from lesbian to gay and the corresponding queer, as opposed to feminist politic, has not yet occurred. This means that the impression of gay ascendance on college campuses is not an actuality here. We have not found common cause with gay male faculty that would increase a gay/lesbian/bisexual visibility. This is perhaps the good news and the bad news. In the absence of a strong gay presence, and after many years of separate agendas, women faculty here are beginning to work together for progressive change, a change encompassing issues of race, class, gender, and sexual orientation. Does this beginning have a future? That depends on many, many, things including the political orientation of incoming women. The scenario does tell us something about the state of lesbians in academia, though: It suggests that on some U.S. campuses it is much easier to be an out lesbian than it used to be though the institutional consequences of that change do not automatically follow.

I, Esther, began my life of being a lesbian and an academic in nursery school. I first fell in love with another girl on the playground when I was four years old. I had my first sexual fantasies of girls when I was in first grade and had a crush on two fourth-grade girls who sat next to me on the school bus. Growing up as a lesbian child in the late 1950s and early 1960s was "easy." My parents liked my "best friends" and allowed me to be affectionate with and spend the night with girls in a way they never would have permitted had I had the same feelings for little boys.

Girlfriends continued to play an important role in my academic life. Carol Gilligan has described the marked changes in girls' development as they become interested in boys and lose their sense of self (Gilligan and Farnsworth, 1995). That certainly does not describe the experience of lesbian girls. As I watched my friends take ballroom dancing lessons and join activities where they could flirt with boys, I continued with varsity basketball and a Latin correspondence course. To some extent, I chose different friends. My high school was one of those in which you could be either "popular" or smart, but not both, so my friends were the academic nerds. I couldn't have joined the popular clique because they were dating, and I had no interest whatsoever in boys.

Each morning in high school during homeroom, I played chess with Maria Poorman. Maria's parents were fundamentalist Christian missionaries; I was Jewish. About once a month, Maria would express concern that I was going to burn in hell because I wasn't Christian. I didn't take her statement to be malicious or condescending, but rather one of friendly concern. Growing up Jewish in Austria, I had heard worse. I certainly didn't tell Maria, nor anyone else, that I feared I might be a lesbian. Years later, when I was first coming out and the occasional heterosexual friend asked me what it was like to be a lesbian, I answered that it was similar to being Jewish in Austria.

Although I came from a very privileged family, I would be the first to attend college. My father consulted his best friend, a college professor, for some reputable "girls' schools" and that's how I ended up at Smith College in Northampton, Massachusetts. This was before Smith became nationally known as the college for lesbians, but I became a feminist as soon as I arrived on campus. It was wonderful to see college women rather than men in all the leadership positions, and I thrived on the presence of this women's community. The handful of male exchange students were referred to as "coeds."

After graduate school in clinical psychology and my internship, I gave up two tenure-track offers to do a postdoctoral fellowship at Yale. I was twenty-five years old and had no teaching experience, so I wanted two years to look older before I stepped into a classroom. Until then, I had pursued my academics—from first grade to the end of graduate school—with single-minded ambition. Now I had two years to sit back and come out. Like many women who self-identify as lesbian from an early age, adolescence had been the period of greatest secrecy. At a time when girls are scrutinized for their heterosexual behavior by peers, parents, and teachers, I knew that my lesbianism would soon be discovered if I wasn't careful. So early adulthood was a time when I could go back to being out about my sexuality to the degree I had in prepuberty.

In 1982 I accepted a tenure-track position at the University of Vermont. I hadn't been in Vermont for a week before other lesbian professors at my university phoned to say they had heard my department had hired a lesbian. They couldn't wait to introduce me to the lesbian community. Our weekly meetings were invaluable to me as a new assistant professor. These women were senior professors, department chairs and administrators. They shared salary information, political issues, gossip. One of the members of that group was Beth Mintz, who had just been awarded tenure. None of us at the time was conducting research about lesbians (although a number of us were doing research about women, which for the time was perhaps even more radical). None of us was out in the classroom, and to some extent we discouraged one another from taking that risk.

Years later, when I chaired the women's studies program, I was curious to meet other female faculty and phoned them to have lunch. I was amazed how often these women told me that this was the first time a colleague from another department had ever phoned them, and some of them were the only women in their departments; they were eager for female companionship. I realized that heterosexual women don't have the same networks.

At the time of this writing, I am out in all the classes I teach, in my research and writing, and to my family, friends, neighbors, and acquaintances. Vermont has a gay civil rights law, and both Burlington and the University of Vermont provide health insurance for the same-sex partners of their employees. Having just divided my sabbatical year between the San Francisco Bay Area and Cambridge, England, I certainly found differences in the political power and proportion of lesbians, but even at Cambridge there are lesbian academics moving up the ranks.

An article citing my work appeared in the *New York Times* and was reprinted in other media across the country. For a while, I was deluged with calls from TV stations and the print media. I also received calls from individuals, including a Mrs. Tom Shannon in Texas. She wanted to know if I had gone to high school in Austria. When I said I had, she asked if I remembered her; her name before her marriage was Maria Poorman and we used to play chess. She had joined a new church, Maria said, a more fundamentalist one. Now she had a husband and three sons, and she was educating the boys at home, using a Christian home study program. She was praying for their welfare. Maria said she had often thought about me and asked what had become of me. I told her that I was a lesbian and an academic. And I realized that, over the years, I as a lesbian had become "mainstream" and her type of fundamentalism had become "fringe." (We still chat on the phone once in a while).

It has been almost two years since we received the first of the narratives in this collection and, as we go to press, we have asked the authors for any changes they would like to make. Many updated their biographies and we were struck by the same mixture of progress and loss that characterized the individual chapters. Since the original writing, many of the women have either been promoted or received tenure; many have been the recipient of academic honors or awards of various sorts; and some have lost jobs or positions in what we call curious circumstances. Our conclusions in overview: Lesbians in the academia continue to occupy an intermediate position between the straight and nonstraight world. With some significant exceptions, the experiences of lesbians are more positive than ever before in history and the comfort levels higher. And yet, these many years later, our locker room conversation still turns to questions of difference as we experience the world around us.

We will now let the women speak for themselves.

References

Academe. (March/April 1996). "The annual report on the economic status of the profession," 82:40–97. Washington, D.C.: American Association of University Professors.

American Association of University Women. (1989). *Women and Tenure: The Opportunity of a Century*. Washington, D.C.

Bronstein, P., L. Black, J. Pfennig, and A. White, (March, 1986). "Getting academic jobs. Are women equally qualified—and equally successful?" American Psychologist 318–322.

Bronstein, P., E.D. Rothblum, and S.E. Solomon, (1993). "Ivy halls and glass walls: Barriers to academic careers for women and ethnic minorities." In J. Gainen and R. Boice, eds. *New Directions for Teaching and Learning: Building a Diverse Faculty* (271–280). Vol. 53. New York: Jossey-Bass.

Chamberlain, M.K. (1988). *Women in Academe: Progress and Prospects*. New York: Russell Sage Foundation.

Dews, C.L., B. Leste, and C. Leste, eds. (1995). *This Fine Place So Far from Home: Voices of Academics from the Working Class*. Philadelphia: Temple University Press.

Gilligan, C. and L. Farnsworth, (1995). "A new voice for psychology. In P. Chesler, E. Rothblum, and E. Cole, eds. *Feminist Foremothers in Women's Studies, Psychology, and Mental Health*. New York: Haworth Press.

hooks, b. (1989). *Talking Back: Thinking Feminist, Thinking Black*. Boston: South End Press.

hooks, b. (1993). "Keeping Close to Home," in Tokarczyk, M. and E.A. Fay, eds. *Working-Class Women in the Academy*. Amherst: University of Massachusetts Press.

Kennedy, E.L. and M.D. Davis, (1993). *Boots of Leather, Slippers of Gold*. New York: Routledge.

Rothblum, E.D. (1988). "Leaving the ivory tower: Factors contributing to women's voluntary resignation from academia. *Frontiers* 10: 14–17.

Sandler, B.R., and R.M. Hall, (October, 1986). "The Campus Climate Revisited: Chilly for Women Faculty, Administrators, and Graduate Students." Washington, D.C.: Project on the status and education of women, Association of American Colleges.

Tokarczyk, M. and E.A. Fay, eds. (1993). *Working-Class Women in the Academy*. Amherst: University of Massachusetts Press.

Williams, O.L.B. (1994). *American Black Women in the Arts and Social Sciences*. Metuchen, New Jersey: Scarecrow Press.

Winthorn, A. (1989). "Dual Citizenship: Women of Color in Graduate School," *Women's Studies Quarterly* 14: 46–48.

Personal
Narratives

Reflections on Being an out Black Lesbian on a Southern Campus

Dawn D. Bennett-Alexander

Employment Law and Legal Studies, University of Georgia

1

Mondays come questions of couples
Where and with whom did you go?
Avoiding the personal pronoun
She hopes it doesn't show.

—Fred Small,
Annie In the Heart of Appaloosa
Rounder Records, 1983

Virtually all lesbians and gays know exactly what gay singer and songwriter Fred Small is talking about. Engaging in the usual mundane Monday-morning workplace chatter about something as simple as what you did over the weekend can be a landmine of explosive secrets for closeted gays and lesbians. Will they find out the same-gender "friend" I went to the movies with on Friday is more than just a friend? Will they suspect that my house-mate is really my partner of ten years? If they do, will it matter? Will I lose my job?" And on and on . . . Henry David Thoreau tells us that "most men [?] lead lives of quiet desperation." I refuse to be in that number. I hate the complex set of feelings "avoiding the pronoun" reflects, more than I dislike the consequences of not avoiding the pronoun, therefore I don't avoid it. That is not an easy thing to do when your teaching career has been spent in two states in the deep south, you're black, and you're in a college or a university that is known for being conservative and even more traditionally male dominated than others. As an out dyke (a term which bothers some, but which I have chosen to rescue from the mouths of villains and conscript into more positive service as a term of profound affection) I teach law in the college of business at a large southern university.

When I first came to the university I was the only black faculty member anyone could remember in the college in recent memory. That, alone, set me apart. I was too *outré* for words: I wear my hair in a very short natural, rarely wear anything other than tennis shoes (sometimes I mention my foot surgery, other times I don't), read a poem at the beginning of every class and (gasp!) wear large "dangly" earrings (no tiny, conservative, sedate pearls for me). Those things may seem mild, or even *passé* to us now, but as short as six years ago when I came to the university, it was positively ground breaking, not to mention, "different."

The significance of it was that I immediately set the tone that I had my own agenda, style, and drummer, so one was not to expect business as usual from me. The South is still traditional in many ways, and one of its traditions is gentility. No one would ever have said anything to me about any of my "behaviors," so I used this to my advantage and merrily rolled along doing my own thing, seemingly oblivious to the raised eyebrows. Not only did I challenge their traditional notions of what a woman is (some of the colleges still have no female faculty members), but also what a black person is. I took my own space in the world, expected to be treated just as anyone else, and acted as if this were all par for the course. In some ways I think that my being such an "oddity" in my college gave me a lot of leeway. I was willing to be so isolated (how can the only black on the entire faculty of over 150 not be?), yet still march to the beat of my own drum rather than conform and assimilate. People gave me a wide berth. The reality is that I knew that for every person who thought I was a breath of much-needed fresh air, there were those who thought I was a bit "out there"—to put it mildly. But, I minded my own business, did my work well, and was pleasant and collegial (with this as my modus operandi, imagine my surprise when I was told by a colleague that the word among the faculty was "Don't fuck with Dawn.")

My research agenda included the full range of employment law issues, which eventually narrowed to race and gender. It was, therefore, completely in keeping with this that I was quickly drawn in as faculty advisor for the Minority Business Student Association, and later the campus chapter of the National Organization for Women (NOW). With this background and the addition of a consulting business on diversity issues (including those of affinity orientation) it was no surprise that I signed on as faculty advisor to the Lesbian, Gay, and Bisexual Student Union (LGBSU). By then I was known as a well-respected, I think, credible, crusader in the civil rights area, because of my professional and personal interests. Being out as a lesbian was only a continuation of my work in this area.

I never allowed myself to really be in the closet. Both times I have moved to a new school, it was clear that my female partner and I, along with my two biological daughters, were a family. (The last time, we were in the middle of adopting a newborn daughter into our family, and that was not kept a secret during the consideration process.) The college even did what they could to try to locate work for my partner (at least they said they did)—all without saying the word lesbian or that we were partners. I also realize that many times people don't connect motherhood and being a lesbian. My experience has been that people (including the kids' teachers) took our relationship in stride when it was presented that way—which is, after all, the way it actually should be.

While I made no secret of my family or feelings on issues, the way I presented it was as an evolutionary process, not a static one. Even though I am out, it has still been, and remains, a changing process. At some point, just allowing people to know I was a lesbian from what they may have gathered during their observations was not enough. I am lucky enough to know precisely when that moment was. After the 1993 march in Washington, D.C., for gay and lesbian rights, I realized it was important to do more than just let people surmise that I am a lesbian. I realized that passively allowing people to conclude that I may be a lesbian was not the same thing as actively making sure they did not think I was heterosexual. I realized that visibility is the only way gays and lesbians could begin the important work of trying to gain the full rights and privileges everyone else in society takes for granted. Studies show people who know gays and lesbians are more accepting of rights for them, but most people didn' t know they knew anyone who was gay. Only we could do something about that. I realized it is important to let people like our coworkers, neighbors, ministers, etc., know who we are and realize that we are OK. I understood that everyone was not in a position to do this, so it was even more important for those of us who could, to do so. I took/take that responsibility very seriously. It isn't a matter of "flaunting it," but, rather, of making sure incorrect assumptions are not made. Thus, for instance, the prominently placed; sign in my office which says, "I am out, therefore I am"—a memento from a National Coming Out Day on campus a few years ago.

When I decided to come out altogether, no holds barred, I did it by way of the piece below, published in the local and school newspapers (we have over 30,000 students). Since it was such a seminal event for me and encapsulates my feelings on the issue of being a lesbian, particularly as it pertains to the academic setting, I would find it difficult to not include it here. I have done so below, in edited form.

As an attendee who saw first hand the recent march on Washington for gay, lesbian and bi equal rights and liberation, I was extremely disappointed with most of the coverage in the press. To look at the pictures chosen to represent the flavor of the march, the march appeared alternately as some sort of "love-in," S&M or body-piercing convention, or an angry lop-sided face-off between marchers and march protesters. What a travesty to have minimized the efforts of so very many people and reduced this important and unprecedented gathering to such a ridiculous and unrepresentative scenario. I can only think that the depictions are either due to insensitivity and ignorance, or the wish to pander to sensationalism.

The fight for basic civil rights for gays and lesbians is much too serious to be trivialized. It is not about sex. It is not about sensationalism, hysteria, special privileges or forcing anything on others. It is not even about religion or morals, for those are something each of us must choose for ourselves rather than have imposed upon us by others. The reason I volunteered my time in helping with the march is because it was about being truthful about who we are and substituting that truth for the myth and sensational pandering which has taken place for so long. I volunteered during the march because it was about millions of the productive, decent, hard-working citizens you know who daily go about their lives quietly, hiding a part of themselves from their families, their friends, and their coworkers out of fear of not being accepted for who they are because of the myths and sensationalism surrounding them. It is about the angst, the loss of job productivity, friendship, and closeness that pretending to be someone other than who you are produces—a loss for us all.

While the fear of nonacceptance is not unfounded, the basis for having it imposed upon us is. Society's reactions to the myths and sensationalism causes most gays and lesbians to hide in cramped, locked closets of fear. This means that virtually the only depictions society sees are the 30-second clips from a San Francisco Gay Pride parade featuring the most extreme elements of the community dressed in drag and parodying the ridiculous media depictions of them. Under the circumstances, society can hardly do less than come away with a skewed sense of who we are. Those elements exist and we embrace them, but that is not all of who we are.

The truth is much less dramatic, much less sensational, and much more compelling. We are simply your family, your children, your neighbors, friends, doctors, lawyers, judges, professors, ministers, trash collectors, research scientists, secretaries, and those who occupy every other job held. You come into contact with us every day and don't realize it. We do not all go around in drag, lisping, making out in public, or recruiting the innocent, impressionable young into our "lifestyle." The unsensational fact of the matter is, there is no "lifestyle." The much less dramatic truth is that there's just a life. Plain and simple. Just like everyone else's. We are millions of people who worry about the same things everyone does: Interest rates on mortgages, how to keep our kids in check, the economy, war, stubborn crab-grass, and whether the car will start. We are people who go grocery shop-ping, get up and shower and brush our teeth in the morning, go to our jobs, and pay taxes just like everyone else.

Boring isn't it? Makes much less sensational copy for a newspaper or magazine, doesn't it? Who wants to do a story about 1.1 million people who look just like every other part of society marching on Washington for basic civil rights like job protection and the right to continue to serve honorably in the military? It is far more sensational, and sells more papers, to feed into the old stereotypes which tug at the deeply rooted ignorance and fear vic-timizing us all. But it is irresponsible if one is a journalist whose job is to accurately report events to those who were not present and wish to find out what occurred. It is also irresponsible to continue to contribute to negative perceptions of a group of people who, as a result, may be physically or emo-tionally harmed by others because of that ignorant perception. Gay bashing and antigay and lesbian sentiment is furthered by such biased reporting. It is also an injustice to the readers who trust the press to be responsible, accu-rate purveyors of the truth, so that they can have solid information upon which to base decisions. These are people's *lives* we are dealing with here. It cannot be reduced to sexual activity or the photo depictions any more than anyone's life can be reduced to that.

I am even more upset when I realize that our legislators, are by and large, as ignorant as the rest of society about gay and lesbian issues, are paused to make national policy based upon the same skewed misinformation the rest of society is subjected to. Having worked at both the White House and on Capitol Hill, I know this to be a very real concern. Media coverage plays a large role in what legislators and the public think they know and operate on the basis of. Therefore, I am not at all surprised that research shows that those who realize that they know gays and lesbians (all of us know them, but many of us do not realize that we do) are much more accepting of them. The fact is, when you know them, you get the real picture of who they are, rather than the sensationalized media version.

While in D.C., I participated in the march's lobby days in Congress. As

I sat in one congressman's office with about twenty other gays and lesbians of color and lobbied for the lifting of the military ban on gays and basic civil rights to protect us from, among other things, unwarranted job and housing discrimination, I was overcome with emotion. Thirty years ago I participated in the 1963 March on Washington at which the Rev. Dr. Martin Luther King Jr. delivered his famous "I Have a Dream" speech. I was only twelve years old at the time, but I vividly remember how strange it felt to have to do something like have all these people come from all over the world to march in order to convince a government that we were human beings worthy of having basic civil rights like job protection and education. Here I was thirty years later, sitting in a congressman's office along with a room full of other bright, capable, accomplished human beings again, feeling like I was on my knees begging for basic civil rights. Here I was, again, trying to convince a national legislator that I was just another human being worthy of the promise of liberty and justice for all, when I am as much of a person as anyone else on this earth. How in the world can it make sense to discriminate against a person based upon the very personal matter of who they feel drawn to emotionally? Or worse yet, who in the world they go to bed with? How significant is who *you* went to bed with last night to your ability to perform your job the next morning? How significant is that to what you are capable of accomplishing as a human being?

As unsensational as it is, and as much as it seems to go against what we've been taught all our lives, sex is such a minimal issue in this fight for human rights as to be a nonissue and I refuse to expend precious time and energy on it. Anyone who attempts to make it more is simply uninformed or mean-spirited. As I sat there on Capitol Hill looking at the faces of these people and thinking about this, the weight of the ridiculousness of the situation was crushing.

Many will wonder why I have chosen to write this. It isn't really a choice. I cannot say I believe in human rights for all, then watch as the media and people like Mr. Chesney wrongfully portray a group in ways which would help to deny those rights to a significant segment of the population. I cannot say I believe in truth and integrity, and not live those lessons myself. I cannot rail out against the media's unfair depictions of gays and lesbians solely as the extremist factions of the community, then not give people an opportunity to know who they really are by being honest about myself. Doing so is not an attempt to proselytize or seek approval. Rather, it is to educate. There has been ignorance about this issue for far too long. Because of that ignorance, lives are being lost through hate-based gay bashing, the high incidence of teenaged gay and lesbian suicide and refusal to face AIDS issues. Continuing to live our lives in ignorance this way, and basing important legal and policy issues on that ignorance is no longer acceptable. I am committed to helping shed light on the issue and it is a commitment which I am compelled to honor.

There is a story from the march that still sends chills down my spine every time I hear it. One of the gay men's choruses which came to the march was riding the Metro subway system to the march and spontaneously broke into song along the way. A couple with a young son was in the car with them. The young boy asked his father what the men were doing. His father looked at the sea of faces singing earnestly in the subway car, turned to his son and said, simply, "They are singing for their freedom." Not one among them could have given a better answer. It greatly hinders this cause to have our accomplishments and who we are trivialized, mythologized, and sensationalized by irresponsible media coverage which is then taken as fact, picked up, then passed on. I do not mind us disagreeing on the issue of gays and lesbians, but we should base that disagreement upon reality, not myth and sensationalized depictions.

I received nothing but positive feedback about the piece. One philosophy professor told me he was making it a standard required piece for his introductory course, as an example of excellent persuasive writing. Another friend told me a year later she had sent it all around the country to friends who were using it as an introduction to telling their parents they were gay or lesbian. For me, it provided a sense of wholeness and freedom that even being the faculty advisor for the Lesbian, Gay, and Bisexual Student Union (LGBSU) or a member of the Gay, Lesbian, or Bisexual Employees and Supporters (GLOBES) at the university does not.

This wholeness spills over into the classroom. Even though I do not make any grand announcements to my classes about being a lesbian, when it comes up in context, and as relevant, I do not avoid speaking of it. In fact, I'm not sure I've ever had a quarter in which I was not included in a school newspaper on the issue, so there is no point in trying to hide it from my students.

For me, education is about teaching our students how to think critically so that when they become actively contributing members of society, they can make decisions that will move us forward as a society. I found I could not accomplish the job of doing that as well as I liked until I felt that I was being totally honest about who I am. They learn to stop simply accepting old entrenched ideas when they are exposed to new ones which somehow fit, though stretch the reality they know. From what they tell me, my being who I am helps them with that. And it has not hurt me with my faculty. In both universities I have been in, I received tenure on the first attempt.

I also feel it a part of my academic mission to further my discipline in these areas. I wrote the first ever employment law book for business students, *Employment Law for Business*, (Irwin, 1995), *The Legal, Ethical, and Regulatory Environment of Business* (South-Western, 1996), and a book on Valuing Diversity (South-Western, due out in 1997). In all of the books, significant space is given to the issue of gays and lesbians in the context of the subject matter. The books all advise stretching our limits of tolerance in order to allow our workplaces to reflect reality. I am happy to say that though the idea seemed quite novel initially, the books have been very well received. I know of no other textbooks in the conservative area of law and business which even begins to discuss such issues.

Being black and female, and thus understanding the importance of participating in the struggle for civil rights for race and gender, made me also understand the importance of doing so for gays and lesbians. I am convinced that being black gives me a sensitivity of what it is to live as a member of a marginalized group, and how important it is not to judge others based upon irrelevant, immutable characteristics. Having that sensitivity, it was only natural that I would extend that same sensitivity to the issue of being a lesbian.

Being a black, female, and a lesbian who publishes in the area of race, gender, and affinity orientation in a largely white, traditionally male, conservative southern academic setting gives me the chance to use my professional research as an opportunity to also provide food for thought for the academic community that benefits me personally. So far, I know of no negative repercussions and am completely glad that I made the decision I did to be out. I think it benefits me and my colleagues and the students.

I knew I was on the right track when I received a note from one of my male students who said, "I have learned so much in your class, not only about business law, but also about life. Your methods have helped me to open my eyes further to other students' points of view and lifestyles. I admit that prior to this class I was, to an extent, homophobic. That whole idea now seems silly. As corny as it sounds, I honestly feel that I am a better person because of this realization."

In, Out,
or Somewhere-In-Between

Christine Cress

Career Services Center,
Western Washington University

2

Racing across the center of red square, I dodge students and mud puddles which have congregated here just a couple of minutes before the hour. My nine o'clock counseling appointment has probably already checked in and I'm late as usual this Monday morning. Today's excuse: my nylons which I tore with my thumbnail when pulling them on. Searching for another pair was fruitless so I grabbed a different blouse and quickly changed into a pair of slacks.

Striding into the office, I throw my mail on the desk while shedding a long raincoat. As the envelopes scatter across the wooden desktop I see that one of them is marked confidential. This catches my attention. Higher education is under a constant barrage of budget cuts and one is never sure when a letter may contain a "pink slip." But it's already two minutes after nine and a male student is indeed waiting for me.

Walking out to greet the student, I notice my slacks have tufts of cat hair on them. I glance around hoping that nobody else notices, but I realize it's the tell-tale sign of a true lesbian. Just two years ago such a situation would have been enough to slightly panic me. Panic me that somebody might find out that there is a reason I never openly discuss what I do during my free time.

"Good morning. How was your weekend?" says the other counselor.

"Oh fine, *I* just went to Seattle. How about yours?" I quickly reply.

"It was great; my wife and I went to Seattle too. Sandy wanted to do some shopping at Nordstrom's and then we hit Pike Place Market. My son Kevin and his fiancee joined us for dinner at the new Pier 7 restaurant. You should try it some time, it was great."

"Yeah, thanks . . . Oops, I'm late for a meeting. See ya," as I run away down the hall.

I know I'm not the only lesbian in America to ever had such an interaction. At times I fantasize a discussion that goes like this:

"Good morning, how was your weekend?"

"Oh, fine. Friday, I went to a k.d. lang concert in Seattle where I met Sheila and afterward we went two-stepping at the Timberline. Saturday, Deborah came over because she just broke up with Nancy, who was seeing Erin. So that night Deborah and I went to Rumors to have a drink but we ran into Janice, who said Diane's artificial insemination worked and. . . ."

"Oops, I'm late for a meeting. See ya," says the other counselor as he runs away down the hall.

Introducing myself, I escorted the student to my office, told him to please have a seat, and we began discussing his reason for seeking counseling. A third-year student, he had completed all of his general university requirements and now needed an academic major. In the middle of our conversation, he stopped and pointed at the sticker that's just above my advising table. "What does that symbol mean?" he asked. He was referring to two upside down triangles, a pink one and black one, encircled by a green border. "It means that this is a safe zone for gay, lesbian, and bisexual students to speak openly about their lives." I went on to briefly explain the historical usage of the triangles in the concentration camps during Nazi Germany. "Oh," he said, and then continued to speak about his confusion of whether to major in physical therapy or graphic design.

I listened to him attentively, but I also flashed back to an anxious moment I experienced two years earlier. The university had received a grant from the American College Health Association to study the quality of life of gay, lesbian, and bisexual students. The research involved focus groups of currently enrolled students as well as alumni. In addition, one faculty and staff group was held—individuals were identified and then invited through an underground phone tree. The night of the focus group I sat in my car in the parking lot for at least ten minutes, shaking. I said to myself, "I have to do this. They've promised me confidentiality. And yet, what if my office finds out?" I remember finally unfastening the seatbelt, unlocking the car door, and easing myself out into the rainy evening.

I was slightly relieved that I knew most of the individuals in the meeting room—custodians, faculty, counselors, activities programmers, and secretaries. I felt empowered and simultaneously terrified. Terrified because even though it was a friendly group, I had to "out" myself to some of these folks. We talked about what it meant to be "out" at Western and what our experiences had been with the administration and other coworkers. Although I trusted the facilitator, I kept looking around the room to see if I was on "Candid Camera" or if men wielding machine guns might storm the room. Just some of your daily safety paranoia that many of us experience, especially women.

Our comments from that evening were summarized into a report that was distributed across campus (Fabiano, 1992). Whether or not a faculty member chose to be out seemed to be highly dependent on whether or not that person had tenure or hoped to get tenure. Some individuals felt pressured by the student population to be out and act as role models. And one member was quoted as sharing, "I probably experienced more direct harassment indirectly because I wasn't out . . . I remember one day in particular when I was in class and I showed a film that was a series of segments of different couples, some male and some female and there were two lesbian mothers who adopted an HIV-positive child. All through that section there were people in the room who were laughing, and acting out . . . I said, 'I noticed that there were some people who were uncomfortable; can you tell me why?' I got the whole list. It's so disgusting, it's so vile, it's against God. I got all the worst things I've ever heard about gay, lesbian, and bisexual people in my classroom, and here I am up in front having to listen to all this—and I'm not out. I just calmly try to be a teacher, and it was awful. It was one of the worst experiences I think I've ever had" (pp. 4–5).

The focus group was the first time in my twelve years at Western that I ever allowed myself to be identified as a lesbian. It was the first time I had ever been given a safe space on campus to talk openly about my life and to experience the camaraderie of others. I struggle daily, as do so many lesbian/gays/bisexual individuals, whether "to be . . . or not to be" out on campus. The focus group became a wedge which began to pry open my life, as well as the overall environment at Western.

By now, the student I was counseling agreed that he needed to further explore his career interests through a series of informational interviews. I showed him around our Career Resources Library and gave him the phone numbers of some professionals to contact in physical therapy and graphic design. It appeared that his indecision over choosing a major was somewhat related to a lack of information about career options and, as he confided in me, he was "afraid of admitting to his parents that he preferred art classes over science classes."

As he left, I thought about how difficult it can be for anyone to make a statement to the world, and in particular to their family, about their interests and preferences. Perhaps that's why I became a career counselor. I can intimately relate to the agony of seeing how one seems to fit, or to not fit, within traditional roles and expectations. I get great joy out of helping individuals find themselves academically and professionally, if not emotionally, psychologically, and spiritually.

While preparing for my next appointment, I reflected on just how instrumental the release of the Focus Group Study in 1992 became for Western in initiating support for gays, lesbians, and bisexuals. With a change in upper administration (a new university president and new vice president) sexual orientation was now included as a part of the concept of campus diversity. The whole mood of the university began to change and it became somewhat acceptable to even say the words "gay" or "lesbian" out loud. And that February, the university sponsored a teleconference organized by the National Association of Student Personnel Administrators (NASPA) titled, "Understanding and Meeting the Needs of Gay, Lesbian, and Bisexual Students." I sheepishly asked my director if I could be the representative to attend from our office—as our diversity liaison, of course.

Among the presenters was Dr. Lee Knefelkamp, chair of the department of Adult and Higher Education at Teachers College at Columbia University. I had long admired Dr. Knefelkamp's work on student development theory but had never before heard her speak. As expected, she discussed the developmental needs of lesbian/gay/bisexual students, but I'll never forget when she declared, "Well, nothing like outing yourself on a national teleconference . . . I guess my orientation has been relatively developmentally delayed." Not only did I laugh along with her at my own delayed development, but I respected her for admitting so via satellite.

My ten o'clock appointment had not yet arrived so curiosity led me to open the confidentially marked envelope on my desk. The letter was from the NASPA Gay, Lesbian, and Bisexual Concerns Network and enclosed was a questionnaire addressing lesbian/gay/bisexual issues on campus. It first asked if our institution had a diversity statement which includes homosexuality.

"Homosexuality?" I said to myself. "I hate that term—it's just so sexual." I marked on the survey: Homosexuality, no. Sexual Orientation, yes.

Next were questions about "outness." "Are you 'out' to the administration and/or colleagues?"

Well, not really. I've never made any statements. But most people assume that I'm a lesbian because I never date men. Of course, I do have long hair and often wear dresses, so that occasionally confuses them. But right now I'm actively pushing the administration to include domestic partner benefits in the Administrator's Handbook, so I guess that makes me guilty by association.

Question #3: "Are you are 'out' to students?"

Some of the students have seen me at lesbian/gay/bisexual functions and some of my student staff knows, but they never ask me personal questions. When I had them over for dinner they did peruse my bookshelves, but so far I haven't added the title to my credentials in the phone book: M.Ed., Lesbian.

Questions #4, 5, 6: "In what specific ways do you feel supported by your institution? In what specific ways would you like to be supported by your institution? And, what are the largest concerns for lesbian/gay/bisexual professionals and students at your institution?"

Whew, these questions required a thoughtful reply. Although I try to maintain a sense of humor about life, I didn't want to make light of the significance of the survey. And I always grapple with how to best represent a collective image of the lesbian/gay/bisexual environment. Pondering my responses, I logged onto the computer to check my email messages. The first was from LesAc, an email line for lesbians in academia and the second was from a domestic partner benefits line. I opened the top message just as there was a knock on the door. I jumped!

"Sorry to scare you Chris." It was my boss. "Oh, that's all right. I was just reading my mail." I turned towards her but from the corner of my eye I could see that on the screen the word lesbian appeared several times. At least 1,000 times I imagined. And the questionnaire was still lying on my desk. I smiled innocently, hoping she'd focus only on my face and nothing else.

She handed me a note and said, "Would you mind calling back Anna. She wants to know if we'll staff an information table during new student orientation."

"Of course," I replied sweetly as she walked away.

I turned back to the computer screen and mumbled to myself, "Why do I feel so guilty?" I knew that I wouldn't have had the same reaction if she walked in and I was reading material on disability or ethnic minority issues. After all, she probably knows I'm gay, but we've never discussed it. Other "out" lesbians on campus have been slightly disgruntled with me because I haven't come out to my director. They've asked me, "Aren't you proud of being gay?" I've told them, "I'm not necessarily proud and I'm not necessarily embarrassed. I'm just cautious because I'm not sure what the repercussions might be. I guess I'd rather be acknowledged as an introvert than be perceived as a pervert."

However, if not leaping out of the closet, I at least flipped on the light a couple of months ago during a staff meeting. In September I had an opportunity to visit Japan for a few weeks as part of an exchange with Bellingham's sister-city, Tateyama. I visited Japan previously when my partner worked there for a year, and now I had the chance to accompany her back and facilitate some intercultural communication training for the other cultural exchange participants. It also provided me with a better title and better role than simply: lesbian love mistress.

When I returned, I shared some of my slides with the staff and when the first slide appeared that pictured Vicky I said, "This is Vicky," and continued on. I considered saying, "this is my partner," but I was too self-conscious. And I decided that saying, "this is Vicky, my friend," was too much of a cop-out. You see, I hadn't yet put pictures of her in my office even though the other counselors have pictures of their families. (Oh, happy delayed development.) I have introduced her to the front receptionist, but let's face it, after three or four decades of carefully concealing personal relationships, it's not easy or even natural to share one's private life with the world. The slides were an opportunity to give the staff a nonthreatening glimpse into the lives of two different cultures—the Japanese sister-city and the American lesbian.

At ten-fifteen I went out to check on the status of my appointment. Hanging up the phone, the secretary informed me that the call was from a student who said she had forgotten about the appointment and so she rescheduled for next week. Overhearing the message from the secretary, Melanie, a student worker asked, "How can someone forget they have no direction in life?" (Melanie's single life ambition since she was six is to become an airline pilot.)

I tell her, "Oh, most of us do a pretty good job of denying reality." And grinning at her I add, "Besides, if everyone knew what they wanted to be when they grew up, I wouldn't have a counseling job."

Returning to my office, I dial Anna, the New Student Programs Coordinator, and tell her we'd be happy to staff an information table during new student orientation. As I put down the phone, I recalled the fall orientation of 1993. I was sitting at one of the information tables with a few hundred students milling around when an acquaintance, Shirley Osterhaus, brought over a new graduate student and introduced her as Monica. Shirley, who's straight, said rather loudly, "Monica wanted to meet other lesbians in the community." Choking in surprise I said, "Oh, nice to meet you." It was the first time, with the exception of the focus group, that I had ever been identified as gay in a professional setting. Although I was shocked, I survived the disclosure and have even become friends with Monica. Now I good humoredly refer to Shirley Osterhaus, as Shirley Ost-her-"out"-her.

The intermingling of our private and professional lives is a challenging phenomenon that often casts us directly into the political arena. Earlier in the year I had contemplated making a full-fledged confession in the form of an all division memo. I felt under duress to take a stand because two initiatives in the state of Washington were gathering signatures that would legalize discrimination against gays, lesbians and bisexuals. I would lay in bed at night and agonize about announcing the next day, "fellow staff members, before you vote for these initiatives, I would like you to know that I am a lesbian and that these initiatives would legalize discrimination against me." The potential ramifications of the initiatives were enormous, even on campus. It could have meant the firing of professional and student staff, the removal of books, library materials, or even employment announcements such as AIDs Prevention Counselor, and as a counselor I would have been forced to condemn any student mentioning homosexuality as a positive lifestyle and encourage the student to seek therapeutic treatment. Fortunately, the initiatives never gathered enough signatures to be placed on the November ballot. However, just as in many states across the nation there is a new people's initiative that would prohibit gays and lesbians from adopting children or serving as foster parents.

It was eleven o'clock and I pulled the diversity committee folder from the file drawer and headed upstairs. Passing the university provost on the way he greeted me with, "Hi, Chris. How are you?"

"Fine, thank you," I said, as I smiled and walked past him.

Just a few steps behind was my friend Tina who works in the Center for Equal Opportunity. She too greeted me with, "Hi, Chris. How are you?"

Still smiling I answered, "Happy and gay today."

"Is that what you told the provost too?" she asked while waving toward him.

"Of course," I answered with a smirk and a wink. "Forget that 'fine' stuff, it's time to bring the complete coalescence of my being into recognition."

"Geez girl, you're sure heady today," said Tina. "Don't get dizzy now from that revolving door on your closet!"

"I'll try not to fall off or throw up," I told her.

Entering the conference room, the diversity review meeting held a large number of representatives from across the division who were discussing the current draft of the student affairs diversity statement. I still wasn't sure who I was supposed to be representing: the Career Services Center? Lesbian professionals? Or maybe campus blondes? At any rate, I was certainly committed to the effort but occasionally felt impatient with the length of time it took to finalize the wording of each and every sentence. At one moment in the interminable meeting a very "out" colleague leaned over and whispered to me, "Do you know why she has such a bad hairdo?" She secretly motioned toward a high ranking official in the division. Glancing at her, I raised my eyebrows and shrugged my shoulders. She whispered again, "Because it's hard to fix your hair in the closet."

I snickered at the comment but tried not to draw attention to ourselves. Since her observation resembled my own state of being, as well as my own state of appearance, I whispered back, "Now I know why my hair always looks so disheveled, it's from jumping back and forth."

She smiled briefly, but I could tell from my colleague's face that she wasn't sure if I was affirming her joke or belittling her assertion. I didn't know, either. But just as I was frustrated at the amount of time it was taking to put together this diversity document, my colleague was also frustrated at waiting for individuals in the community to get every detail in place before they would come out. She was tired of being alone in a crowded room.

After two hours of slow but sure progress, the meeting finally concluded and I returned to my office to get my umbrella before going to lunch. Forgetting to check in at the office signboard, the receptionist asked, "So are you in or are you out?"

"What?" I said, and stopped instantly.

She repeated, "Are you in or are you out?" She pointed to the signboard. "I wondered if you were in a meeting, at lunch, or back in your office."

"Oh, sorry Teri, " I said. "I forgot to move the button from the 'in' position to 'returning at 1 o'clock,' but I'm going to get something to eat so I'll move it to 2 P.M." I reached up and shifted the button.

"That's all right," replied Teri. "It's just that you got a phone call and I didn't know if you were in, out, or somewhere-in-between."

Chuckling, I responded, "You should know by now, Teri, that I'm usually somewhere in-between," and stepping outside to go to lunch, I closed the door behind me.

Reference

Fabiano, P. (1992). *Community building grant: Summary of faculty and staff focus group*. Unpublished report, Western Washington University, Wellness Program, Bellingham, GA.

Coming Out
and Coming In
A Kind of Homecoming

Mildred Dickemann

Professor of Anthropology, Emeritus;
Sonoma State University

3

To those who haven't lived it, the nature of that state of being clumsily termed the "closet" is difficult to convey. Central to most closeted lives is a conspiracy of silence, a tacit contract between oppressor and oppressed never to name or to manifest the secret state of being gay. Having been crossgendered, or body-dysphoric, since at least the age of four (family photos prove it), I had plenty of time to learn where the boundaries were, and which I dared, or was even encouraged, to cross. I was the predictable childhood tomboy, partially encouraged by my parents, though the times and my timidity caused me great uncertainty about who I dared be. During my sophomore college year, I dated men, had a boyfriend, ironed my skirt every morning and combed my hair before every class. I hated dating, dancing, necking, men's piggishness and sexism, but the social pressure was intense and I knew no other gays. Yet I had long since abandoned lipstick and was never without some kind of involvement with a woman. One professor gave me support: we met often after his literature class, he read my dreadful poetry, and encouraged serious reading. I didn't understand quite why. I only felt dimly what I now know: he saw me for who I was, being himself gay. My survival technique of amnesia and denial kept me from focusing. The very *existence* of other gay people was both exhilarating and frightening. I could never tell him, "thank you, I need you."

During graduate school, we heard rumors that at eastern women's colleges, jeans were allowed on campus. Not so with us. On campus I was nicely skirted and sweatered, while off campus I slunk around in jeans and a long raincoat, a disguise which was still an emergence compared to earlier days. But even this little liberation drew criticism from suspicious male peers. One political science major asked sarcastically if I was trying to be like "those girls during the Weimar Republic." I knew what he meant, but shrugged and evaded. In a last period of guilt-ridden dating, I was told many times that all I needed was a good screw by the gentleman in question. However, two screws didn't fix me.

More congenial was my first gay group, a foursome including a gay male couple and my new partner, all grad students. We discovered a bit of San Francisco. Finocchio's drag show, though jammed with tourists, was a revelation to me. But in school, I was devoted to academic success, seen as bright but shy, intellectually assertive but emotionally fragile. From other students I learned that the faculty believed I had been seduced by my more formidable partner. In fact, she was without previous lesbian experience: I had courted her determinedly with conversation and poetry. More significant was my professors' discussing my personal relations behind my back with other students. It was years before I uncovered my outrage at this behavior.

Gradually I met other lesbians, mostly graduate students. We socialized in our apartments, but never discussed seriously the nature of our lives as hidden gays. We took the closet for granted and joked about Kraft-Ebing. My brief exploration of the gay bars during the 1950s was ended by a series of police raids. Nor did I join Mattachine, One, or the Daughters of Bilitis, all then forming in San Francisco. I was too terrified. I read Radclyffe Hall, Donald Webster Cory, many atrocious and harmful psychology books, furtively bought lesbian pulps at the corner smokeshop, and dreamed of a sex change that I considered impossible. *We Too Are Drifting*: The sad romanticism of novelist Gale Wilhelm was exactly my mood.

I tried therapy. For three years an insecure male psychologist encouraged me to acknowledge a sexual attraction to men and thereby be "cured." He even kissed me. But he didn't get it. I have always been sexually attracted to men: I don't *fall in love* with them. It was always women I sought, cared for, needed, wanted to trust and share with. I had no change of heart.

Returning from a year in the field, I learned that a professor with whom I had become a student friend had been forced to resign from the department. He had been solicited, in a nearby city, by an undercover policeman in a men's toilet. My professors rushed up to me, expressing regret. "We did all we could," they lied. Why to me? Because their guilt at their failure to protest needed absolution from a gay person. Thus they revealed their awareness of my status for the first time.

At graduation I was still in disguise, wary, and rather blind. Nevertheless, during my first teaching years some lesbian students recognized me, by evidence I was unaware of. Some students, I was told, labelled me "merely bisexual," apparently attempting to defend me. Others came for advice and support, teaching me the raw reality of their lives. A young lesbian couple was in despair: The mother of one was threatening to intervene. I was sympathetic but ineffectual. A few years later I encountered each of the young women separately. The mother had committed her daughter to an institution where she received electroshock therapy. When I met her, she was no longer in school but living at home. She was listless, and seemed almost mentally retarded. This frightening experience confirmed for me the need for secrecy.

My social life remained private, consisting principally of dinner parties or evenings drinking and dancing in each others' livingrooms. Crossdressing was indulged in only in such private arenas: it was best to sneak in and out of one's car in the dark. Liquor, hangovers, and drunk driving were a normal part of our lives. But as was true of many gay men and women in this period (Martin Duberman and Andrew Kopkind come to mind), my inability to manifest and defend my own identity probably intensified my involvement in the fight for others' rights. My liberal sympathies were old, but not manifest until graduate school and early teaching years. I protested the McCarthyism of the university in a Student Civil Liberties Union which I helped to found, but signed the U.C. loyalty oath to become a teaching assistant. At a racially mixed junior college, I was patiently educated by African-American students about their lives and concerns, leading me to later civil rights work in Louisiana and long-term involvement in affirmative action and ethnic studies. At the University of Kansas, I was one of three politically active faculty members who organized a chapter of C.O.R.E. and a Vietnam teach-in.

After several years in the Midwest, I returned to California, mostly due to personal loneliness. I had never met another gay person, nor had I the courage to look for gay bars in the nearest metropolis. Successful in teaching, beginning to undertake research, politically active, I was emotionally shrivelling. I returned to Berkeley, a locus of greater liberalism where I had acquaintances, straight and gay. It was my home town of choice. I bought a house but had no job. Many interviews and a year later, I obtained a position at Sonoma State, north of Berkeley, a new institution emphasizing the humanities and liberal values. There I found myself involved in faculty politics in a small, growing institution of great tolerance. Though still closeted, I was known as gay to close associates. After serving in various faculty governance roles, I was elected to the chair of the academic senate. I am sure my demeanor must have become more "masculine," as it certainly became more confident, in that context of trust and authority.

Partway through my career there, two professors whom I knew well, and with whom I had worked in faculty politics, approached me regarding the necessity for some sort of antidiscrimination policy regarding sexual orientation. Of course they had come to me as someone with a personal interest in and knowledge of this issue; this was left unsaid. I was evasive and unhelpful: out of the best of motives they had blown my cover. My illusory disguise was disintegrating.

An aspect of my academic life, one that is often overlooked, was the masculine privilege that accrues to butch women in heterosexual contexts. Most people react unconsciously to the stereotypic signals, in dress, manner, and voice, of masculinity and femininity, no matter by whom displayed. So, in a largely male context, as were most of our meetings above the departmental level, as a woman in men's dress, engaging in logical, analytical, assertive discourse, forceful and firm, willing to take command, expressing concern for general principles, efficiency and responsibility, I was treated as "one of the boys." This was especially the case in bureaucratic settings where familial issues are of secondary import. As a masculine woman, I avoided much male sexism; my arguments were more often heard and my leadership more often acceded to than those of more feminine women, whether homosexual or heterosexual.

These interactions had for me a positive feedback quality: The more I gained respect in such contexts, the more self-confidence I gained. Like most individuals cross-gendered from early childhood, approval and acceptance of the felt, desired but thwarted gender identity was central to my self-esteem. This process certainly played a central role in my increasing ability to manifest my identity and abandon my disguise. In addition, toward the end of my teaching career I entered intensive psychotherapy, initially because of a failing relationship. This also was significant in my gaining greater self-acceptance.

Having been imbued in childhood with my parents' extreme gender stereotypes, I was, early, a male chauvinist pig, but many experiences conspired to reduce my sexism. For one thing, I got tired of opening doors and planning entertainments. Only marginally aware of 1970s feminism and feminist anthropology, I was persuaded by student interest and the disinterest of other anthropology faculty members to teach a course on the anthropology of women. It was a revelation. I was able to examine my sexist beliefs on an analytical, historical level, while for the first time being acknowledged by openly lesbian students as their sister. Self-acceptance as a woman, also important in my therapy, was necessary to my self-acceptance as a lesbian, a cross-gendered person and a body-dysphoric man.

This self-description may sound peculiar, as our language, insofar as I know it, does not allow precision in matters of identity and persona. My own gender identity, like others', has been and is being constantly constructed out of opportunities, accidents, aspects of the current environment, and at the same time recovery of memories and feelings from my past, previously subject to denial, amnesia, and neglect. The contradictions in previous paragraphs must be taken as a crude representation of states, composed of all extremes and in-betweens: in short, queer.

Late in my career, I became involved with another professor, a married woman with children, who divorced and joined me. Though we were circumspect, our relationship could not be secret on our small campus. Yet I heard no negative comment other than the report of one secretary's remark. At this time, I was elected a second time to the academic senate chair, with a difficult charge; to constrain or to initiate the removal of an arrogant and destructive president. (Failing at the former, I did the latter.) I was now fully crossdressed and well known on campus. It was a moving endorsement, and a measure of the merit of that rare institution, that I was elected.

And so I acquired the courage to offer a course on the anthropology of homosexuality, the first in this discipline in the United States, as far as I can determine. It was a high point of my teaching career, but also productive of many amusing and revealing stories. For example, the photocopy business that had done many previous readers for me strangely left the course title off the cover of this one! A secretarial assistant's accomplished typing fell apart as she got well into my course outline. But I myself had amazing reactions: for some weeks I imagined a heart problem as I climbed the stairs to my classroom. It was only anxiety.

In mid-career, during my late 40s, I underwent a transition familiar to those of my generation, which I term "coming in." After years without contact with any gay community other than the small private world of gay friends, and hearing little of the transformations of the gay community since 1969, I was finally able to act on my own behalf. My first act was to join the (then) National Gay Task Force, safely done privately by mail! The excitement of receiving that modest newsletter is unforgettable. I soon moved rapidly into the local gay world, assuming leadership positions in several organizations, and cofounding the U.C. (Berkeley) Gay and Lesbian Alumni Association. The feeling of welcome, acceptance and solidarity were entirely new, a homecoming. This affected not only my academic politics but my scholarship as well. Learning of the upcoming 1987 International Conference on Homosexuality in Amsterdam, I grabbed my chance and wrote a paper to gain attendance. The conference was a marvelous introduction both to the state of gay research and to its participants. My research focus then shifted to homosexuality and gender, as I finally integrated my scholarly and personal life. I became a leader in our discipline's Society of Lesbian and Gay Anthropologists, which is actively involved in efforts to combat discrimination in our field.

To this fundamentally positive account I must add two caveats. To discover and unite with one's community of identity is to discover a long-lost family. After the first bloom of validation, one realizes that one's kin group is composed of people like any other, and divided by deep fissions, cliques, and feuds. Some of these conflicts reflect fundamental disagreements regarding criteria for membership. Stigmatization and exclusion occur within such families, falling upon any who deviate from the currently popular gay or lesbian norm. In my own case, the old butch is often a species rejected, misunderstood, or merely invisible. Disillusion sets in. And yet, for me the queer family still remains a site of return and renewal.

Second, acceptance of a queer identity means alienation from some parts of heterosexual society, in which one formerly moved in disguise. The closet is preferred by some not only for safety's sake, but as a guarantee of greater access. In my own case, increasingly cross-gendered appearance has meant loss of access to the closeted higher academe where I now do most of my research, namely U.C. Berkeley. It's a cliché that there's no rejection like that of a closeted peer. Now retired, I have not found congenial intellectual colleagues outside of our annual national meetings. Then too, leaving the silence of the closet exposes one to stereotypical condescensions of one's "liberal" colleagues. Having become both obvious and active in my discipline, I chanced to pass a colleague with whom I had once collaborated closely. He stopped me to ask for my help: He was now teaching a course on human sexuality. Could I please tell him about the children of gays? I have never worked on this topic, yet he assumed that all gays know all gay research. This phenomenon is familiar to all those "deviants without closets," of race, disability, or other undisguisability.

Maneuvering one's way through the shoals of a divisive gay community, the shallows of interactions with brothers and sisters with whom one shares nothing but one's identity, and the sometimes accepting, sometimes rejecting waters of heterosexual academe, one must develop a high tolerance for loneliness, often enhanced by the queerness of one's research. Disciplinary gay caucuses, institutes, and fellowships are critical for one's survival. But something more is needed.

The Silent Partner Finds Her Voice

Penelope Dugan

The Writing Program,
Richard Stockton College of New Jersey

4

On the wall above my desk, a postcard dated March 12, 1991, reads, "Be of good cheer, my plucky Penel. Win or lose, we have each other. Our love has been strengthened by struggle. All my love, Flower." We did win the struggle of March 1991. But a year to the day later, my beloved Flower was diagnosed with an inoperable malignant brain tumor. For the next fifteen months, we fought brain cancer. I look back on our struggles during the twelve years we shared our lives with one another grateful that we waged them, so we could be together until Flower's death on June 7, 1993.

For the first four years of our life together, we worked at the same college, a college where I had taught for five years before my partner's arrival. We were compelled to work with each other closely at the end of her first semester when the local congressman forwarded to the college president a letter written by the mother of a freshman student protesting my assignment of Rita Mae Brown's *Rubyfruit Jungle* and James Kirkwood's *Good Times Bad Times*. The mother thought it was an outrage that "such filth" should be taught to impressionable eighteen-year-olds at a tax-supported college. The president referred the whole matter to my not-yet partner who was swamped with learning a new college and learning how to be a dean. I lightened her workload by writing my own defense which went out over her signature. She loved my writing first and then me.

Two years later, we bought a house, which colleagues helped us move into, where we entertained numerous faculty and student groups. While we did not announce our relationship, we were not secretive about it. After an administrative reorganization, my partner became my division chairperson, a position she was elected to by the vote of the entire college faculty.

Because of our relationship, my partner never recommended me for awards or any special recognition. Had we been husband and wife, I do not believe this situation would have been different. It was a productive time for us both. Working as a team, we secured grants for the college and instituted new academic programs.

In our third year together, the college hired a new president. In December, 1984, the president fired my partner for "institutional considerations." Prevented from getting another administrative job because the president and vice president were giving her bad recommendations, my partner sued in federal court (with funds raised by the college faculty), securing a settlement whereby the college administration would say she resigned and would give her good recommendations.

My partner was hired as an administrator at a college in another state, eight hours by car from my college. I bought out my partner's share in our house, so she could buy another house in the rural area where she was moving, and made out a will leaving her our former house in the event of my death. She did the same with her new house. Although we were domestic partners in fact and commuted 830 miles a week to preserve our relationship, that relationship was not legally recognized, so every aspect of our lives that married couples take for granted had to be specified in some legal document or another—will, power of attorney, and so on.

When my partner moved to her new college in August 1985, I was surprised when a straight couple, close friends of ours for several years, asked if I would look for a new lover now that my partner was so far away. I asked if they would divorce if either of them had to get a job several hundred miles distance from their home. They replied that they wouldn't, but their situation was different. And, of course, it was. Neither one of them would be fired because of their relationship. The unemployed partner in their relationship could be covered by the major medical benefits of the other. The employed partner could try to find a position, openly, for his or her spouse at the new college. With rare exceptions, lesbian couples are not able to do this.

For the next six years, I spent nearly every weekend and every vacation at my partner's house. Even though I was included in most personal invitations (but never official invitations) she received, my partner was still invited by colleagues to join their singles' clubs. My presence was acknowledged but not our relationship.

Tired of commuting and wanting to find a place where we could be together, I went on the job market. We decided I would look only in large cities with a number of colleges and universities to increase the likelihood of my partner being able to find an academic administration job in the same area. When a large university in a midwestern city asked me to interview there, I asked the chairperson of the search committee, whom I knew and trusted, what the environment would be like for a lesbian couple. She replied that the administration would protect me as long as I didn't engage in advocacy in the classroom, but I should be aware that the state was conservative. She also said that the university had a placement bureau which aided faculty spouses in finding jobs, but she wouldn't recommend that we use it. Not wanting a repeat of our previous bad experience, I declined the on-campus interview.

A position opening at my partner's college appeared in the October, 1990, Modern Language Association job listings. I applied for it immediately since the advertisement read as if it were written for me. It wasn't, of course. It was written for the husband of another administrator at the college. Although he has not been professionally active for years, he was currently teaching on an ad hoc basis for the department with the vacancy and was well liked there. However, he lacked my experience or credentials.

Read by a search committee that did not know me, my dossier rose to the top of the 200 or so other applications. Invited for an on-campus interview in February 1991, I accepted it readily. By the time I arrived on campus for the two-day interview, my relationship with my partner had been discovered. For the first time in my life, I was treated like a faculty wife. Even though I had driven hundreds of miles for the interview, I was not provided with lodging or taken out for dinner at the end of the first day. I was not given a tour of the area or even a campus tour. No effort was made to familiarize me with the college or the department where I was interviewing to teach. Only six members of the sixteen-member department appeared for my lecture. In short, my candidacy was not taken seriously.

A week later a member of the department called to apologize for my treatment which had differed so greatly from that given other candidates. He said that he didn't think it was fair because I was the most qualified candidate. He said he felt awkward going public with any of this because of my relationship to my partner. Still smarting from my treatment, I replied that the sole reason I had applied for the position was *because* of my relationship with my partner, and that the college had never failed to find jobs for the *husbands* of women on the faculty and staff. That being the case, I would prefer to be regarded as the moral equivalent of a husband, not a wife, and have my credentials to do the job taken seriously. Thus began the struggle of March 1991. While I declined interviews with Big Ten and Ivy League universities, the department of this upstate state college tried to extend their search. My partner, upset about what was happening, accepted a nomination to apply for the provost position at an urban midwestern university.

Figuring I had nothing to lose, I wrote an account of my treatment by the search committee to the academic vice president of the college and suggested an affirmative action suit might be in order if the job were offered to anyone else. The vice president told the department they would lose the line if they could not produce a candidate from their existing pool with better credentials than mine. Finally, I was offered the job in May 1991. At the age of forty-five, with twenty years of college teaching experience, I accepted a tenure-track assistant professorship and a fifteen thousand dollar cut in pay. My partner declined her offer from the urban university to be provost. We rejoiced that my commuting days were over, and we threw a big party to celebrate our tenth anniversary and her fiftieth birthday. Having been outed, we offically announced our relationship.

In the first week of the new academic year, a member of the department came to tell me that she had nothing against homosexuals. In the second week, another member came to ask me if I could request money for a speakers' series from my partner. I suggested he follow the usual procedures for securing funds. In the first department meeting of the semester, the minutes of the last department meeting of the previous semester were distributed for approval.

There I read the department's discussion of my candidacy. Members of the department who hadn't seen me during my two-day interview characterized me as "noncanonical" and "ideological." I was "too nontraditional" and "lacked authority." I wasn't "a good institutional fit." One member warned of departmental business being relayed to the adminstration through "pillow talk." A member of the search committee said that she had heard from the dean the salary he planned to offer me and asked other faculty to go with her to the academic vice president to protest my salary. I was stunned that all this was in the minutes. After they were approved, I raised my hand and asked if the group protesting my salary had already gone to the vice president because if they hadn't I would like to join them in protesting it. Nobody laughed.

My first semester was stressful. To my surprise, I missed the long weekend drives that had given me time to think. I missed the rhythm of living alone during the week and cramming all my work into a four-day period. I missed the loving nightly telephone calls. Finally, we were together again, but it felt like we talked less and made love less. We had to relearn the rhythms of daily life together. We had both made professional sacrifices for our relationship, but I had come to a place that belonged to my partner and felt like it would never belong to me.

Now included in all my partner's official invitations, I remained a pariah in the department. At administrative receptions and dinners, I was seated with the wives. In the department, I was treated as an unwanted, over-age junior faculty member. I learned how to talk with administrative wives about schools, children, and where their husbands had previously held positions. I learned—but couldn't master—the deference behavior expected in the department.

In my first year review, the department personnel committee wrote that my course in American literature before the Civil War deviated from the departmental syllabus and contained "too much social justice" for a course required of majors. They asked for a written assurance that I would conform to the syllabus before teaching the course again. I wrote back that the departmental syllabus was written in 1971, that lots had happened in literary scholarship since then, that I didn't know what constituted "too much" social justice, and that "social justice" should not be confined to elective courses, as they suggested. The committee did not acknowledge my letter and sent to the dean their reservations about my lack of conformity to departmental curriculum standards. I was reappointed for a second year and third year.

In March 1992, when my partner's brain tumor was diagnosed, the campus community rallied to support us. The administrative wives sent cassaroles; the secretarial staff assisted by driving my partner to appointments that conflicted with my classes; flowers and cards from faculty and staff across the college arrived on a daily basis. Even the secretary in my department and the faculty member who had blown the whistle on the search acknowledged my partner's illness and offered their help.

The rest of the department which initially had made an issue of our relationship now pretended it didn't exist. The chairperson asked me to take on the additional responsibility of directing freshman composition. I declined. Later, he asked me to coordinate placement testing in the summer. I declined. Still later, he asked me to be faculty advisor to the student literary journal. I declined. He asked how I expected to be tenured if I continued to decline invitations for greater participation in the department. I replied that my teaching received high scores on the student evaluations and my publication record was solid. If that weren't enough, then I wouldn't be tenured, but it did seem as if his invitations for extra responsibilities, at a time when he knew I couldn't undertake them, were unreasonable. He placed a letter in my personnel file charging me with insubordination. My energy was directed toward caring for my partner. I was in the contracting world of our present and could not think about my own future.

My partner died in our home, nursed by lesbian and gay friends who came from all over the northeast, as well as by administrative wives, women's studies faculty, and secretarial staff from the college. They formed a circle of love around the two of us.

The memorial service at the college Newman Center drew five hundred people. I spoke at the service of our life together. Women held hands as they went up to the altar to light memorial candles. Probably for the first time, the word "dyke" was spoken from the pulpit. The service ended with every-one signing "We Shall Overcome." Still standing in their places, the crowd broke into spontaneous applause. I ducked out of the Newman Center immediately after the service. The college president, who kept my partner on full salary until her death, caught up with me. He shook my hand, saying he knew I was having a hard time with my department. I answered I was having a hard time with the loss of my lover and thanked him for his kindness to her.

The following semester, my last at the college, I came out—for the first time ever—in all my classes on National Coming Out Day. There was nothing to lose, no one to protect. I told my students that I had been a nun, that I had been married to a man, and that I lived in a loving relationship with a woman for twelve years. I said that life was short, and we never knew in what directions it would take us. I asked if there were any questions. One young man asked if I were still a lesbian now that my partner was dead. I said yes. He blurted out, "But you could fit in now." I said whether or not I "fit in" did not have much to do with whether I was a lesbian or not but what other people decided to do with the fact.

At my current institution, where I have tenure, I come out in the con-text of class discussion. I continue to include works by gay and lesbian authors in my required course assignments. I continue to challenge admin-istrations and colleagues when it is an appropriate use of my energy. Life is too short to do otherwise.

Out
in the Heartland
Lesbians, Academics, and Iowa

Michele J. Eliason

College of Nursing,
University of Iowa

5

The place was an undergraduate classroom: Introduction to Child Development and the class just viewed the video, "Gay Youth." The teacher stated, "At the end of the last class, there were two questions submitted to me about lesbian, gay, and bisexual issues. They were, 'What do you think causes sexual orientation?' and, 'Are you a lesbian?' I am going to answer both of these questions." The lecture hall became completely silent—250 eyes riveted on the teacher. She spoke at some length on the first question (secretly relishing the rapt attention of the students—so rare in a big lecture class). Then she said, "Regarding the second question, yes, I am a lesbian. I tell you this because many of you indicated that you did not know any gay, lesbian, or bisexual people. You probably do, but are not aware of it. I believe that it is important for us to be visible, so you can see who we are and learn that we are just like the other people you know. I would be happy to answer any questions." There were no questions. Anonymous class evaluations at the end of the semester were overwhelmingly positive, with many students thanking the teacher for including lesbian, gay, and bisexual issues in the course.

The occasion was the first faculty meeting of the semester in the College of Nursing. Faculty members were asked to describe the university committees or groups to which they belonged. Most of these generated some discussion as to the purposes or goals or activities of the committee or group. At the end of her litany of mundane committees, one woman added, "And I have just been elected cochair of the University of Iowa Lesbian, Gay, and Bisexual Staff and Faculty Association." There was a moment of stunned silence, then the supervisor quickly asked the next person in line about her committee involvement and the meeting resumed.

These two experiences from 1994 typify the reactions to my campus activism, my teaching, and my research on gay, lesbian, and bisexual issues— approval from students and silence from colleagues. I have rarely encountered overt disapproval or negative comments from my faculty colleagues (although I have from some staff members), only a sense of discomfort and a "please don't say that 'L' word again" look. In this essay, I would like to further explore the reactions I have encountered from colleagues and students, and what I have learned from these encounters. But I'm getting ahead of myself. No lesbian account would be complete without the "coming out story."

Like many lesbians I know and have read about, my coming out was a long, gradual process that began in childhood with the recognition of difference from my friends. But as a conscious process, I generally consider my coming out to begin in 1980 when I decided to stop dating men. From 1980 to 1984, I used a form of denial strategy to cope with feelings of difference. That is, I threw myself into my graduate studies. Every time I felt an attraction to a woman or had a fleeting thought about my own sexuality, I hit the books. I suspect that the strategy of academic overachievement is used by a number of queer people—someday I'll collect data on this. But I digress from my story. Near the end of 1984, I had finished my doctoral work, was progressing nicely through a postdoc, and had run out of energy for studying. When the choice was to pursue a second degree or face up to my sexual identity, I chose the latter. So I "came out" to myself and a few close friends. As any good academic would do, I educated myself through reading about sexual identity, and went through many of the reactions noted in stage theories or theoretical accounts of coming out—questioning and disruption of stereotypes, anger at societal prejudice, relief, and pride. I eventually decided to label myself as a lesbian. I slowly came out to the people who were important to me. But at that time, I was working in a pediatrics clinic with very conservative coworkers. I had heard antigay jokes and comments from secretaries, lab techs, social workers, psychologists, and physicians in this setting over the years. Once the head secretary handed me a phone message with the remark, "Some goddamn faggot called you today." It did not feel safe to come out at work, so I led a double life for about three years. I gradually stopped any social interaction with coworkers, worked through lunch breaks, and made excuses for the occasional after work social gatherings. In the meantime, I continued to educate myself about sexuality issues and started taking women's studies courses in the evenings. I was getting politicized about the processes of oppression as they apply to many groups and finding it increasingly difficult to sit by silently when racist, sexist, and homophobic remarks were made at work.

In 1988, a position in the Nursing College opened—as a registered nurse and Ph.D. psychologist, this seemed the perfect opportunity for me so I applied. At the time, nothing in my vitae or my appearance indicated my sexual identity and I saw no reason to reveal it in my job interviews. I got the job as a half-time tenure-track position, so I needed to continue to work half-time in pediatrics as well. The double life persisted for a time. But I began to meet more lesbians in academia and felt a need to do research on lesbian, gay, and bisexual issues. The first study involved nursing students' reactions to lesbian patients and coworkers. I can clearly remember my anxiety when I read the project summary to a class—how difficult it was to say "lesbian" for the first time in front of a large group of students. I was dripping with sweat and was sure I would stutter or maybe even drop dead if I uttered the word. This first research project was published in 1991 in a major nursing research journal, after being rejected by two other journals without a peer review. I consider this first publication as my coming out at work. Publications are prominently displayed on a bulletin board in a high traffic area in the building and are also listed in a monthly newsletter. Interestingly, my article disappeared from the bulletin board several times—luckily I had many copies and kept replacing them. I still don't know whether they disappeared because someone found the topic too distasteful, or whether several people wanted to read it but were afraid to ask me for copies. At any rate, I began to perceive a change in the way my colleagues related to me. Instead of being that nice pediatrics person, I was now some radical activist whose research was politically motivated. I learned firsthand the curious phenomenon about lesbian, gay, and bisexual studies—you must be one if you study them. This assumption is not made about any other topic (save perhaps studies of racial issues). My colleagues who study children are not considered childlike and no one assumes that the expert on bedsores has had one herself. However, because I was (am) a lesbian, they thought that my research must be personally and politically motivated.

Regardless of the negative reactions I got from colleagues, I found this study so personally satisfying that I decided to shift my research program. I knew it would be very difficult to remain in pediatrics as an out lesbian, and my best clinic contacts were leaving, so the time was ripe for a change. I asked a number of senior faculty in my college and outside of it for advice. Here are a few of the comments I got:

"Don't do it until you get tenure. It doesn't look good to shift your research focus mid-career."

"It's great to study lesbian issues, but make sure that your vitae is balanced and that you have one or two articles on other topics for each one on lesbian issues."

"Be careful who you choose for research collaboration—some people on campus are not respected."

"It's OK to do that, just don't put it on your vitae."

"There is no need to study homophobia (or racism, sexism) in health care because we teach our students to treat everyone equally."

"Can't you tone it down a little? It makes our profession look bad."

These comments, aimed at discouraging me, had the opposite effect. I was doubly motivated to engage in this research, as these comments indicated how deeply ingrained homophobia was. In the meantime, I was becoming more political. I was involved in campus politics. I was involved in a campaign to educate the campus about sexual harassment and was on the Human Rights Committee, which hears complaints related to civil rights issues and does educational programs for the campus. I was a member of the Campus Homophobia Committee which conducted a university-wide random survey of attitudes of staff and faculty toward lesbian, gay, and bisexual employees (my name was on the survey letter—another way to "out" oneself in a big way and as a result, I did receive some threatening letters). I belonged to the Lesbian, Gay, and Bisexual Staff and Faculty Association, and became chair of an advisory committee to develop a sexuality studies program. I developed a slide show presentation about lesbian, gay, and bisexual issues and have made this presentation to over fifty groups on campus in the past two years. I felt that I was really actively engaged in providing service to my university and truly felt that my efforts would be appreciated. However, at my next annual review, I was told that I had chosen questionable service activities that could count against me in my tenure decision.

In 1992, I began teaching Introduction to Lesbian, Gay, and Bisexual Studies, a course offered in the evenings, taught on overload, and paid by funds outside of my college. My superiors made it clear that this was something I could choose to do with my own time, but that it had better not interfere with my "legitimate" duties. In spite of my superiors' perception that this has nothing to do with nursing, several nursing students enroll in the course each time it is taught. Student evaluations from this course are among the most positive I have ever received. But again I heard, "Don't include these evaluations in your review materials."

Recently (fall of 1994), we hosted a national lesbian, gay, and bisexual studies conference on our campus with 1200 academics, artists, and activists in attendance. The three-day event included academic papers, panels, workshops, art exhibits, readings, and performances and brought much acclaim to the university (and money to the city). I was one of the media spokespeople for the event and was quoted in local and state newspapers and appeared on a local TV newscast. Only two of my colleagues acknowledged this fact—most looked at me in a different way, or avoided eye contact. One made an effort to be supportive and said in front of a group, "I saw you on TV last night. The conference sounds really great. It must have been a lot of work to pull it off." No one else commented.

(By the way, the most common question that reporters asked was, "Why Iowa?" They often made some comment about rural Iowans being extremely conservative and that they would certainly not approve of having this conference in their state. When I pointed out that I was born and raised in rural Iowa and had the support of my family and friends, they were always quite surprised. They seemed to think that all lesbian, gay, and bisexual people in Iowa have been imported from one of the coasts. Dealing with the media was another good learning experience for me, and because of the media exposure, the conference was another major coming out event.)

Now that I have related part of my coming out story, I want to discuss some of the things I have learned from students and colleagues. I call this section "The Good News and the Bad News." First, the good news. Students have been great, and I truly believe that without student support, I would have given up on academics years ago. A few of the lessons I have learned from teaching "straight" and lesbigay courses include:

1. Most heterosexual students are willing and eager to learn about lesbian, gay, and bisexual issues. As there is more open discussion of these issues in the media and people feel freer to come out, most students have a lesbian, gay, or bisexual friend, relative, or acquaintance and they value the opportunity to learn about the issues in the classroom. They also value having open lesbian, gay, and bisexual role models among the faculty. I have felt more respect from students as an out faculty member than I ever experienced as a closeted faculty member.
2. Most lesbian, gay, and bisexual students are hungry for open, affirmative presentation of our history and issues in the classroom, and they desperately need role models in academics.
3. Teaching "straight" classes, such as child development, lifespan development, and human sexuality is a wonderful opportunity to

educate straight students. Early on in my teaching career, I had only one lecture devoted to sexual identity in each class. This lecture stood out, seemed very awkward, and I felt I had to defend it. But as I learned more, I began to integrate issues of sexuality into the entire course. For example, when discussing prenatal development and genetics, I mention research searching for a "gay gene." When discussing family structures, I include research on gay and lesbian parents. When I discuss peer pressure and social group formation in adolescence, I mention the potential alienation of gay and lesbian teens. And of course, no discussion of teen suicide could be complete or ethical without inclusion of sexual identity. I always try to frame discussion of sexual identity issues in the most "objective" and "clinical" terms, such as prefacing my remarks with, "Research indicates...." or, "The evidence is quite clear that...." This method highlights the fact that the study of sexual identity is no different than the study of moral development or parenting styles. I always stress to students that we look to research for our conclusions, not conjectures or popular opinions.

4. Teaching "gay" classes with a mixture of students of all sexual identities, including the undecideds, is a real challenge. I have learned to balance the needs of the heterosexual students who are there because they really want to learn the issues, but may have very little knowledge, with the needs of lesbian, gay, and bisexual students who also vary widely in their knowledge, but have personal experiences that influence their thinking, and the needs of undecided students who are exploring their own sexual identities.

The heterosexual students often feel that they must be silent, because they don't know enough; feel silenced by gay, lesbian, or bisexual students who talk too much; and occasionally say things which upset the lesbian, gay, and bisexual students. The atmosphere is different from that of a "straight" class. One male heterosexual student wrote on his evaluation, "For the first time in my academic career, I felt I was in the minority. I felt I had very little to contribute to class discussions." This was particularly interesting since the composition of the class in that semester was twenty-seven heterosexual, thirteen gay, lesbian, or bisexual, and three undecided students, so he clearly was in the majority. What he felt was probably not related to the number of different kinds of students in the classroom, but the fact that lesbian, gay, and bisexual issues were the center of the course rather than a marginal or invisible issue.

The lesbian, gay, and bisexual students may also lack knowledge, but some of them think that their personal experiences are universal and general to queer people, or they are early in their own coming out process and still believe in some negative stereotypes. Some have been "heterophobic" and resent the heterosexuals in "their" class. Others expect to get good grades solely on the basis of being lesbian, gay, or bisexual, or they expect differential treatment from me as their teacher on the basis of a shared sexual identity. I have also discovered that the sexuality studies classroom can be an "academic erotic zone" as Barale noted in her contribution to *Tilting the Tower: Lesbians Teaching Queer Subjects* (Routledge, 1994). Students may enroll in the class with the express purpose of meeting other lesbian, gay, or bisexual people to date, or they may develop attractions to classmates or faculty members. When topics of discussion involve sexuality, the classroom environment is a very different one. In my experience, these classes are much more intimate than the usual course, because students do share personal experiences which create emotional bonds within the class. These bonds can be good and bad—sometimes emotions get in the way of learning, sometimes they facilitate interpersonal relating and understanding of oppression.

Then there are the needs of the students who are actively exploring their own sexual identity. They may be in real turmoil and at risk for effects of internalized homophobia such as depression, suicide, substance abuse, and unsafe sexual activities. Their personal confusion may interfere with their academic progress and sometimes these students need to be referred to a counselor or support group to deal with their issues. Sometimes they think the sexuality studies class is the place for this personal work and say things that are inappropriate for the setting. These students must be monitored closely, but are sometimes the most rewarding.

Now the bad news. What I have learned from colleagues has been primarily a message that promotes secrecy, shame, guilt, and fear. The bottom line for some of the most well-intentioned colleagues is, "don't advertise your sexuality" and "don't study issues of sexual identity—this is not legitimate research." Some of the lessons I have learned include:

1. Some faculty members are hopeless—don't waste your time with them.
2. Choose your battles—it is so easy to become the one trouble-maker in the department. I tackle the issues that touch me at the ethical level and let the others go.
3. Colleagues need to be educated, but you can't do it all. The most

effective education has often come from the outside. You can arrange to have speakers, panels, or films to do the work for you. If they hear it from other sources, you sound more legitimate in the future.

4. Play the academic game only to the extent that it doesn't harm your own self-esteem and ethical value system.

5. Find a mentor. This can be someone within your department or college or outside it. The important thing is having someone you can trust to talk about the things that happen to you. Someone who can recognize homophobia.

In conclusion, here is where I stand at this writing, in August of 1995. I am up for tenure review this fall. I have among the highest student teaching evaluations in my college, have had six funded grants (three federal, three institutional), and have 41 articles in peer reviewed journals (14 in nursing journals, 15 in pediatrics journals, and the rest in sexuality studies areas), ten chapters in books, and a book in progress. This level of productivity is higher than any faculty member who has received tenure in the past ten years, yet I expect a battle. In fact, I have been told by a ranking official that I will probably be denied tenure at least at one level of the process. My brief experience as an out lesbian academic has been nerve-racking at times, exhilirating at times, but mostly, has been personally satisfying. I feel more integrated as a person when my sexual identity is not a secret, and more fulfilled as a researcher when my work feels ethically responsible—like I am giving something back to the community that sustains me in life. I have chosen the path that feels right for me—to engage in research on lesbian, gay, and bisexual issues, to integrate my teaching with sexual identity issues, and to educate my campus to make it a safer place for us all. The costs may be very high; I might even lose my job. But the benefits to my own personal value system are far greater than any particular job.

Living Outside the Center

Kathryn M. Feltey

Department of Sociology,
University of Akron

6

In my graduate program there were a lot of lesbians. When I took notice of this fact, I was living with my infant son and his father. Several of us who were the feminist contingency in the Sociology Department (lesbian, bisexual, and heterosexual) spent hours talking about the politics of sexuality, the meaning of relationships, and our future research plans. These three topics became intricately intertwined for me, with my research serving as a map of direction and change in my life.

My dissertation examined female-headed-family poverty across communities. I was, at that time, trying to figure out how to leave the relationship with my son's father. I was more afraid of stepping out into the world alone with a child, than I was of the poverty I was researching. But, it was clear from my findings, and from my fear, that manlessness was a condition to be avoided, especially when one has children.

I did, however, leave the relationship, and entered fully into a network of support, my lesbian feminist sociologist friends who were family to me and my son. I remember one summer evening looking around my home, seeing one friend out in the garden picking flowers, smelling dinner as it was being prepared by two other friends, and hearing my eighteen-month-old-son's laughter as another friend was giving him his bath. We were building a community, and in that context I began a relationship with a woman who was to become my partner and coparent for the next five years. Her thesis research on lesbian mothers later became the basis for our first coauthored article in which we explored the politics of lesbian motherhood and the construction of family in lesbian community.

As I finished my dissertation, I prepared to move into my life as an assistant professor of sociology at the University of Akron. I had interviewed for the job while still living with my son's father. By the time I actually started the job, my whole world had changed. I arrived in Akron, to a department with seventeen men and one woman (who was on leave that semester) on regular faculty. There was no one I felt safe telling the truth about my life. So, I lived two lives: one in the department where I struggled to make the transition from graduate student to assistant professor and the other at home as a single parent through the week, waiting for the weekends when my partner and I could be together.

I was very lonely, and very scared. I wanted to tell someone that my life had changed since the interview, that I had met someone wonderful and was looking forward to sharing my life with that person, and that that person happened to be a woman. But, I looked around my department and found no one. So, I contacted the director of women's studies and, confiding my dilemma, was advised to "fake it" if I wanted to keep my position. Although I had a clear feminist consciousness, and worked and marched for feminist and gay rights, I had a lot of fear around personal exposure. Not just in terms of sexual identity, but in all ways. I had been in therapy for several years working on family of origin issues, and I was attempting to challenge the ways I "hid" as a child. I was working and dealing with the ways that hiding behavior permeated my adult life and relationships. But, I didn't feel I could risk challenging the conservative environment of the university when my future as a professor of sociology seemed to be at stake.

So, I fought homophobia and heterosexism in the curriculum and the classroom, and developed a workshop that I conducted with my partner for different organizations and conferences. And, I proudly put my first "good" publication on my vita: the article on lesbian motherhood out of my partner's thesis. And I cried the whole way home when the chair of the retention committee told me to remove that article from my vita, counseling that "we all look back on articles and research that we are embarrassed by, so save yourself that experience and don't claim it." I translated this to "don't claim who you are, don't embarrass yourself, or make us acknowledge who you really are."

My nonlesbian research in my early years at Akron focused on the problem of homelessness. It seemed to be a natural extension of my earlier work on female-headed-family poverty: How much poorer can you get than without home? But, I think the real question I was struggling with was how one finds and keeps a home. I felt homeless, moving between worlds, fairly adept at maneuvering identities to fit the moment, but never feeling settled or at home. One homeless woman I interviewed described homelessness as "just being out in the world" without an anchor or sense of belonging. Her words played back to me, as I struggled to integrate all of the parts of me, to have them all together in one place at one time.

In my next project I analyzed interview data with women in prison who had killed abusive partners. During this time I was angry about the ways that I had experienced abuse in my life, and for the ways that I had been silenced and prevented from telling my own story. I came away from that project feeling that silence is deadly for women. All of the women had tried to reveal the nature of their experiences in these relationships, meeting resistance, often violent, to their efforts to voice their truths. They described their use of violence as the only option left; it was a "kill or be killed" voiceless. Trying to make sense of all this, I felt violent. I could not find my voice.

I spent the next several years in a frenzy of work, focused on the tenure decision. It took my attention away from home, from my partner, from my son, from our family. I felt justified, I had to secure my position in the department and in the profession. I worked day and night, often until daybreak. I was exhausted and scared and lonely. I thought if I received tenure and was promoted, it would balance the sacrifice. I wrote in an academic voice, felt separate from the data I had collected, felt separate from the analysis I was conducting. I was promoted and received tenure.

Nothing much changed. Looking back, I think I was emotionally and physically depressed in the aftermath of all the energy expended in the years before tenure. Within months, I was hospitalized with an undiagnosed illness, later identified as Chronic Fatigue Immune Dysfunction Syndrome (CFIDS). It took several years to regain anything approximating my former energy level. My current research includes a study of the relationship between identity, outness, and health outcomes for lesbians. I'm still looking for answers to questions about my own experiences, my own life story.

Within a year of the tenure decision, my relationship with my partner ended. I had not cared for the relationship (as in care-giving). In fact I acted out a lot of my anger, denial, and frustration, extracting from her a level of commitment that was unreasonable and abusive. I wanted our relationship to serve as a remedy to the splintering I was experiencing in my life. I expected her to be the cure. When we separated, and later broke off communication for the better part of a year, I lost not only a partner, but a coparent to my child.

A few people at the university and in the department knew. No one gave condolences, no one offered support. I felt unreal, as if there was some sort of shield between myself and others. I felt like I could will myself into being and then out again, it felt like I had a lot of power to control perceptions of who I was and who I could be. It was a strong and painful reminder of the invisibility and voicelessness I had experienced at other points in my life. The shielding or hiding behavior was still with me, an integral part of self that was paradoxical in that it served to protect at the same time that it destroyed. I have been planning my next research project: a study of the effects of homelessness on children. I've approached this work, and then avoided pulling together the pieces to develop a comprehensive research plan. I don't think I'm ready for the answers yet, or perhaps I haven't finished formulating the questions.

My teaching over the years has shifted in style and substance. Early on, as a graduate student, I was personable and approachable and encouraged students to establish relationships within the classroom and with me as teacher/facilitator. Later, as an assistant professor, I continued in this vein. I enjoyed the classroom, feeling competent and creative and responsive there. Students responded to the attention and to my invitation to come more fully into the material by making connections between the sociology they were studying and their own life experiences. Toward this end I required journals for almost every class, suggesting that students use this opportunity to reflect on the ways that theories provided a framework for understanding what they saw and felt in the world around them. I stopped requiring journals several years into my teaching career, however, when the material that I was reading became too personal and the sense of responsibility to the students too great.

Part of my teaching dilemma was the asymmetrical nature of the classroom relationships. I required students to integrate self-reflection as a learning method; I revealed very little about myself and my politics. I felt guilty when students chose to come out to me, often as one of the first "authority" figures they risked telling, and I supported their story without offering any of mine back in return. I talked about being a mother, using examples for lectures on gender socialization and role overload. But, the rest of my life remained privatized and privileged information.

In many ways I don't regret the decision to maintain this privacy. Given the conservative university environment, it was self-protective to maintain some structured distance between myself and students. The first time I brought a gay and lesbian panel into a class (including the mother of a gay son), students pulled out bibles and began reading together aloud and praying for the salvation of the panel members. Unprepared for this action, I was warned of the severity of antigay sentiment on the campus.

I have had the opportunity to mentor individual lesbian students, who had previously gone unnoticed by faculty who were unaware of their isolation and lack of opportunity. This has been gratifying, as I have been inspired and motivated by the courage of young women who refuse to hide who they are for the sake of surviving in academia. I know there is a generational effect, but I also feel that the presence of women like myself makes it possible for younger women to believe in their ability to create space for their presence in institutions like academia. The mother in me is anxious for them, but I believe that their uncompromising position moves the boundaries for all of us.

Part of the dilemma for lesbian academics is that we are isolated from one another by department and discipline. Without community, there is no context for moving from strategies of survival to celebrations of difference that create a richer, more encompassing academic enterprise. I have felt grateful for isolated incidents of acceptance, but they do not accumulate into a home for those of us who are different from our colleagues. I've witnessed my difference being used as evidence that diversity is alive and well, without any awareness or understanding of my isolation and pain.

Another way that we are hurt is by each other. As women trying to fit into structures that at best ignore us, and at worst persecute us, we divide against one another as a strategy of survival. I've experienced this divisiveness on the basis of sexuality, with heterosexual women distancing for safety. I sat silent while the women's studies faculty, in the early years of the program, discussed ways to protect their image so that they would not be perceived as "man-hating lesbians." In finding my voice, and trying to advance an agenda for inclusiveness, I find myself included as a representative of the lesbian perspective, as if my race and class privilege are muted by my sexuality.

As lesbians in academia we have all, to some extent, internalized the expectations that we discard our sexuality when we enter this domain. But, I am encouraged by the ways that we are quietly, without great fanfare, making our presence known. I heard recently that a faculty member from another college, in conversation with a dean, came out in response to his observation that he had never met a lesbian. In another university in the area, a new untenured faculty member, hearing that rumors about her sexuality were circulating in the department, came out to the department chair and shared her concern about the ways that this information might be used to harm her relationships with students and other faculty. These individual acts of courage do accumulate, bringing sexuality out of the closet in academia, forcing those in the center (and others precariously close to the edge) to evaluate their perceptions, prejudices, and methods of protecting the status quo.

My struggle in academia has been how to integrate who I am as a mother, a feminist, a lesbian, a survivor of childhood abuse, and a sociologist into a meaningful whole. Pieces of who I am are revealed in my research (homelessness, women who kill their abusers, lesbian family, and lesbian health), but I have never, in a public forum, connected my identities to what I do as an academic sociologist. I am constantly challenged in a discipline where it is only safe to research, teach, and make public statements about lesbian and gay life when one is clearly and indisputably heterosexual with a career-path not marked by a primary interest in life outside the center. I am frustrated by the rules of sociology that dictate an objective, impersonal, detached approach with room for exceptions only if the status quo is not too seriously challenged or compromised. And I long for a context where fear in academic institutions is replaced by a collective willingness to challenge and change structures that place almost everyone outside the center. Making connections between who I am and what I do has been an effort to contribute to this challenge and to future change.

Out
in the
Maine Woods

Maggie Fournier

College of Nursing,
University of Southern Maine

7

I was born a lesbian. I am very happy about my life now, though this was not always true when I was growing up. At seventeen, I fell in love with a beautiful woman. Our love was natural and spontaneous. My lover and I worked as lifeguards and we lived together during the summers. We went to different colleges, but we spent our weekends together, often at the expense of my studies. I was happy in a way that I had never imagined. I didn't have a grasp on what was happening to me, at first, because in my home the topic of homosexuality was strictly taboo. Growing up French Canadian and attending Catholic schools for twelve years gave me no context in which to frame this new relationship. I had never heard the words lesbian, gay, and homosexual. I didn't care for these labels and, on some level, I wanted to distance myself from naming what I was experiencing. In the early months of this new love, a parish priest told me that I must stop my feelings of love for another woman. With that, I left the confessional and left my religion, too. I was so much in love and, at the same time, experiencing profound loneliness. I knew that my love was a secret to be guarded above all else. Who would ever accept this kind of love? Who would ever support me and understand? I was cut off from sharing my happiness with friends and family. Even my church had abandoned me.

With a fake I.D. I gained entrance to and I danced in clubs with names like *The Continental* and *The Pink Triangle* (such a strange name for a bar, I remember thinking). I felt kinship to all of the women I met in those smoke-filled lounges. We were socialized into closets and committed to subtle codes and secrets amid the haze and darkness. I grew accustomed to lying to those who must never learn the truth. The Stonewall Rebellion which occurred during that period meant very little to me. Those people must be crazy, I thought. It seemed so safe and rational to stay hidden. Why risk the rejection of being found out?

The love affair with my girlfriend ended after three years and left me feeling devastated. My neighbor, Cheryl, comforted me in my grief. Over time, she would become the true love of my life.

In 1972, we started our life together as a couple. Upon graduation from college we began our professional lives as nurses. Like newlyweds, we decorated our first apartment with new furniture and dishes. We worked and paid for all of our housekeeping possessions as there were no bridal showers and wedding gifts to help us on our way.

At twenty-five, I became the youngest faculty member at the University of Southern Maine. My partner was offered an administrative position in Maine, and although we considered offers in Alaska, Maine won out because it had always been special to us. It was 1976, and I was fresh out of graduate school. As my academic preparation is in public health and gerontology, I assumed a position teaching courses in these areas. In 1982, I was awarded tenure and promoted to the rank of associate professor.

Our first home in Maine was a tiny apartment over a garage which had the most glorious view of the Atlantic. We would swim right outside our front porch in the summers and, at night, the lighthouse provided us with a revolving stream of light. During those first few years, we lived quietly and did not have a large circle of friends. We considered ourselves to be private people and thought it best to keep our life somewhat guarded. Besides, we didn't want to upset anyone, particularly our families and coworkers. As for Cheryl, I referred to her as "the woman I live with." I assumed that if my colleagues were open, they'd figure out that we were gay (never the word lesbian) or if they were more comfortable thinking of me as a heterosexual, then so be it. It never occurred to me that I felt shame about being a lesbian and at the time, I would have vehemently denied it. But the truth is, I was ashamed of myself. Today, I understand the high price I paid to be in the closet during that period in my life. I hope that no young person will ever hold inside them the beliefs that were so depressing and hurtful to me as a young woman. I thought that, in some way, it was dishonorable to be a lesbian and that others would not want to be my friend if they knew about me. I believed my family would hate me if they knew the truth. And, I believed I would never have a child of my own to love and to hold.

In the early eighties, I met a wonderful gay colleague while working on an interdisciplinary project. He coaxed us out into the lesbian and gay political world of Maine. We soon discovered the Maine Lesbian and Gay

Political Alliance (MLGPA) and I started volunteering at the newly formed AIDS Project. We made new friends and drew courage from their abilities to be open. Coming out is a process. Once started, the layers peel away and you become genuine; in my case, I became a happy person again. It was such a relief not to hide. Coming out encouraged Cheryl and me to revisit an important issue in our lives. We would often speak about how we thought we'd be great parents. Yet, I was tormented that I would never have a child and tried to accept this as a consequence of being a lesbian. We thought that it would be unfair for a child to have lesbian moms. We were certain that our families would never accept the idea and we weren't sure that we would find a physician who would assist us in the process. Every obstacle seemed insurmountable until we found the courage to follow our hearts. It took a great deal of courage to decide become parents. The turning point in this matter came when we both understood the responsibility we had for living our own lives. It was during my pregnancy that I discovered the strength to come out of the closet completely. I vowed never to go back. In order to raise healthy kids, you cannot live a lie. The best legacy we can give to our children is one of truth. In 1986, I gave birth to our daughter Emily.

My colleagues reacted to the news of my pregnancy with a certain degree of amazement. I was more than a little nervous sharing this information with the dean. To my great delight, she arose from her desk and hugged me. It was a truly memorable moment for me. She later related that while many of the office staff were surprised to learn of my pregnancy, the reality of this event brought a new sense of openness to the group and went a long way in combatting homophobia. Over the years, my coworkers have come to know Emily and Cheryl. I am generally regarded as a garden variety parent, often joining in on discussions of softball games and school projects. Since the birth of our child, we are frequently invited to speak on campus. The increased interest in the lives of lesbians, particularly those who have conceived children through donor insemination, is astounding.

In my role as a professor of nursing, I pay close attention to how family is being handled in our curriculum. At meetings, I raise questions and make comments as to how our classes address issues of diversity. I am invested in assuring that lesbian and gay persons and families are included when we teach family theory and reproductive health in the classroom, and I monitor to what extent discussions about HIV are free of bias and homophobia.

I've come to believe that homophobia on campus is insidious. At times, I am aware of a feeling of coldness or indifference toward me which I suspect is rooted in bigotry. As it is generally not politically correct for bias to be overt, it is sometimes difficult to read behavior which is excluding or demeaning. Once, early in my career, a department colleague questioned my ability to teach nursing based on the fact that I was a lesbian. She made this comment to a friend of mine who later related it to me. I confronted the former and told her that I would take legal action (as if I were really protected) if she ever discussed the matter again. It never came up again. In general, though, my lesbianism does not seem to be an issue for most faculty and students.

While I do not generally discuss my personal life a great deal with my students, I am comfortable sharing that I am a lesbian. I am careful not to use the classroom as a soapbox for my political beliefs. However, in the process of delivering a lecture, if I mention my partner or child in an example in the same way a heterosexual colleague might, it is likely to be noticed. I will raise the issue of homosexuality if it is relevant to class and judging from comments offered, many students feel inspired to hear a lesbian faculty member speak out. However, amid generally positive evaluations, occasionally I'll receive students' comments that I am too political and/or too "feminist" in my approach. Some students (often men) mention that too much is made of feminism in our curriculum. One student remarked that he found visiting me at my office to be intimidating because of the material I have chosen to hang on the wall: an article on domestic partnership, another on including children of gay and lesbian parents in holiday festivities, a poster from the march on Washington, and pictures of my child. Even more troubling is that this student, like so many others in our society, was offended by what they perceive to be "flaunting it." It is our role as faculty to teach the truth and to enlighten and we are entitled under academic freedom. My students are the future nurses who will encounter homosexuals in their practice on a daily basis. I am not threatened, nor will I be silenced from helping them to understand diversity.

In 1987, the board of trustees of the University of Maine System added sexual orientation to the protected classes in their nondiscrimination policy. This action, which drew little attention in the press was well received by lesbian and gay employees. We believed that the university acted courageously in promoting the policy. We felt that our rights were protected. I was soon to discover that it meant very little.

Early in 1990, my partner lost a lucrative position as a vice president of a health care consortium. This came as a devastating blow to us emotionally and financially. Soon, we would have to buy a single health insurance plan for her which would cost approximately four hundred dollars a month.

Given our increasing financial concerns, I decided to enroll her in my family insurance plan through the University of Maine System. After all, I was aware that the university had a clear policy on nondiscrimination on the basis of sexual orientation in all matters of university affairs and that it self-insures, thereby controlling the rules. I surmised that some reasonable accommodation would be made given the board of trustees' nondiscrimination policy. I hit the proverbial wall when I challenged the University System on the matter of my health insurance benefits.

First, I filled out the necessary forms to add a family member to the existing plan. While I did not expect this to be processed unnoticed, it actually caused quite an uproar. This was the first time anyone tried to test the resolve of the nondiscrimination policy. No one wanted to take responsibility for granting me this right under the policy. In fact, for months my request was bounced from one office to another until it finally came to the attention of the chancellor who, in turn, backed away from the issue by saying it was a campus matter (which clearly, it was not). I became a campus activist fighting for my rights and those of my sisters and brothers. Immediately, I contacted the affirmative action officer on campus. Because lesbians and gay men do not have legal protection in Maine, she was of little practical help. It is my opinion that the university's nondiscrimination policy on sexual orientation is deceptive and meaningless. The university refused to stand by its word and grant me the same consideration as my married colleagues. The policy clearly discriminated against me and my life-partner of twenty-two years.

A call to Gay and Lesbian Advocates and Defenders (GLAD) in Boston was met with great interest. GLAD is a public interest law firm serving the gay community in areas of civil rights matters. Mary L. Bonauto, Esq., Civil Rights Director at GLAD, represented me in filing a grievance with the Associated Faculties of the University of Maine System (AFUM) against the University System. She assisted me in building a system-wide coalition of lesbian, gay, and friendly activists called Advocates For Equality in Family Benefits (AEFB). Bonauto was instrumental in convincing AFUM to take my case to arbitration. I lost in arbitration because the arbitrator refused to take the high ground and do the right thing. The evidence was there for her to rule in my favor. She ruled that the provisions for domestic partner benefits needed to be spelled out clearly in the union contract. Nonetheless, this setback did not discourage us. During the last four years, we have worked diligently with the union's bargaining council and its general membership to change the language in the contract to reflect parity. Primarily, the strategy has been one of education.

As a result of our efforts, the faculty union developed a standing committee on lesbian and gay concerns and employees of the University of Southern Maine organized a lesbian, gay, and bisexual employees association. In 1994, the president of USM appointed a Lesbian, Gay, and Bisexual Task Force to study campus climate and other issues of concern and AFUM and the University System agreed to a joint committee to make recommendations for domestic partner benefits for employees. I served on all of these committees for a period of two years. In January of 1996, the joint AFUM/University committee completed its work. It unanimously recommended that same sex domestic partners be considered the equivalent of spouses for purposes of University policies and benefits. The University System now joins approximately sixty colleges and universities nationwide who offer benefits to partners of lesbians and gay employees.

I am proud of the journey which has brought me to this point in my career and in my personal life. It's been a trip well worth taking. I love my partner and daughter, and I love myself, too. I've found that being "out" at this university has meant that I can fight for our rights, teach the truth, and make true friends.

As lesbians and gays, we have much more to accomplish with respect to education, parity, and acceptance. I hope that, someday, none of us has to fight for our jobs, or benefits, or the basic freedoms that heterosexuals enjoy. I'd like to believe that my university will play a significant role in this struggle for parity and acceptance.

Out in Academic Psychiatry

Nanette K. Gartrell

Department of Psychiatry,
University of California, San Francisco

8

I was the first out lesbian physician on the Harvard Medical School faculty. I was at Harvard as a psychiatric resident (1976–79), as an instructor (1979–83), and as an assistant professor (1983–87) on the full-time academic track. I had come out selectively in medical school, and I was out as I applied for residency in 1974. Having already published several articles as a University of California medical student, my prospects for admission to a top program were good.

I had been wooed by Columbia and essentially assured of a position there by the psychiatry chair during my interview with him. My final interviewer was Robert Spitzer, architect of the *Diagnostic and Statistical Manual of Mental Disorders (DSM)*. He began by inquiring if I thought my lesbianism indicated I wanted to be a man. He then asked if I was butch or femme (fifteen years before we reclaimed these terms). I replied that I did not see the relevance of these questions to my application for residency. He then discussed the elimination of the pathological diagnosis of "homosexuality" from the *DSM*. I told him that I objected to the diagnosis "ego-dystonic homosexuality," (a new diagnosis, referring to homosexuals who were dissatisfied with their sexual orientation) because the *DSM* did not include the parallel diagnosis "ego-dystonic heterosexuality." When he questioned the usefulness of such a diagnosis, I said that I had come across many radical feminists who were extremely dissatisfied with their heterosexuality and would have been delighted to convert to lesbianism. I felt that his ques-

Nanette Gartrell would like to thank Joan Biren, Mary Eichbauer, and Marny Hall for their assistance in the preparation of this article.

tions were inapproproiate and that he did not conduct an interview which was pertinent to my application to the program. Several weeks later, I was informed that I had been rejected at Columbia.

My undergraduate mentor, who had recently become the psychiatry chair at Duke, contacted the chair at Columbia to inquire about my rejection. My mentor learned that I had been rejected because of my lesbianism. Columbia, he was told, had a psychoanalytically oriented department with very traditional ideas about lesbianism. The admissions committee had decided that my comfort with my lesbianism (that I did not consider it a problem)—rendered me incompatible with Columbia's training program. Consequently, I ended up at Harvard.

During residency, my visibility as a lesbian was dramatically increased after I came out to a woman supervisor who rarely kept confidences. As I had anticipated, she informed the entire department. Her disclosure saved me the effort of coming out to each person individually. Thereafter, if new residents or faculty made heterosexist assumptions about me—typically through questions about my marital status—I laughed politely and said matter-of-factly, "Oh, no! I'm a lesbian. But I'm involved in a committed relationship—if that's what you are asking." I would not make any effort to allay the inquirer's embarrassment, because I had learned years before that such care-taking typically made me feel worse rather than better. Those efforts to mop up others' *faux pas* gave colleagues license to unleash hefty doses of well-intentioned homophobia (such as advice on how unsafe it was to be out at Harvard), which I found aggravating and invalidating. A matter-of-fact response to mistaken assumptions by new acquaintances allowed me to assert myself pridefully without getting stuck in the quagmire of a colleague's homophobia.

My academic career progressed more rapidly than those of most of my psychiatry peers at Harvard—despite my lesbianism and political activism. I went from residency to a full-time academic position as an out lesbian psychiatrist. I taught in various sexuality courses, lectured on and off campus about coming out, and supported colleagues in their struggles to come out. I organized lesbian physicians locally and nationally. I served on the Harvard Medical Area Joint Commission on the Status of Women. I established and coedited the first newsletter for Harvard medical area women.

At regular intervals efforts were made to silence me, but I resisted. For example, my very conservative department chair at Beth Israel Hospital objected to most of my projects—from organizing the American Psychiatric Association's ERA boycott of unratified states, to advocating blind review by the *American Journal of Psychiatry*, to exposing sexual abuse of patients by psychiatrists. I had always been impressed with our hospital president's sensitivity to issues of discrimination, and I decided to approach him about the obstacles that were being put in my path. I explained that I was wasting valuable time and energy butting heads over my political work with my chair, and that I needed to know if his resistance represented hospital and medical school policy, or merely his own attitudes. The president assured me that my work was not incompatible with hospital policy, and said that I should use my institutional affiliation whenever I spoke to the media. His backing allowed me to take on new crusades with greater vigor, unimpeded by concerns that I might be fired for my activities. Also, closeted lesbian and gay colleagues began coming out themselves after hearing my account of his support.

Although my department chair had been unhappy with my politics since I had joined the faculty, I was not treated differently from outspoken heterosexual women in the department. We were all subjected to the same sexist double-standard for promotions. When I became eligible for promotion from instructor to assistant professor, the chair refused to nominate me until I had twice the number of publications required of male peers. Several straight white male physicians who wrote promotional letters commended my efforts to educate the medical community about homophobia, and described me as a role model. Although I never obtained inside information concerning the promotions board meeting, I suspected that my promotion was sustained—despite the lukewarm support of my department chair—because my lesbianism was presented in a straightforward manner rather than charged with secrecy.

My partner of twenty years, Dee Mosbacher, began her psychiatric residency at Cambridge Hospital in 1983. When she was applying, she was open about her wish to rejoin me in Boston. We had been commuting from Boston to Houston for the four years that she had been in medical school at Baylor. Her lesbianism fortunately proved no obstacle to being admitted to one of the most popular training programs in the United States.

While I was at Beth Israel Hospital and Dee at Cambridge Hospital, we occasionally attended each other's departmental social functions. Although we never felt unwelcome at any of these events, we were the only lesbians in attendance. Neither of us particularly enjoyed this work-related socializing. We considered it more work than pleasure. However, it is possible that our experiences might have been different if there had been more diversity in our respective departments.

After Dee completed her residency in 1987, we moved to San Francisco. I was thrilled to be returning to California, but I was sad to leave my position at Harvard. I had contributed substantially to increased lesbian/gay visibility at Harvard Medical School, and it was difficult to leave the supportive environment I had worked so hard to create. I took a position as associate clinical professor at the University of California, San Francisco. Dee became the medical director for Mental Health for the County of San Mateo. We were both completely out in accepting these positions.

At UCSF, I teach feminist theory and ethics. I come out during the first class of the feminist theory course I teach with friend and colleague Karen Johnson. We ask students to introduce themselves and invite them to tell us something about how their racial, ethnic, class, or religious background, or sexual orientation has affected their feelings about themselves. We model answers by listing our various identities and discussing their importance to us. Karen discusses her working-class background in relation to her professional identity. I state that I am a lesbian and talk about my early education in oppression as a result of my lesbian identification. The first time I came out in this fashion, approximately twenty students got up and walked out. Since they never returned, we presumed that they had dropped the course. I had mixed feelings about their departure. Partly I was hurt and angry at such a blatant demonstration of homophobia. At the same time, I was surprised to find that I felt empowered by my ability to scatter people so effectively simply by saying the word "lesbian." I rationalized that those students would have been disruptive had they stayed. It is sad to realize, though, that they were the individuals who needed our course the most.

Some students objected to identifying their sexual orientation. Although such disclosure was never a requirement, they considered even optional mention of it an inappropriate invasion of privacy. Complaints reached other faculty, who relayed their own disapproval of our teaching style by passing on the criticisms. For example, a colleague who considers herself a friend said, "Your ears must have been burning during our meeting last week. I know that your course is very popular, but I understand that many students are very upset about the way that you teach it. Do you think it's a good idea to force students to come out in class?" In such instances, I feel obligated to defend my teaching techniques as well as respond to my colleagues' homophobia. They would never consider it invasive for heterosexuals to state marital status or race/ethnicity, and so on. I explain that we establish a learning environment in which individual experiences of discrimination can be shared as a way of understanding feminist theory. Regardless of the apparent impact of this explanation, I feel disheartened after such encounters. Karen and I talk, and she reminds me that efforts to suppress us sometimes focus on criticizing our teaching. At other times, they target some aspect of our marginal status—my outspokenness as a lesbian, or her advocacy of a women's health specialty. We discuss the obstacles we have overcome in teaching feminist theory within a white, patriarchal institution. We reiterate our accomplishments and bolster each other for the next round.

For the last three years, no students have departed during the introductions; each student has chosen to identify her/his sexual orientation, and we have received glowing evaluations at the end of the course. We consistently hear that ours is the most meaningful and memorable course in students' entire medical education (our students come from the medical school, graduate nursing program, school of pharmacy, and various science doctoral programs).

I consider myself a fringe faculty member at UCSF. Although there is no dearth of collegiality concerning lesbian/gay issues, my views on feminist therapy and women's healthcare are considered too progressive by most colleagues. I feel more of an outsider because of my feminism than my lesbianism. In recent years I have been willing to collaborate with colleagues only if they share my political beliefs concerning the project at hand. Such choices may contribute to some professional isolation, but they engender much less frustration, and they significantly enhance my productivity. For example, in my recent study of physician sexual abuse, I put together an interdisciplinary research team of prominent UCSF faculty. I selected non-homophobic individuals who were willing to speak out about sexual exploitation by physicians.

I am currently conducting a multicity, prospective, longitudinal study of lesbian families. My research team has been following 154 mothers and their children since the mothers became pregnant by donor insemination (DI). We will continue to interview the families at designated intervals until the children become adults. Topics of investigation include: the impact of having a child on the mother's relationship (if coupled) or dating (if single); coparenting issues and concerns; the impact of donor choice on the child; the child's growth and development; the demands of motherhood versus career; legal and contractual arrangements; child care and school decisions; and the impact of homophobia on the family. This twenty-five-plus-year study began in 1986. As with most of my research projects, it is funded entirely out of our own pockets. That my academic career has advanced through publications derived from unfunded research projects distinguishes me from most of my colleagues at Harvard and UCSF, where investigations are typically supported by governmental or other agencies. However, if we had delayed the launch of this project until institutional homophobia was no longer an obstacle to obtaining funding, we would have lost the opportunity to document the first generation of DI lesbian families.

As I look back on my academic career, I find that being out has given momentum and purpose to my work. I have educated students and colleagues about diversity and homophobia. I have smoothed the way for others to come out without repercussions to their academic careers. Certainly I have had to face more obstacles than my white, male colleagues, but that is to be expected for any outsider to the dominant culture. I feel good about my career accomplishments, believe that I have achieved as much or more as my straight colleagues, and am proud to have maintained my integrity as a lesbian in the work that I have done.

Becoming
a Lesbian
in Academia

Barbara W. Gerber

Counseling and Psychological Services,
State University of New York at Oswego

9

I began college teaching in 1961, as a doctoral student. At that time I was a married mother with a three-year-old child. I came to my present campus as an assistant professor in 1965. I didn't really know I was a lesbian until early 1972. However, the woman on the 1965 hiring committee told me later that she had been sure that I was "one of us." She told that story in social gatherings later on, maintaining that she knew before I knew.

That first realization of being a lesbian was the result of logic; I figured that because I was in love with a woman that I must be a lesbian. Having decided, I went forward with my life accepting this as the case. However, I was out to very few in those days as my lover and I were both still married to our spouses! Coming out happened slowly as I was also developing a growing awareness of the effects of homophobia in our culture and within myself. By 1975 several colleagues knew, and now I am open with most everyone—although I do not always bring it up.

In 1989 I began volunteering in National Coalition Building Institute workshops, workshops which are designed to address issues of diversity and oppression. We did a weekend workshop in which I was a leader of a small group, and in which there was a mix of faculty, staff, and students. Several were students in my department. The workshop trainer asked me to come forward to share a story of personal oppression with the larger group, and I agreed to share an instance of homophobia. Later, after thinking about that situation and that one of those students might well remark to the department chair about my homosexuality, I decided to tell him directly. I described the workshop and the request to testify. Then, I said, "So, if someone comes to tell you about me, I want you to be able to say that you already know." I concluded, "So, I am a lesbian; you heard it from me." He responded, "Are you sure? You know, you might be wrong." I left his office stifling my laughter; I was pretty sure he would not understand it.

I spent several years as an administrator in the late 1970s and early 1980s, during which time I was increasingly out with more and more colleagues. Shortly after returning to full-time teaching in 1985, I began presenting research results, and doing local and state level workshops on gay, lesbian and bisexual students' concerns and needs to school counselors and others from agency and private settings.

Shortly after the end of my first semester's return to teaching, a student from my psychology of women class came to tell me of Wayne, whom she had overheard telling others that I was a "dyke, and a man hater." His "proof" was that he got a lower grade than his female friends had. I invited Wayne to my office, and told him that he had been overheard talking about me, and that indeed he was correct about part of what he had said in the laboratory. "I *am* a lesbian, but you are wrong about why you got that grade." I went on, "I want you to look at my gradebook and the syllabus, and take note of where your total score falls." At that point, flustered as he was, he recognized that his final grade was actually higher than what his average would have dictated. I found this whole conversation difficult, because until then I had been reluctant to be so open, and I had believed that such information was not to be shared gratuitously with students. I do come out in the classroom when it is appropriate, and I use it to promote the goals of the course. I see this as an ethical issue, and do not feel that "coming out" is ethical behavior unless it also serves the course objectives. This is received quite well by most of our graduate students.

Since then, I have used that experience with Wayne to illustrate to other students how easy it is for misperceptions to arise and be extended. These days, I approach those situations differently. My contention is that folks need to know because otherwise they could, and likely would, assume otherwise. As I teach developmental and educational psychology, I often speak about my own children so I can see that it would be easy for students to assume that I could not possibly be a lesbian. I now create a classroom where it is appropriate for me to come out. This does not always occur immediately, but certainly no later than a third of the way through a course. I am delighted to say that it has resulted in very good feedback from students of all orientations. The gay and lesbian students often already know because I advise BiGALA on campus, but they are thankful because it gives them room to also be forthright. The remainder of the students respond sometimes with admiration and they often share thoughts about their family members—seldom with negative commentary. In the past several years I have had only one student challenge me in class: her conviction was that homosexuality is sinful. I was able to suggest to her that while I believed in her right to hold that conviction, I didn't believe homosexuality was sinful. That was difficult, to be sure. I gave her some material to read on gay, lesbian, and bisexual teens and their anguish. It was interesting that she raised the issue as I knew she was planning to work in a religiously conservative school.

I have never been treated badly, to my face anyway, regarding my coming out. Back in the early 1970s I was welcomed by my psychology department colleague, the one who always believed I was a lesbian anyway. My general experience is one of being openly welcomed by other gays and lesbians whether or not they themselves are out. Today "straight" folks are sometimes surprised but often quite accepting—which I attribute as much to their good sense as to the fact that the acceptance and respect I have earned in the thirty-plus years I have been on my campus. There are of course still folks whose response is not at all positive and I am resigned to their approach to life but I am thankful that they are a minority. There are also folks who do not really know that I am a lesbian, and wouldn't believe it if I told them myself. Some of these folks are simply not sensitive to their environment nor the people in it; others cannot conceive of a woman being a lesbian who has been "married with children."

I think that cultural antipathy, the resultant fear of harm, and one's internalized homophobia lock each of us firmly within the closet. We tell ourselves that if we come out our friends will disappear, our families will disown us, we'll be fired; but each time it becomes easier. The "thank-you's" from younger people serve as great reinforcement and encouragement. Most of the obstacles to coming out, I think in retrospect, are tied to the need human beings have to belong, to be accepted and loved by family and friends.

I was thirty-six when I began coming out to myself. I feel fortunate to have been a late bloomer, in that I did not personalize societal homophobia during adolescence when we all need so much to belong. I think it took until my thirties to discover because the culture during the late 1940s and early 1950s offered little or no information about any sexual issues. Retrospectively, I recognize my attraction to other women in adolescence and young adulthood, but it never occurred to me to question marriage. I certainly do remember people on the school bus talking about queers, but they were boys referring to boys. Mostly, I suspect that what slowed me up in the recognition of myself as a lesbian was my own ignorance about possibilities, and the estrangement from oneself that came as part of the female socialization in the post-World War II environment.

Because I only came to know myself as lesbian in the 1970s, I think my experience was probably quite different from others of my age who were certain of their sexuality at a younger age. I never accepted that there was anything wrong with me, even though my psychologist husband tried valiantly to convince me that I needed therapy. There were times I was afraid that being a lesbian would interfere with with my career. Perhaps it did, but not in a manner that can be easily assessed. Being a woman was probably a larger interfering factor than being a lesbian because of the rampant misogyny in our society. I am convinced that many male colleagues liked it that I behaved in a manner that desexualized our work situations. In the mid–60s men complimented women by telling us, "What I like about you is that you think like a man." I believe that message contained within it the subtext, "I feel comfortable, not sexually challenged, working with you." I think that feeling prevails among many men, even today; they more easily work comfortably with lesbians because they are not confused about the interpersonal messages; that sexual tension, often described by straight folks, simply does not exist. These days I am able to tell male colleagues that I think they are neat, or that I love working with them, without causing them great confusion. That of course is not only a benefit from being known as a lesbian; such privilege also comes with age. Women who are obviously "older" are seldom treated by their male colleagues as sexually attractive, and flirtation is minimized.

When my partner and I began our relationship we worked in different locations. She is a librarian and archivist and I am a psychologist and counselor educator. Since 1980 we have both been privileged to work on the same campus. We team-taught a women's studies course for four semesters in the 1980s. We are now team teaching an honors program course.

My research and writing have always been limited by my teaching load, and in my early years, raising children. The research I have presented, on gay, lesbian, and bisexual teens' perceptions of high school counselors, was begun several years ago. I used the preliminary data to extract narratives to share with counselors in workshops. My plans for further and more extensive data gathering were shelved when no local school districts granted access for the questionnaire distribution. I am part of a campus-community group that is committed to working against all oppressions. We do prejudice reduction workshops on campus, and for schools and other groups in the community. I am one of the group leaders and always work as an out lesbian. I also advised the campus Bi-GALA group for several years; in fact I helped get it started in the early 1970s as a support group when I was working half-time in the College Counseling Center.

I have been politically active on our campus on lesbian/gay/bisexual issues, although not extensively. I helped work on the "ROTC question" a few years ago; we got the faculty governance and administration to support a resolution to ban ROTC from our campus by 1996. In 1977 I was one of over a hundred women who started the Lesbian Caucus of the National Women's Studies Association (NWSA) at the constitutional convention.

The male Bi-GALA advisor and I tried to organize a faculty-staff lesbian/gay/bisexual group in 1991. We did not get a good response, probably because there are just as many folks who are afraid to "come out" as there are those of us who are out—actually likely more. We did succeed in lobbying the student services division to appoint a staff member as advocate for lesbian, gay, and bisexual students.

Since I first came out, I have been twice promoted—to professor in 1976, and to distinguished service professor in 1992. These promotions required documentation of my work as teacher and researcher, as well as in campus and community service. Especially in the most recent promotion, my work was subject to the scrutiny of colleagues and administrators beyond our campus. Testimonials were required from past students and colleagues from local and other campuses. That I am a lesbian could not have been hidden.

I was, like many lesbians of my age, heterosexually married. Being married was a somewhat uneasy time for me; I never really felt settled about it. When I fell in love with my partner, it was then clear to me why I had felt uneasy, and just as my mother had said, "I knew it!" My partner and I have been together for twenty-five years. Our three children have grown up and are all in their mid-thirties. One is a partnered lesbian, two are married and raising families.

I view myself as still in the process of becoming a lesbian in academia and other settings. When my daughter was a toddler she once told us, "I'm being the best Jaime I can!" I follow her lead in being the best I can be as each day comes along.

Out on a Small Southern Campus

Charlotte L. Goedsche

Foreign Language Department (German),
University of North Carolina at Asheville

10

It is not true, as some say, that I came out at the chancellor's wife's tea party my first year on the faculty of the University of North Carolina at Asheville. She was serving coffee. I was an assistant professor, was very glad to finally have a tenure-track position at a liberal arts college, and was absolutely thrilled at the prospect of spending the rest of my career in the beautiful Blue Ridge Mountains of western North Carolina with my spouse, Cynthia.

After chatting around the coffee pot at the chancellor's residence, the twenty or so of us (new faculty women and wives of new faculty men) were asked to take seats in the circle of chairs. I happened to sit about one-quarter of the way around the circle to the left of Lin, the chancellor's wife, and am convinced that my life might be very different if I had happened to sit on her right.

Lin announced that we would now introduce ourselves to the whole circle, and asked that we also share something about our families and our interests. She began, and then turned to her right. I watched and listened as, one by one, the women mentioned their husbands, their children, their hobbies, and again and again voiced their hopes that they could get to know the other women better. I was touched by their obvious sincerity, and, as my turn came closer and closer, slowly realized that I could not—and would not—lie any longer about who I was, even by omission.

I don't recall exactly what I said, after beginning with "I don't know how to say this," but I do remember speaking of moving back from Germany five years earlier to be with Cynthia, the love of my life, and of our moving south together to Asheville so I could accept the German position.

And then, fully "out," but not knowing how to wrap it up gracefully, I blurted out: "And I hope I get tenure!" The woman whose turn it now was patted me on the arm and said, "And we hope you do, too."

I was as surprised as anyone else in the room that day in March, 1986. I was born in 1944, and I grew up in the closet and didn't even know it had a door until I was in my mid–thirties. My coming out to my parents and, years later, at Lin's party, was motivated, I believe, by a deep-seated and strong desire for integrity; integrity not simply in the ethical sense of telling the truth, but truly in the sense of being whole. I have come to believe that a lesbian cannot achieve a sense of wholeness until she embraces herself completely. Every step out of the closet is a step into self-integration, toward wholeness.

Even with such a dramatic coming-out party, it wasn't always easy at first to come out to the next person and the next, but in general, the more I came out, the more support I received, and the more my sense of self-worth was corroborated. As my self-esteem grew, the more positive I appeared when coming out, and thus the more positive the responses grew. My coming-out snowballed. Being open about who I am, both on and off campus, very soon became a habit—I rarely think about it anymore.

Coming out is said to be the most powerful political act a gay person can make, and it is essential for promoting tolerance and acceptance. In fact, research has shown that "personal contact with a gay man or lesbian is a powerful predictor of heterosexuals' attitudes toward gay men" (Herek and Glunt, 242). Clearly it initially takes courage for a person from a reviled group to be honest about who they are, so by coming out, a lesbian or gay professor offers straight students a role model, too. Thus a professor's coming out is beneficial to all students, regardless of their sexual orientation. "Homosexual Professors Owe It to Their Students to 'Come Out,'" as John D'Emilio titled his article in the *Chronicle of Higher Education*.

Being out has enabled me to serve as a role model both on and off campus; an advocate for lesbian, gay and bisexual students and youth; a resource for colleagues, students, and citizens of all sexual orientations; and a catalyst for political and social change.

It is in this spirit that I will share a number of my experiences as a lesbian professor, describing in some detail how I have come out to my classes and to the faculty as a whole, and some of the consequences of my being out. I will also speak about working for change in university policies and organizing in a national professional association.

Three attitudes have been essential to my progress. These are, first, a willingness to come out; second, a cheerful determination to turn negatives into positives; and third, wakeful sensitivity to emerging opportunities for educating and for influencing policymaking. I hope my story will encourage others to discover what doors they can open at their own institutions.

Since reading D'Emilio's article, I have made it a point to come out to all of my classes. Unlike my initial coming out at the party, I always wait until I have built a good rapport with the class, and the students have a sense of what I'm like as a person. This takes some weeks, and the timing usually works out well for me to come out to my first-semester classes on 11 October, National Coming Out Day. (For more information on NCOD and on coming out, see Rob Eichberg's excellent book, *Coming Out: An Act of Love.*)

Since every class has its own collective personality, I come out to each class differently, but generally I begin by giving the history of the pink triangle. (I have several rose quartz triangle pins that a friend made, and I wear one every day on my blazer.) The majority of students still don't know that homosexuals were arrested in Nazi Germany and interned in work camps. I often draw parallels between the Nazi's attitudes toward minorities and the bigotry expressed in our country today toward religious, racial, ethnic, and sexual minorities, among others, and talk a bit about prejudice as a defense mechanism in people with low self-esteem. I usually mention the lack of civil rights protection for lesbians and gays in the United States and in North Carolina, of which most students have little awareness.

In any case, I always close with something about my spouse and our long-term, mutually supportive relationship, and with something thoroughly nonthreatening, like our hobbies of birding and listening to classical music. In elementary German class I conclude with family photos, and we practice *Bruder, Schwester, Onkel,* and so forth, with pictures of Cynthia's siblings and their children. Although history provides a convenient rationale for coming out in German class, I'm sure a hook can be found in any discipline to initiate faculty's coming out.

At first I allowed about five minutes for coming out, but now I ask the class if they have any questions, and in some instances we have taken the full hour to talk about prejudice, civil rights, gay parenting, and any number of other issues the class brings up.

Of the several hundred students I've come out to by now, only two have let it be known through their posture that they disapproved. There have also been a few negative comments on the evaluations the students fill out at the end of the semester, but this is a very small price to pay for the obvious benefits to the other students and to society. (One student objected that

I talked to the class about my "sex life"! I don't know if he/she had a very vivid imagination or a very narrow mind.) Far outweighing the negative responses have been the very gratifying positive ones.

Sometimes coming out to students has had unintended and far-reaching consequences. In the fall of 1989 I arranged for the student newspaper to interview me for National Coming Out Day. After the article appeared, Marlon, one of my freshman advisees, came to my office. He came out to me and told me of the untenable situation at his parents' home, where he lived. His mother was a Christian fundamentalist and rigidly antigay, but for financial reasons Marlon had no choice but to live with her. It was only later that he told me details of the pain, both emotional and physical, which his parents had caused him since learning some years before that he was gay.

In March of 1990 Marlon attempted suicide. Afterwards, as he was just about to be released from the hospital, his social worker phoned me to say that she would have to release him to a homeless shelter, as his parents had refused to take him back. His mother had even threatened both the social worker and Marlon's counselor at the University of North Carolina at Asheville with bodily harm, blaming them for not "fixing" Marlon's homo-sexuality. I quickly consulted with Cynthia, and then drove to the hospital to pick him up. Thus began a three-year period of parenting a college student.

Cynthia and I watched Marlon's development with parental pride. He learned to channel his anger and energy into positive action. At the begin-ning of his junior year, Marlon cofounded the Gay and Lesbian Association, the first gay student organization at UNCA. GALA applied for and received funds to sponsor several panel discussions which were very well attended by students as well as by interested parties from outside the university.

Being out has led to my being asked by students to serve as faculty advi-sor for their campus groups, first GALA and then its successor, Sexual Minorities on Crusade for Equality (SMOCE), a group for all sexual minori-ties as well as for supportive straight students. SMOCE's first project was undertaken in October, when they handed out little bows they had made of purple ribbon for National Coming Out Day, and others of red ribbon for National AIDS Awareness Month, and asked students to sign banners that read: "I support equal rights for everyone." They collected over two hundred signatures; the banners were hung in the student center. Surely this is a sign of increased acceptance of lesbians and gays among the students of UNCA.

Some time after my coming-out party I came out formally to faculty in the scope of the faculty forums, monthly luncheon meetings where a faculty member could present their latest research, talk about their vacation in an exotic place, or about their hobby. I titled my presentation "Positively Gay," after Betty Berzon's book by the same title. My forum was well attended, and I received welcome support in the form of comments and a few notes in campus mail.

Since then, faculty members have used me as a resource, and some have invited me to speak to their classes. Others refer gay students to me as someone they can talk to about issues related to sexual orientation. Recently more and more students, both gay and straight, have been coming to me for suggestions or help on research papers and projects they have chosen to undertake for other professors on gay-related topics. This increased interest in gay issues on campus is a welcome development.

In my university service work, being out enables me to be politically active in matters of concern to sexual minorities. In 1989 I was appointed to the Minority Affairs Commission (MAC) by the Faculty Senate. The commission had been formed to improve the quality of minority life on campus, with "minority" understood according to the federal guidelines. For most of my first year on MAC, all meetings were devoted to African American issues, and I participated eagerly. As soon as there was a breather from our main task, however, I raised the issue of sexual minorities, quipping that I wasn't sure if I had been appointed to MAC as a minority representative or not. The vice chancellor for academic affairs was quick to assure me that I had not been appointed for that reason, but the issue was now on the table. I utilized the self-made opening for regretting that the vast majority of UNCA students were never exposed to facts about homosexuality. The vice chancellor was very surprised to learn this and suggested that a unit on homosexuality be offered in a course required of all undergraduates, called Health Promotion.

The director of health promotion encouraged me to develop a unit on homosexuality, which I presented the next academic year to seventeen health promotion classes. The health promotion curriculum has been revised, and the instructors now cover sexual orientation themselves.

At my suggestion the Minority Affairs Commission formed a subcommittee on gay and lesbian issues. Both gay and supportive straight colleagues, as well as a gay student, were invited to join the subcommittee. The first item on our agenda was to propose a nondiscrimination policy for UNCA. The chancellor of UNC at Chapel Hill, the flagship of the sixteen-school UNC system, had already issued a policy of nondiscrimination on the basis of sexual orientation for UNC. We tailored that policy to our institution, got the full committee's approval, and presented it to the faculty senate, where it passed unanimously. The policy appeared in the university catalogue and the student handbook the following fall.

In an effort to make the antidiscrimination policy system-wide, I drafted a resolution which our faculty senate passed unanimously, requesting the sixteen-campus faculty assembly to resolve to urge the president of the UNC system to issue a directive to all campuses to adopt a policy forbidding discrimination on the basis of sexual orientation of faculty, staff, and students. At its next meeting, the faculty assembly passed a somewhat altered resolution with the same intent, and at the beginning of the next semester one of our sister institutions in western North Carolina adopted a nondiscrimination policy.

The next step for gay and lesbian faculty at UNCA is to obtain health insurance benefits for our spouses. We have already succeeded in adding "domestic partner" to a new policy on faculty leave at our institution, and I am now serving on the UNCA Employee Insurance Committee and learning more about insurance than I ever wanted to know.

My being out has also had positive consequences for a professional organization. While attending my first Women in German (WIG) conference in 1990, I recognized a need for a lesbian support network within the structure of WIG, to provide support for lesbians working in gay-hostile environments, and to share information on gay-related issues on our campuses. I convened the first meeting at the conference, and the response was overwhelming. Like so many things, it was mostly a matter of being *out* in the right place at the right time. I understand that another lesbian in WIG had been interested in establishing a network for years, but the time hadn't been right. Now lesbian Wiggies were ready to come out. Two of us gave short presentations at the opening session of the 1991 conference (mine was called "Professional and Personal Identity as a Lesbian") to bring lesbians to the attention of the straight majority in WIG. At the 1994 conference I was delighted to see a proud, out, self-confident and self-identified "dyke" who had come out to me confidentially four years earlier.

Nine years after my coming-out party, I am a tenured associate professor of German at UNCA, an elected member of the faculty senate, serve on the Academic Policies Committee and the Employee Insurance Committee, and am chair of the Faculty Grievance Committee. But I am no longer *the* campus lesbian—there are at least three of us on the full-time faculty, and gay and lesbian faculty and staff who have life-partners now list their partner's name under "spouse" in the university directory.

My spouse, Cynthia, has just been promoted to research director at the Area Health Education Center (AHEC) in Asheville. We both enjoy attending UNCA and AHEC functions together, but have never had more fun than when we slow-danced together, along with other lesbian and straight couples, at the AHEC Fall Fling last year, attended by most of the other 250 employees.

Being with whom you love and be fully yourself, no matter where you are—let that be our ultimate goal.

Works Cited

Berzon, Betty, ed. *Positively Gay*. Los Angeles: Mediamix, 1979.

D'Emilio, John. "Homosexual Professors Owe It to Their Students to 'Come Out.'" *Chronicle of Higher Education*. 28 Oct. 1987: A52.

Eichberg, Rob. *Coming Out: An Act of Love*. New York: Dutton, 1990.

Herek, Gregory M., and Eric K. Glunt. "Interpersonal Contact and Heterosexuals' Attitudes Toward Gay Men: Results From a National Survey." *Journal of Sex Research* 30.3 (1993): 239–44.

The Making of a Lesbian Academic, 1974–1995

Nancy Goldstein

Department of Women's Studies,
Harvard University

11

Part I: Early Warning Signs; Three Vignettes

#1: Joseph and Betty Harlam United American Hebrew Congregations Camp, Poconos, Summer 1974:

I'm twelve when I stand on my bed in girl's bunk ten and declare to a dozen or so assembled campers that everyone is born bisexual. My first lecture. No one freezes, screams, or stops asking me to tickle their backs to put them to sleep at night. Success.

#2: South Campus High School, Abington, Pennsylvania, 1979:

I'm seventeen and a high school senior. Although it has been two years since I transferred from the standard high school in my area to the hip experimental high school miles away (where I take courses in physical anthropology and in film, and read the collected Castaneda for English credit), I'm still in love with a woman from seventh grade homeroom. Each morning I steal my mother's car from the Jenkintown train station parking lot (I don't have a car *or* a license) and drive across town to South Campus High School to sit in on her honor's English class.

The teacher appears to be touched by my feeling for literature, evidenced by my daily commute; no fool, she's also wise to my real motive for attending her class so faithfully, evidenced by who I sit next to each day. Never mind. She lets me stay so long as I do the course work.

I read Austen, Dickens, and Hardy for the first time.

When we read John Fowles' *The French Lieutenant's Woman*, I'm thrilled to discover Sarah Woodruff, the heroine, fast asleep in bed with her arm flung over the body of another maidservant in the employ of Mrs. Poulteney, the novel's villainess. Lest I get the wrong idea, the narrator coolly informs me that Sarah sleeps with Millie out of compassion: the younger woman has nightmares, and most often she creeps into Sarah's bed uninvited, where she is not even noticed by her sleeping companion until the next morning. In the Victorian era, sex between women is unknown, unthinkable, says the narrator, claiming that even had Mrs. Poulteney come across the two entangled bodies, she would "simply have turned and gone away—more, she might even have closed the door quietly enough not to wake the sleepers." And if the suspicions of even the despicable Mrs. Poulteney are not aroused then surely, the narrator implies, I can and should keep a lid on mine. "We may describe this common Victorian phenomenon of women sleeping together far more to the desolating arrogance of contemporary man than to a more suspect motive" he intones, as he closes the passage with a rhetorical question that is more flourish than inquiry: "In such wells of loneliness is not any coming together closer to humanity than perversity?"

Even as an adolescent I'm no stranger to narrative strategies of titillation and denial, arousal and deferral. For example, I know better than to accept my beloved's invitations to sleep over at her house or her offer to share her bed. I'm too worried that I'll roll over and put my arms around her in my sleep and too wise to imagine that my narrative will play itself out like some heterosexual love plot, where attraction is as inevitable as the closural convention that demands formalized unions. No, although she seems pleased to see me and the small gifts I bring her, she still devotes most of her time to singing in the church youth choir, petting on her parents' couch with a succession of local boys, and trying to get into the South Campus High School Honor's Society.

She graduates that June and the following year goes to Princeton to date smarter, richer boys, major in architecture, play rugby, and agonize over her social standing and academic performance. I, in contrast, am rejected from my top four college choices, (since neither getting toasted, following the Grateful Dead, nor watching foreign films seem like acceptable extracurricular activities to their admission departments). I decide, in desperation, to go to Boston University.

#3: Boston University; Boston, Massachusetts, 1981–1985:

In all fairness to the admissions departments that reject me, I *am* kind of a wreck at seventeen, and my alternative high school education *does* have some significant flaws: I am for instance, the only person in my American history class who sits on the edge of my seat waiting to see who will win World War II; it's news to me that Ireland is predominantly Catholic. I have seen *Persona* four times and can identify all the painters in the Impressionist wing of the Philadelphia Museum of Art, but I cannot write a standard expository paper.

College is as revelatory socially as it is academically once my family doctor trumps up some excuse about an allergy to meat that secures me a much-sought-after card for the vegetarian dining room. It's there amongst the members of the women's long-distance running team, the theater arts students, and the computer nerds that I find my first circle of lesbian and gay friends. We occupy a large round table flush up against one side of the salad bar where we can check everyone out. We flirt, dish, flame and talk loudly about "breeders." We sneer at rumors that the college president refers to the Women's Center as the "lesbian lounge" and considers the English Department "a damned matriarchy." I take to wearing a pink triangle and a heart-shaped pin that says "deviant."

When we vegetarians tire (and we do, *early* in the semester), of the kitchen's endless variations on tofu we give up on dinner altogether. Each evening we meet to down big bowls of cheap gummy institutional ice cream drowning in coffee and talk, talk, talk; afterwards we go to Burger King for Whoppers and fries. Sometimes we go to the 1270 Club on Boylston Street to dance until 2 A.M. Other nights we cruise the Fenway—me with my black leather jacket zipped up tight over my breasts and a cap on my head.

I finish my first semester at Boston University with two incompletes and a note from the dean saying that I'm on academic probation.

Things improve dramatically the very next semester when my undergraduate advisor casually mentions that no one will ever notice if I slip into upper-level classes at this university the size of a small nation. I break my vow never to take a 9 A.M. class when a Virginia Woolf seminar is offered— it's the first time in my entire educational career that a course devoted entirely to studying a single woman writer ever *has* been offered and I quickly decide that Woolf is the greatest writer of the twentieth century. Such intelligence, such intuition. How does she know that I will know what she means from those vivid clusters of words which are no more moments of being than John Singer Sargeant's blobs of white are a little girl's pinafore?

I love the intensity between Jacob and his school chums in *Jacob's Room* and am intrigued by the connection between Mrs. Ramsey and Lily Briscoe in *To the Lighthouse*. I'm delighted when my professor mentions Woolf's affair with Vita Sackville-West; it's the first time that I have ever heard anyone referred to as lesbian or gay in the context of a classroom—anyone whose work we were reading, that is. I am overjoyed. I celebrate by spending several days in the library reading Woolf's and Sackville-West's letters to one another in order to ascertain the exact date of first seduction; each night at dinner, I entertain my friends at the vegetarian cafeteria with progress reports on my research.

Sometime between December 15th-twenty-first, 1925 at Long Barn, Weald, Sevenoaks, I decide.

I declare an English major.

I am shocked to learn that there are teachers of mine who want to see me go on for the Ph.D.

"But I'm not nice enough to be a professor," I tell one.

"You don't have to be nice," she replies.

"But I'm a lesbian," I say. "Are there any lesbians in academia?"

She smiles and names a full professor at Harvard.

I've never heard of the professor, but I have certainly heard of Harvard.

I apply to graduate schools, am rejected from Yale for the second time, am offered a full tuition scholarship by Brandeis and go there against the advice of all but my favorite advisor who tells me to look up a newly-hired feminist theorist and Victorianist

Part II: Graduate School

I become a Victorianist in my third year when the professor who had been recommended to me tells me that she thinks I'm a natural. "But how can you say that?" I reply. "I've never read any nineteenth-century novel besides *Jane Eyre*." "Because," she retorts, "you like realism and you like girls."

When I entered graduate school in 1986, there were eleven other students: six women; five men. Three of us consider ourselves lesbian or gay, although others will later tell me about their same-sex affairs. I'm the only one who's out. I ask my new advisor about my future in academia. Is it time consider going back into the closet, where I haven't been since my late teens? "No," she says. "Just don't put the word "lesbian" in the *title* of your dissertation."

But by the time I go out onto the job market for the first time, things have changed. Poststructuralism and postmodernism have already swept into the academy; Eve Sedgwick's *Between Men* has long since inaugurated the gay studies movement; the job market that my undergraduate advisors had predicted would improve got much worse.

Still, I decide to do the job market semiclosed that first year, mostly because I don't know and can't find a single out lesbian or gay man who had initially gone out on the job market as an out lesbian or gay man to tell me what it was like. Sure, tenured faculty members who had been closeted until their tenure decision, or who had come out after tenure, tell me that my being out as a lesbian on the job market won't hurt me a bit, but I need more, and more current, reassurance than that.

I made up three c.v.'s and three job letters: out, straight, and read-between-the-lines. "This is surreal," my advisor says.

In the end, it didn't matter. I didn't get any interviews at MLA that first year; the next, I got interviews but no job. (When I tell my friend Joel that Yale has blown me off for the third time in as many degrees, he suggests that I start telling people that I enjoy an ongoing, consistent relationship with their English department). Like everyone else, I listened to my advisors mumble soothingly about why a bad job market was no indicator of my potential; like everyone else, it made little difference and I was depressed for months.

In desperation, I just decided to go ahead and do what I wanted to do. I was angry about having to perform this academic exercise in which I was expected to write a two-hundred-page-book-report complete with a zillion footnotes to show that I'd read what everyone else on earth had written about my subject. And I know that I was irritated that I couldn't use my natural voice or say anything about myself, especially since so many tenured professors were starting to do both. It seemed grossly unfair to me that the reward for finishing this Augean-scale task would almost surely be unemployment. And I know that I was angry and scared: angry that I had been willing to sell out my sexuality for a job; scared to realize that even selling out my sexuality, an important part of my identity, wouldn't guarantee me one.

I decided to hell with it. I refocused my dissertation to ask how the novel had aided in the shift from the deployment of alliance to the deployment of sexuality—or, more simply put, to ask how it was that culture came to need, and came to supply itself with, an endless supply of willing-to-be-married straight girls. I pursued in writing about women and AIDS. I exhumed everything on my cv that I'd closeted.

Maybe it was timing. Maybe it was luck. Things changed after that.

Sure, writing the dissertation was still miserable, and I still felt lost and lonely a lot, and I still worried about money, the quality of my work, and whether I'd ever have a job or a steady girlfriend, but at least I was no longer afraid that if I got hit by a car on my bike the next day that I'd have to admit to myself and God that I'd wasted the last three years of my life.

After over a year of searching for an academic job, after sending out over one hundred applications, and after spending just over a month waiting on functions at Rowe's Wharf Hotel in downtown Boston—I decided that if I couldn't pursue my career of choice, I'd rather make the good money I'd made all through school waiting tables than no money working at some bookstore—my first teaching job—as an adjunct.

I was researching and writing about lesbians and HIV when I was supposed to be finishing my dissertation because the most recent fiasco on the job market had left me with a terrible writer's block on my Jane Austen chapter, my last. I gave up on *Emma* and focused on lesbian health issues instead for a breather. Finding ways to get articles from medical journals without a paying a library fee and then trying to familiarize myself with the discourse of an unfamiliar field was challenging, absorbing, and sometimes disheartening, but it was the change of field and topic I needed. I went from feeling an inadequate English doctoral candidate to feeling like someone who was pretty smart about public health issues given my background in literature.

Getting my first real academic job—albeit a part-time one—and getting it as an out lesbian, broke my writer's block. Delivering my paper to an interested audience and discussing my ideas with them renewed my faith that someday someone somewhere might actually read what I was writing. It was July of 1994, and heat wave that hit Boston was so intense that dogs couldn't even bark. I used the check my father gave me as an early graduation present to buy myself an air conditioner, set up a palette in the living room by the fan, and wrote my final sixty-page chapter and a thirty-page introduction in five weeks to finish. September 1 I dropped off the manuscript to be photocopied for my advisors, then commuted to Connecticut, the scene of my first adjunct job: two hours later I was being introduced to my students as Professor Golfstein.

The next month I defended my dissertation the week before my birthday. The month after that, I changed my Visa card to read "Dr. Nancy Goldstein."

Part III: Teaching

On my best days, I adore teaching. On my worst days, I try to remind myself that at least I don't come home every day smelling like grease and with food on my clothes.

Some of my students would probably be happy to overlook my lesbianism, relieved if I never mentioned it. But I think that feeding into a "don't ask, don't tell" dynamic reconfirms the status of lesbian/gay sexuality as shameful secret—a defect that polite queers don't mention and polite heterosexuals ignore. So I come out for several reasons: in order to act from a position of strength that clearly places the burden of attitude adjustment on them; and because I want my students to know I'm not afraid of the administration finding out that I'm a lesbian—that in fact they have hired me not only in *spite* of my lesbianism, but in part *because* I teach sexuality and gender issues from a queer perspective.

By coming out, I also want to send an unmistakable message to the students in my classroom who are lesbian/gay, or thinking about it, or who have queer relatives or friends: I want them to know that in my classroom and in my presence they will not be ignored, elided, or considered defective on account of their sexuality. I hope that they will be able to draw some encouragement from seeing that living life as an out lesbian I still have a job and friends and colleagues who will talk to me and let me play with their kids.

I don't mean to depoliticize this, to imply that coming out is like some Nike ad where one only needs the proper attitude and the right sporting goods equipment to just do it. It's not that easy. But I want my students to know that there may be options other than pretending to be just like straight people, or drinking and drug themselves to death, or resigning themselves to lives of isolation. And I can't be a viable proponent for any of these positions unless I'm out, so I am. Period.

Coda: October 1995, a year later.

A year and numerous courses later, some of my ideas have shifted since I first wrote this paper. For example, I no longer believe that I have to make a choice between being a moving target and an open secret. Formally coming out has come to seem to me to constitute a confession, an *apologia pro vita sua*, that I'm not interested in making. Announcing my lesbianism in primarily straight undergraduate classes too often lends itself to a response wherein my students assure me, whether verbally, in their papers, or implicitly in their reports for the class—that my being a homosexual is "OK" with them—and then there are, of course, the usual homophobic accusations of bias or "unprofessional" conduct every so often. Neither response represents the kinds of ideological change I'm pushing for when I come out. Rather, in a reversal that exemplifies the ability of dominant culture to reincorporate opposition, my gesture comes, in this setting, to appear confessional rather than assertive, while my straight students' response reconfirms rather than dislodges their most deeply held beliefs: that all people are either straight or gay, that all people can comfortably be assumed straight unless they announce otherwise, and that they themselves are neither prejudiced nor queer.

Perhaps I shouldn't be surprised. Images of straight men playing gay men appear on movie screens throughout the country these days, and my students boast to me that even their parents loved *Priscilla* and *To Wong Foo*. Still, I still find myself astounded by the extent to which dominant culture has adapted to consume queerness—a feat it performs without experiencing any indigestion whatsoever, and for which it sometimes pats itself on the back a great deal more than is warranted considering the material conditions of lesbian/gay existence.

I think of my refusal to come out formally, all the while continuing to live and teach as a distinctly and unapologetically lesbian person, as a means of intervening in the formulation of false assumptions: that whether one is openly or furtively queer must all come down to a matter of personal character and personal choice rather than political and social conditions, that being out must be a fairly easy matter after all, and that the presence of identifiable homosexuals signals the arrival of an age when homophobia and prejudice are no longer with us.

Is "Out" Now "In"?

A Letter to a First-Year Lesbian Professor

Batya Hyman

Department of Social Work,
Arizona State University West

12

Dear newly hired Assistant Professor,

Welcome to the other side of the desk!

This has been a difficult letter for me to write. Searching for inspiration, I've sung along with Meg and Chris, have read Audre Lorde, and have talked with friends. Why am I having such difficulty? Because I am writing about myself—my successes and worries—not my research findings. What can this quantitative researcher say, based on just one person's experience, about life as a lesbian academic? Which of my experiences as a forty-two-year-old first-year assistant professor will you find useful?

For me, one of the joys of being a lesbian is the freedom to devise my own rules. My status as an outlaw allows me to invent, with the women in my life, the social structures we consider necessary to the ordering of our interactions. Yet, sometimes I wish I might draw upon the wisdom of a lesbian pioneer who has successfully navigated these waters. This longing was particularly acute last summer as I made the transition from postdoctoral research fellow to assistant professor. Quite frankly, I felt both exhilarated and terrified as I imagined myself moving into my new office or standing in front of a class or attending a faculty meeting. Also, I felt the opportunity and challenge inherent in entering this job as an "out" lesbian. So, though I certainly do not view myself as a pioneer, I am writing to you about some of my experiences as a dyke in academe.

I am the oldest child in a Jewish family. Because we were, at that time, the only Jewish family in a small Maine town, I quickly learned how it feels to be different from other people in my environment. I was tagged with stereotypes—loud, pushy, smart—by teachers and classmates. I was treated as though I represented all Jews, and had to learn not to assume responsibility for how those around me viewed my religious group. In fifth grade, I got into big trouble. The teacher spent weeks preparing for Christmas and teaching us to sing Christmas carols. Liking to sing in large groups, I sang along with my classmates. But, on the first day of Hanukkah, the teacher asked me to tell the class about the significance of the holiday and how it is celebrated. I asked her why it was her job to teach about Christmas, but my job to teach about Hanukkah.

I came out to myself at eighteen and chose to attend a women's college. Women students and our thoughts were highly valued. I thrived on the challenges posed by smart strong women professors who cared about their students and expected us to develop our abilities to think and lead. Within this vital academic climate, I learned about power, oppression, and opposition. I also learned this was not a safe environment in which to be out as a lesbian. During my first year, a lesbian couple was told their "sexual experimentation" would not be condoned and they were thrown out of the dorm. Everyone knew that many students and faculty were lesbian, but this was never discussed publicly. I watched some junior faculty worry about how far "out" they could be and still get tenure. These were the same teachers who were best liked by the students they so clearly valued. This women's college endeavored to produce capable and resourceful women, but didn't dare directly challenge heterosexist assumptions. The argument against such challenges went something like: If some lesbians come out, all women who choose to attend or teach in a women's school will be labeled dykes and, as we know, this is risky business. So, I learned about heterosexism from lesbian feminist women who, in the name of the women's movement and women's education, put aside their claims as lesbians and put forward the claims of women. Nonetheless, I'd glimpsed a world in which women's ideas and words were valued and would never choose to settle for less again.

My experiences in social work school, a few years later, were disappointing. We learned concrete helping skills, but not how to think about our new profession or to shape theories that might inform practice. After obtaining my MSW, I worked in a variety of social service settings as a clinician, administrator, advocate, and trainer. During a period of reflection, following many years of direct practice, I realized that I was again hungry for the intellectual stimulation and vitality of the academic setting.

At age thirty-eight, I was privileged to enter a doctoral program in which my research interests and wish to teach were taken seriously. My savvy and accomplished women classmates and I supported one another, and together we celebrated each successful step on our roads to the degree.

The many lesbians among us gathered for the occasional potluck (what else?) to share stories, validate our relationships, and bring our partners into our school-related lives.

Determined to investigate the possibility of a link between childhood experiences of abuse and labor-force participation for adult women, I searched for data to analyze as part of my dissertation work. Not surprisingly, labor economists don't gather data about childhood experiences of victimization, and child-abuse researchers have not gathered much data on the woman survivor's labor-force participation. However, I discovered the National Lesbian Health Care Survey contained the variables required to build and test my model. My experiences trying to convince faculty of the appropriateness of testing my model in a lesbian sample prepared me for some of the objections I now encounter when I discuss my interest in researching lesbian life. For example, I was asked repeatedly whether the ways in which lesbians differ from heterosexual women were likely to limit the generalizability of my findings. Rarely did someone suggest that studying these questions in a lesbian sample might be, in and of itself, interesting or important. Others did not recognize the serendipity of being able to investigate the association between abuse and earnings in a sample of women who were, most likely, highly motivated to support themselves. Instead, they consistently focused on heterosexual women and external validity. I defended my dissertation, based on this lesbian sample, at age forty-one.

While completing a postdoctoral fellowship, I interviewed at several schools of social work in different parts of the United States as an out lesbian. I never questioned whether to come out during the application process. Because social workers encounter and advocate for diverse groups of people, I expect graduate social work students to examine their experiences of privilege and oppression. If I ask this of them, I must be prepared to model this process for them. Therefore, I was determined to work in a school that would support me as an out lesbian. (I imagine that you, too, have wondered about whether, when, and how to come out to your potential or new colleagues.) After some debate, I decided to mention my interest in teaching lesbian/gay content in my application letters and to come out more directly during on-campus interviews. I cannot know how many hiring committees took any action on my application, positive or negative, based on this particular piece of information. But, I do know that I was invited to several campuses. In some instances, I came out to my contact person at the school; in other situations, I came out to the dean in our discussions at the end of the day.

During my visits to several campuses I encountered a number of closeted lesbian faculty and deans. Most of these women were "out" to some degree; that is, people in their schools were aware of their lesbianism, but they didn't talk about their partners, nor did they come out to students. Over and over again, I was reminded that we may be everywhere, but we are still invisible. One woman, a highly respected successful dean, told me about sitting in her car by the side of the road as her lover and several students from her school marched proudly past her in the local gay pride parade. I wanted to cry as she described her delight in watching these women participate in a community she feels unable to claim. Whether or not this woman truly needs to remain closeted in order to protect her job, she believes this deception is necessary. During my interviews with faculty, some people seemed genuinely confused about how to respond to my coming out. As one heterosexual woman said to me, "we're so accustomed to ignoring Dr. X's (a closeted senior faculty member) sexual preference that we're unsure of how to respond to you."

I was offered several positions and am now one of twenty-five tenure-line faculty in a large, urban graduate social work school. So, if you're worried about applying for your first academic job as an out lesbian, I hope you find this news heartening.

Relations with colleagues. Based on my experiences as a student, I expected some "politics"—the taking of sides in sometimes silly disputes—among faculty, but I also anticipated occasional animated interactions with engaging colleagues about our students and our research. Sadly, this has not been my experience. Worries about tenure, self-interest, overwhelming demands, and a host of other factors diminish opportunities and energy for such encounters. We do, however, manage some lively exchanges, often in hallways, about current events, someone's health, a new restaurant, a play or movie, or our travels. When necessary, we have collegial talks about students or course content. Very rarely has anyone asked about my research and I've learned not to ask others about their work.

I've made some unflattering and disturbing observations about the interpersonal dynamics in this community which are not, I assume, limited to my school. The president of the university rules with an iron fist. Faculty have little power to influence the behavior of the administration or the structures of the institution. Like members of other powerless groups, some faculty engage in a variety of behaviors that demonstrate and reinforce their powerlessness such as scapegoating, ostracizing, and "us vs. them" thinking. Junior faculty, ever aware of the need for senior faculty support at tenure time, imbue the white-haired fellows with more power than they actually have. Thus, we are hesitant to challenge their behaviors and assumptions. In-groups and out-groups are formed around ever-changing dichotomies—researchers vs. clinicians, old school vs. young blood, quantitative vs. qualitative, supporters of the dean vs. critics. Apart from the sheer waste of energy and time, I am concerned by this behavior because prejudice is both a consequence of, and a reinforcement for the existence of in-groups and out-groups. Because prejudice kills Jews and lesbians.

Survival strategies. Fortunately, I have found a few heterosexual feminist allies with whom I am able to discuss some of these issues. Each woman has had reason to consider carefully her privilege and her membership in oppressed groups. Each woman is passionate about ideas, research, and teaching. Each woman brings her understanding of the dynamics of power into her classroom or her research. We appreciate and discuss our differences as we challenge, support, and encourage one another. Although we are very busy people, we find time to share bonds that are nourishing.

Though I am acutely aware of the ways I differ from some of my colleagues, my daily interactions with students and colleagues are rooted in common ground, not our differences. Ostensibly, we all care about disenfranchised people, social welfare, learning. Most often, I choose to push the differences into the background and concentrate on shared goals and activities. This is, I think, a common survival strategy. But, I do wonder how to define my roles as an out lesbian in this school. Many of my colleagues are unaccustomed to considering and speaking about their privilege as well-educated, middle-class white people. Sometimes I question whether I'm mentioning lesbian/gay issues too often to suit some. One colleague says she doesn't want to think about gay people. What can I say to her? I've looked at the curriculum, syllabi for other courses, and the Council on Social Work Education's mandate to "present theoretical and practice content about patterns, dynamics, and consequences of discrimination, economic deprivation, and oppression" about lesbian and gay persons. Students often enter the program knowing little about lesbian/gay people and, unfortunately, lesbian/gay content is not included in most courses. Aware that lesbian women and gay men tend to congregate in large urban areas, I want us to teach about the lesbian/gay community, our strengths, and our likely needs for services. Is it my responsibility to enunciate these needs and push for their implementation? Will it always be my responsibility to teach about Hanukkah? And, if my colleagues come to rely on me to raise lesbian/gay issues, am I relieving them of the responsibility for examining their heterosexism? How do I weigh the risks and benefits of being out and, more importantly, challenging the heterosexist assumptions and behavior of students and faculty—as a junior faculty member? This is similar to the old feminist debate: Do we gain more by risking being seen as confrontational and troublesome women or do we try to "get along" and work more gradually toward our goals?

I've found support in connections with faculty at other institutions, often through the Internet or a conference. A few lesbigay faculty have generously shared teaching strategies and have encouraged me to push on. Looking beyond the walls of this school has helped to provide me with a context in which to place my concerns and actions.

This is my first year. I want to grow into a better teacher and I have a substantial research agenda. During the next few years, I hope we, the faculty, acknowledge and embrace our diversity and then move forward to integrate material about lesbian/gay people into the curriculum. I want to be able to write a different sort of letter after my third year, describing the process of working with others on this shared goal, instead of this statement about the loneliness of working in a setting in which coming out is still an issue.

A piece of advice: In every job, we choose to put up with a person or dynamic or task we don't like because we are basically happy with the other people, dynamics, or tasks. During the interview process, we try to gather as much information as possible with the goal of estimating the tradeoffs inherent in a given position. But, we cannot truly know what these tradeoffs will be until we are actually in the setting. I encourage you to think carefully about the tradeoffs you are and are not able to make.

A final word: As I sat down to write this letter, I spent a minute wondering whether I'm jeopardizing my chances for tenure by writing about my experiences as a lesbian academic. I'm sorry to tell you that this is a consideration. Some of my colleagues have suggested I wait until I secure tenure before writing a letter such as this. After all, they say, investigating the issues of lesbian academics might be a legitimate research activity, but writing a personal statement has no place in academe. To choose not to write this letter would be to silence myself. Such an act would be antithetical to my values as a feminist and a social worker and a tradeoff I will not make.

Double Vision

Lesbian Twins in Academia

Sherrie A. Inness

Department of English, Miami University

Julie C. Inness

Department of Philosophy, Mount Holyoke College

13

"You're one of the twins, aren't you? Which one are you, Sherrie or Julie? It's impossible to tell the two of you apart. I don't know how your mother can do it!" As identical twins, we experienced a doubling of vision from the earliest moments of our lives, when friends and even family members sometimes proved incapable of distinguishing between the two of us. It is impossible for either of us to fully imagine what it would be like to be a "single," since our doubleness has helped to define who we are. One source of our doubled vision came from our experience of each other—each of our perceptions was accompanied by a shadow, the world as seen by the other. From cookies to clothing, people to politics, we were never distant from each other's point of view, a perspective incorporating both sameness and difference. We did not always agree with what the other thought, but we always had to be aware of that other perspective.

At the start of our lives, our closeness as twins found expression in our shared use of a partial twin language, a language shared only by us in an intimate community of dialogue. No one, not even our mother, could understand many of our words. As we aged, the language we used turned into the common tongue, but we remained bound together in our world. Sensing our sameness and difference, questioning soon became second nature. Loving cake, one would have to question why the other loved pie. Appreciating the countryside, one would have to question why the other desired only the city. Adoring reading, one would have to question why the other shared this passion. Raised in the same family, sharing so many physical similarities, yet different people all the same, we were both necessarily plunged into wondering about identity and difference, questioning which features marked the vital yet puzzling boundaries between individuals.

Another source of our doubled vision rested with those around us. Seeing us, even close friends would mistake us for each other, going so far as to warmly kiss the wrong twin in a moment of enthusiasm. Neither one of us could make a friend without the inevitable plethora of questions about our apparently fascinating twinhood: What does it feel like to be a twin? Can you tell what the other one is thinking? Did you ever switch places in your school classes? Which one is older? Do you ever not want to be a twin? Did your mother dress you the same when you were young? These questions were asked to us interchangeably, for we had become "the twins" in the eyes of others, a curiously composite being. Even when being introduced, we would often be announced as "the Inness twins" or "one of the Inness twins." Yet this temptation to create one being from two people on the part of others was always accompanied by an urge to distinguish us; from teachers and acquaintances to friends and lovers, people continually asked, "Who's who?" Faced with this reiterated question, we had to constantly explore our two identities, inscribing and reinscribing our differences and similarities. Learning to question endlessly due to our inescapably doubled vision, perhaps it is not surprising that we both became lesbians and academics—lesbians question the status quo of heterosexuality and academics question the world.

When we first came out in high school, some of our friends took our shared lesbianism as "proof" that lesbianism was purely biological (ignoring our shared upbringing). But they were wrong. For us, being twins and becoming lesbians were intertwined, yet neither of us embraced the idea of biology as destiny, our shared genes pushing us into a common future. Rather, being twins made us question basic dichotomies such as nature/nuture and self/other. Looking at each other, we were never far from a reminder that shared genes did not equal destiny. Remembering our different lives, we could not forget that variety could develop from a common substance. And this set us free, making us ontological rebels of a sort. If we could become such different people, surely the world was a malleable place, a place where one's being was shaped rather than given. Locked in adolescence, during which free choice often appears an impossibility, we knew that choice did matter. While many of our high school peers were embracing heterosexuality as "natural," we had only to look at each other to remember that "natural" was a fiercely contested category. Yet, if heterosexuality were not "natural," what other hold could it have on us? Having read much feminist theory during high school, we knew the answer: Heterosexuality was a guise for power relations. Bound together by our politics rather than our genetics—Simone de Beauvoir, Betty Friedan, Audre Lorde, Charlotte Bunch, and Adrienne Rich rather than our chromosomes—we knew that we could differ from others because we differed from each other. Being twins gave us access to a subversive vision that led readily to the subversive vision of lesbianism and, ultimately, academia.

Does Aristotle allow for lesbians? What does it mean to write a lesbian text? By the time we entered the same college together, both fully out as lesbians, we knew to question received wisdom, reaching for the hidden subtext. As lesbian twins, such questioning, although difficult at times, was almost second nature. As twins, we had the constant challenge of acknowledging each other's standpoints, in the process permanently undermining received stories about what it meant to be the same or different. As lesbians, we knew that things were never as "natural" as they seemed. As we read canonical literature, whether Chaucer or Plato, Shakespeare or Descartes, we remained aware of the stories that were not being told. Talking with each other late at night, eating cold pizza and drinking too many cups of strong coffee as we covered reams of paper with writing, we reminded each other what a small role lesbians played in the received truth about English or philosophy, our respective majors amplifying our individual questioning through the sounding board of another who was both Other and self. Perspective was either falsely universalized or ignored in our two fields: One could choose between an all-knowing, "neutral" and "gender-free" position or silence. Yet as lesbian twins, we knew that perspective was vital—navigating between our own closely linked worlds had taught us this, as well as piloting between homosexuality and heterosexuality. Rather than giving way to despair, we decided to enter academia, taking the questioning skills we had learned from each other into the realm of teaching and scholarship.

The classroom, however, was not always a place where lesbians—twins or not—were welcome. "Homosexuality isn't natural." "Homosexuals are perverts and should be put in jail to rot." "Gay men with AIDS deserve what they get because they haven't followed nature. Nuke them." "Lesbians are sick and shouldn't be allowed around children." "All fags deserve to die. I'd like to run them over with my truck, then back up and run them over again." These are only a few quotations from essays that we have received from our students. Many students enter our classes yearning for the stability of knowing that certain things are "natural" while others are "unnatural," clear-cut divisions that delineate the permissible and impermissible. They have little or no desire to be told that the "truths" they have held for many years might not be as absolute as they has assumed. Sometimes they lash out in anger and dislike at anyone who challenges such deeply held beliefs, terrified about losing their well-worn certainties.

Encountering such students, it sometimes feels overwhelming for any educator. Where does one turn when one needs advice or support about such a student? How does one teach a student who refuses to hear that her worldview might not be the only acceptable one? How should one deal with personal anger? We have learnt to call each other, renewing our shared understanding that teaching as lesbian twins involves showing students how to question their preconceived notions, teaching them to recognize that an invocation of "nature" often conceals power imbalances. So we share insights, trading tips on everything from coming out to a classroom full of students to responding to a student who has just stated categorically that he hates homosexuals. As we talk, we discover how being twins and lesbians continues to shape us as teachers—trying to explain things to each other, we learn how to teach our students; remembering being lesbian, we continually question whether we are excluding stories that need to be told in the classroom.

Since we have always been marked as Other, bearers of the paradoxical difference of sameness, we bring a keen awareness of deference to our - classrooms. Even today, we can never even take a walk together without strangers staring at us, separating us out with their glance. Such attention is seldom malicious—people are curious, and they inevitably look at us closely, noticing the unmistakable similarity. Some individuals are content only to stare; others are more direct and ask, "Are you twins?" The boldest inquirers enter into dialogue with us, doing everything from telling stories about twins in their families to inquiring about how our mother tells us apart. When we are together, we cannot escape such close scrutiny. People are clearly driven to "figure us out," so driven that inhibitions about questioning strangers vanish. We have come to understand this sustained intense curiosity as reflective of people's uncertainty about their own identities; asking us about what makes us "the same" or "different," they struggle to delineate these troublesome categories for themselves, striving for clear-cut and stable divisions in an often chaotic world. But twins ultimately prove to disrupt identity stability, being both the same and different in one confusing melange—walking examples of deconstruction. It is the feeling of always being a perplexing Other that has helped us to become better teachers. We recognize what it means to be set apart as oddities that fundamentally challenge the status quo; thus, we encourage our students to question how and why they make or fail to make distinctions between themselves and others, reminding them that identity must be more than skin deep.

Even as adult twins, we are repeatedly reminded of the confusion that exists surrounding our identities, a confusion that is often very visible for us. For instance, a few years ago, one of us spent a semester doing research near the other's campus. We would frequently walk about the campus separately, leaving chaos in our wakes. Colleagues were uncertain who was who; students were bewildered, mistakingly believing that their professor refused to answer their greetings or accept their papers. One friend suggested in frustration that we should wear name tags, neat markers to both advise and warn the insufficiently informed. Another person insisted that the visiting twin show him her driver's license because he thought that she was only his colleague who was pulling a somewhat curious joke on him. Yet another teacher ate dinner with the visiting twin at a college gathering, failing to recognize throughout the entire meal that this person was not the colleague whom he knew. People around us wanted clarification about our identities, often to the point of demanding it. This sort of identity confusion has followed us all our lives and shall continue to do so, forcing us to reconsider and reinscribe the lines that distinguish us, always asking the questions, "What makes me myself?" and "What makes her herself?" The answers to these questions continue to elude us, teaching us that identity is a process rather than a destination. Even now when we are teaching at institutions that are hundreds of miles apart, it is still impossible for either of us to escape our twinness, a force that continues to make us question the meanings given to identity. Yet, as we have discussed, this confusion has ultimately proven a boon rather than a bane; moving back and forth between our own worldview and that of another, we have learned to see double at an early age. Understanding our own individual viewpoints as not universal, it has been a simple step to envision a multiplicity of viewpoints in the world, a perspective that has deeply informed us as both lesbians and academics.

Way Out at Saint Michael's College

Carey Kaplan

Department of English,
Saint Michael's College

14

When I arrived at Saint Michael's College in the fall of 1972 I was twenty-eight years old, fresh out of graduate school, approaching my first full-time teaching position. I had come straight (in any and all senses of the word) from the comfortable, radical, rioting, anti-Vietnam world of the University of Massachusetts at Amherst where everyone was so politically up-to-date that I felt no responsibility to develop even a feminist—never mind a lesbian—consciousness. I looked forward to a predictable, typical academic career. If I was attracted to women, I did not know it.

Saint Michael's in 1972 was a revelation. Under economic pressure it had become a co-ed institution just a year before. There were thirty young women on campus, 1500 men. Ninety-five percent of the faculty was male; there were two tenured women, both married to male faculty; other women faculty were junior, like me, or adjuncts. Perhaps 20 percent of the ninety or so faculty were priests, nuns, or brothers; 85 percent of the faculty and the student body was Roman Catholic. The school was sponsored by the Society of Saint Edmund whose primary activities involve social and human rights work primarily in Latin America.

I had known all this when I accepted the job, but I had not understood how I would react. The attractions of the position for me were that it was in Vermont where I wanted to live; it was one of only two jobs in my field, eighteenth-century British literature, in New England that year; Colchester abuts Burlington, a town much like Northampton and Amherst where I had blissfully spent the previous four years; the University of Vermont has a good library, as does Dartmouth, an hour and a half south, and McGill, two hours north; and the English Department at Saint Michael's seemed congenial, collegial, and ecumenical.

Moreover, a Catholic environment was comfortable to me because my mother was Catholic, even though my father was Jewish and I had been raised as a Jew. My upbringing and education (at Barnard, University of Chicago, and the University of Massachusetts) had been 1950s liberal. The two sides of my family, Jewish and Catholic, had learned not merely to coexist, but to love one another, and to share holidays and family occasions. Additionally, I had never to my knowledge encountered anti-Semitism, sexism, or anti-Catholicism.

Almost from my first day at Saint Michael's, the women students were in my office asking me to advocate for them: There was no gynecological care available; there was no women's sports program; male professors ignored or humiliated women; there was one women's toilet in the whole classroom complex (at least five for men); in the cafeteria, when women came in for meals, men held up cards rating their appearance from one to ten; sexual pressure and harassment were endemic; and all the women were housed in a dormitory a mile from the main campus. These young women were only a few years younger than I; I identified and empathized with their feelings of exclusion and abuse.

To compound my burgeoning radicalization, I was placed on the Student Life Committee, chaired by a young, well-meaning priest who unwittingly uttered one abysmally sexist remark after another when I raised some of the issues of women students. By the end of my first semester, I had metamorphosed from a mildly leftist, passively egalitarian graduate student to an enraged and politicized feminist assistant professor.

Within a year I was also a lesbian, separated from my husband, and deeply conflicted about whether to leave Saint Michael's, where despite my changing politics I was happy in my department, happy in my teaching assignments (which included encouragement to design a women and literature course), and convinced that I was an important role model and advocate for the increasing number of women on campus. About that time, I fell in love, discovered the large, complex Burlington women's community, and decided to stay put. Twenty-three years later, I have no regrets.

I cannot explain how or why I so suddenly became a lesbian because consciously I was enthusiastically heterosexual from, say, age fifteen to age thirty. Then I was suddenly equally enthusiastically lesbian and have remained so. I assume some combination of time, place, people, politics, and physiology account for the change, but experientially all I can say is that I felt one way for a long time and then I felt differently.

I was not officially out at Saint Michael's until six years ago. I did not hide my sexuality; Burlington is too small a town for a covert life and my lover was a high profile person. Furthermore, I attended all the women's events I could find, and danced, sang, and marched with all the energy of those early, heady years of feminism and gay pride. Being gay or lesbian on a Catholic campus is not easy and there were rarely openly gay or lesbian students, but from time to time students who were homosexual or were confused about their sexuality would talk to me about their problems. I usually came out to such students.

When I went to conferences with colleagues, I came out to them so that I would not feel uncomfortable if I were travelling with my lover or attending gay and lesbian events and panels. As far as I could ascertain, some of my colleagues did not know I was a lesbian until I told them, while others did; to none did it seem to make much difference. I was happy about being a lesbian, excited about it intellectually and emotionally, and fascinated by the new lesbian and gay scholarship, so I was not comfortable being closeted. On the other had, I did not feel Saint Michael's was a safe environment in which to be officially out until six years ago.

By then I had been chair of my department for close to a decade, I had won three distinguished teaching awards, had published several books and articles, was a tenured full professor, and had been elected and appointed to significant committees. I was accepted, respected, and liked by most of my colleagues. During a sabbatical I talked with friends who were out at their campuses, asked about repercussions and about how they actually came out, and searched my soul. I felt that I was in a uniquely powerful situation at Saint Michael's and that if I came out, others—colleagues, staff, and students—would feel more free. It was time, I thought.

The course in which to come out was logically my critical theory course, because positioning oneself in relation to texts is essential to my critical stance and my pedagogy. For years I had been uncomfortable with my hypocrisy when gay and lesbian issues would come up and I heard myself saying, "Lesbian friends tell me. . . ." I decided to take the advice of a friend who would address a large lecture class, explain the role of situating the subject in relation to her/his critical stance, and then situate himself somewhat as follows: "I am a middle-class, highly educated, black gay male," and so forth. His classes, though, had over a hundred students and Brandeis was a biggish, urban university, not a small, intimate Roman Catholic school.

In September of my return from sabbatical, I made my speech to a class of twenty-five students, many of whom had taken other classes with me, many of whom I knew well. I was *not* cool and poised: I blushed painfully and stammered. After all, I was forty-five and announcing my sexual orientation to a group of hormonally frantic and profoundly curious twenty-year-olds was not my idea of fun. I wanted to be out, I wanted it to be possible for others more vulnerable within the institution to be out, and I wanted the potential for candid and open discussion. But none of those considerations made my announcement easy. I am a private person and, while my coming out was primarily a political decision, I knew my students were most interested in the personal aspects of my lesbianism.

One class erupted in questions, which I answered as honestly as I could even when they were like one woman's, "As a lesbian, do you feel like a woman?" And, in fact, the open—and basically friendly—discussion helped me relax and even admit to my unease.

Since that occasion six years ago, I have come out in my critical theory courses in the first few class sessions and in other classes if it seems relevant. Sometimes discussion happens, sometimes not. Once I realized the difference between slipping one's sexual orientation into a lecture to a hundred anonymous students and announcing it in a group of twenty-five young people I know, I have changed my approach. I now say a few things about myself, including that I am a lesbian. Then I explain that it is hard for me to talk about something as intimate as my sexual orientation but that I have political and ethical reasons for doing so, which I elaborate. Finally I say that I am willing to take time now or in any future class to answer questions.

My students are interested in gender issues and sexuality. I try to address these interconnected matters continually in whatever I teach. In critical theory I devote about a month to gender theory, gay and lesbian theory, and feminist theory. My pedagogical effectiveness has increased since I have come out.

I remain a respected member of the college community. Right after I came out I was asked to head a committee to raise money from the faculty for our first capital campaign, and achieved an amazing 90 percent participation. I continue to be elected and appointed to committees. I have been invited to tour with the president of the college to conduct seminars with parents and young people who are thinking of attending Saint Michael's. The academic vice president has even asked me to design a course on gay studies.

My partner is an elementary school associate principal in a town about forty miles from Burlington. She has not had the luxury of being out, given the Christian conservatism of her town—although of course there are many who are aware she is a lesbian. She nervously enjoys being out in the context of Saint Michael's. We go to social and cultural events together on campus, she participates when I entertain my seminar students in our home, we entertain and are entertained by colleagues with no strain or awkwardness that I notice, and I have even asked her to address a seminar class about her experience coparenting two alternative insemination children.

Beyond my teaching, my informal support for and counseling of gay and lesbian students, and my continuing self-outing, I am not active on campus on lesbian and gay issues. My lack of activity does not signal lack of interest, but rather of time. As soon as I came out, so did two members of our student counseling service as well as several young faculty, initiating a visible gay and lesbian campus presence that permits me the luxury of doing what I do best—teaching and writing.

My writing has always been feminist; in the past three years I have begun to write and lecture on lesbian issues. A 1993 article in *Signs: Journal of Women in Society and Culture*, coauthored with Ellen Cronan Rose, "Strange Bedfellows: Feminist Collaboration," makes an analogy between ideal feminist collaboration and an ideal lesbian relationship. In that article I am explicit about my sexual orientation. Ellen and I have also written two follow-up essays that discuss and theorize the friendship and work experiences of a lesbian and a straight woman. When asked to be a keynote speaker at the annual convention of the Vermont Council on the Humanities in 1994, I outed myself as part of my talk. As with my teaching, being out in print and in public gives me a sense of freedom and allows new depth and authenticity in my scholarly work. And, as with my teaching, my institution has welcomed my work, giving me an award for scholarship, and asking me to present my recent work at a faculty colloquium.

Demographics have changed during my years at Saint Michael's. The faculty is now about 46 percent Catholic, has 30 percent tenure-track or tenured women, and few priests, nuns, and brothers teach. Aggressive hiring has given the school about 6 percent African American and Latino faculty. The last three presidents have been lay; this year for the first time in the college's ninety-year history the president of the board of trustees is not an Edmundite but a lay person. There is a gender studies program. The student body is still 85 percent Catholic, but the college has made and is making efforts to attract minorities, especially African Americans and Latinos.

I have been fortunate at Saint Michael's. The Edmundite tradition is committed to peace, justice, social equality, and academic freedom. While there are many at Saint Michael's with whom I differ ideologically, the stated and active mission of the college is to ethical, honest teaching even when such teaching is at odds with Roman Catholic doctrine. Indeed, Saint

Michael's is one of very few Catholic colleges or universities to include a "nondiscrimination on the basis of sexual orientation" clause in its mission statement, contracts, and job advertisements. The school is currently debating domestic partnership benefits and appears to be leaning in the direction of granting them. As one of the vice presidents remarked to me the other day, "We do not think of these issues until they are pointed out to us because they are simply not part of what we are used to."

Certainly there is tokenism in the generosity of Saint Michael's toward my sexual orientation, but I have accepted tokenism as part of my role. I am still one of few Jews on the faculty or staff; sometimes I feel that anti-Semitism is more pervasive than homophobia so I try to be as openly Jewish as I am openly lesbian. As a feminist and leftist, I also represent minority attitudes. But growing up as I did in a family that was not at all clear about its cultural identity, celebrating Christmas and Hanukkah, Easter and Passover, I am comfortable on the margins. I live with tokenism, assured after all these years that the institution is largely benign and even educable.

Is it Homophobia, Heterosexism, Sexism, or Can I Pass?

Sandra M. Ketrow

Department of Communication Studies,
University of Rhode Island

15

I didn't know I was a lesbian. I was a midwestern farmer's daughter. Sexuality was not talked about; one was assumed to be heterosexual, and it wasn't until I was in junior high and the other children began using the words "queer" and "fag," that I thought about it at all. I was raised as a heterosexual, and until my late twenties, played that role. Although I had vague stirrings for a gym leader in high school, and a very close attachment to a woman in college in my junior year—we ended up wrestling frequently, but she repudiated me when I later came out to her—it was not until years later that I began to examine the nature of the attractions I had felt for women, and to struggle with my own homophobia. Coming out is a process that never ends, and has only a small beginning. A colleague and close friend tells me that unless she knew, she would not believe that I am a lesbian. I guess that means I can "pass" for straight, and that is a tempting possibility. Because of my earlier experiences, including a five-year marriage to a man, and the belief that for me, being lesbian is truly a preference rather than an orientation, I still struggle, sometimes celebrating lesbianism, sometimes wishing for a more acceptable lifestyle. My father's words still ring in my ears: "I abhor your lesbianism, and you embrace it!"

Three themes emerge regarding my being a lesbian in academia: 1) coping with multiple and conflicting roles; 2) managing a public "face" that passes as sexless or even more straight in a society and university community that is not necessarily accepting of lesbians; and 3) handling the fear that permeates one's life. My life seems defined less by my sexual orientation than by the challenges of juggling multiple roles successfully, a problem shared by many women, persons with families, or single parents, including males.

Entering academia was one challenge to my relationship with my partner. My partner sacrificed her early career path to follow me and she supports me as I develop my career, in or out of academia. Mary has been a mainstay and a comfort when I have faced upheaval or difficulties in teaching or research, or just with life. She has often made her own choices secondary to mine, and we are in the process of changing that. I am pleased that she persists in seeking her doctorate in experimental psychology despite the travails of her disabilities. In my first year in this academic post, Mary suffered a major head injury. Without downplaying the impact of identifying as a lesbian on my "self-hood" and self-presentation in the public of my university, one consuming issue, then, has been how to deal with a chronically ill/disabled partner and maintain a professional career. This entails, among the joys of academia, earning a living adequate to pay for healthcare bills. In addition to establishing a presence in my research community and trying to keep up with a teaching load of four courses a semester (one "extra" for additional income), I cook, clean, shop, do laundry, manage finances, take care of the plumbing, paint, mow the lawn, and care for cars. My partner Mary's disabilities are such now that she can fully share chores, and sometimes she has taken on more than her portion. In my first year in this academic post not only did Mary suffer her first head injury, but I began to deal with the anguish of my own incest experiences, and at the urging of my therapist, I struggled with getting clear of chemical dependencies. Disclosure of this sexual abuse to my family created a tremendous rift and pain over the last seven years. If I were not in academia, and had we not moved far away from both of our families, we might have more help with our needs. While our circle of gay and straight friends have been generous with their support, there are limits to how much one can ask or expect. Also, despite my university's policy of nondiscrimination toward persons in various categories, including sexual orientation, and the university president's public proclamations toward promoting diversity, gays and lesbians at my university are not provided domestic partner benefits. The stress of dealing with these personal and family problems, and the limited support available is constant.

Actually, I feel less constrained in academia than I did when employed in private industry. That may be a function of growing older, being settled in a job where I have achieved tenure, much autonomy about my schedule, and a modicum of job security. However, since I was employed in academia, "stopped out" for a career stint in marketing computers, and then came back to academia, I have some measure of comparison that allows me to note a difference in acceptance. Or should I say tolerance?

My first supervisors were female and lesbian for the position I last held in private industry, and the faculty position I currently hold. Marianne, a director of operations, was very closeted and terrified of being found out. I took my cues from her, since I knew that the owners of our small company were at least racially bigoted. When there were company events or socializing at local bars when we were on the road with promotional events, I appeared as "single," passing as a heterosexual, while discouraging romantic attention from the males and deflecting conversation about my true private life. When I was hired eleven years ago in this small, predominantly Roman Catholic state my department chair was a very out, tenured lesbian. I was nervous and closeted with anyone outside my own department faculty. I did not attend faculty social gatherings with my partner for a couple of years; I did not appear at my partner's psychology department (she is a doctoral student) social events until I had been granted tenure.

The degree of my "outness" seems to hinge upon my perceptions of safety, either physical, psychological, or career. Even when I was in doctoral studies, I only had my nose peeking out of the closet; my close friends and my only sister knew, but I had told no one else. At the end of my second year of coursework, my partner of almost three years terminated our relationship, telling me to "get out." I will not detail the breakup, but obviously I was emotionally devastated. I also knew that the relationship was destined to end because I was tired of living in such a closeted way. At this juncture, because of the change in my living arrangements and because I was tired of living a lie, I gathered my family and came out to my parents and my sole grandparent. While I had not been vocal about my sexual orientation to my professors, I tearfully approached them and asked for incompletes because of personal problems, that my relationship had ended. I did not identify being lesbian. However, my major professor came to know my current partner Mary of fifteen years. He and I have been good friends, and he always asks about my partner when we talk or meet. One twist to this relationship in the last few years is that despite his knowledge of my being lesbian and in a committed relationship, at certain conventions in private meetings he has indicated what I perceive as sexual interest. I find that odd, and have taken to meeting with him only in very public places. I suppose that I thought being out with heterosexual males, being in professional relationships with them, and getting older precluded that kind of sexual attention.

Job interviews were a particular source of worry about being openly lesbian, as I moved to faculty positions from graduate school. I declined an offer from Louisiana State University, as the dean and other administrators with whom I interviewed displayed deep-seated racial bigotry, and I was convinced that such prejudice linked with sexism and homophobia. Mary and I worried about what being lesbian in the deep South would be like, and, at that time, I would never have queried faculty or administrators to determine an answer. Nor were lesbian/gay communities easy to locate.

At the next university in Florida, I decided it would be the kiss of death to be out, so I carefully developed an answer to the expected illegal interview question, "Are you married?" Was I flustered when the question came as, "Will you be coming alone?" Although I did not ever state that I was a lesbian, nor did I introduce my partner with "this is my partner," we were always invited as a couple to faculty social events. I appreciated that Mary joked about being a "faculty wife," and that she was a good sport about supporting me emotionally through the first years of my early academic career. Life in Florida was quiet for the most part, except that we were isolated, serving as each other's social support system. We never did locate a resident lesbian/gay community; our lesbian friends were limited to women I played rugby with for the first two years of our stay there.

I did not identify myself openly during interviews over subsequent years except once about four years ago, when I was asked to interview at a small private university where I had been a visiting professor. Most of my former colleagues knew I had a female partner; they invited us as a couple to social events. I never openly identified myself as a lesbian, nor did I introduce my partner as such at the time I was employed as a visiting professor. During this interview, I asked about some medical issues and resources because of my partner's needs, and their response was supportive. The faculty conducting the search provided names of doctors, clinics, and other such resources. Later, the department chair told me that they would be making an offer, but instead to my surprise I got a letter telling me that they had selected a male candidate. I still attribute that loss to my being open about my sexual orientation.

Tolerance in academia seems marked by display of attitudes both positive and negative by administrators toward gay faculty at my university. About a year prior to my consideration for tenure and promotion, I had taken a position coordinating several task forces, thinking that it would be relatively safe and gain me some visibility and access to decisionmakers in the tenure process. One afternoon I stopped in the provost's office to make a brief report. As we ended our discussion, he mentioned how concerned he was about his daughter, who is gay and was apparently having some struggles. This, I thought, was the Lady or Tiger choice. Did he know that I am a lesbian? A moment of crisis—if I identified myself as lesbian openly, I ran the risk (I thought) of not being promoted and tenured. If I did not, and chose not to express understanding of his daughter's dilemma because I had experience, then I would—and did—suffer the cognitive dissonance of not being open or totally honest. I admit to the coward's decision. In the long run, that choice with him had no effect since we gained a new provost the next year when I went up for tenure/promotion. I still feel sad that I did not have the courage to be open in that moment. Such a dilemma is one nadir of existence as a lesbian—safety versus courage in the face of risk.

The most disturbing part of this process were the hurdles in my tenure and promotion process. I knew that if there was a sticking point it would be at the dean's level, although I was not worried about the dean. Our associate dean made the recommendation for tenure but not promotion. After an involved battle ostensibly over my number of publications, I was tenured and promoted. I still have a bitter taste in my mouth from that associate dean, and my dean, regardless of the friendly relationship. I think that in the former case, the associate dean was being at least sexist and at most homophobic (we have a history of such problems for women at our university). In the latter, my dean was, I believe, not maliciously sexist and certainly not blatantly homophobic—my personal relationship with him got me farther than I would have expected otherwise. So, I have an unconfirmed suspicion that my difficulty lay in my gender more than my sexual orientation.

On the other hand, I have two friends who were teachers in public schools and were terminated when someone outed them; and another friend who has lost two jobs in academia because she is a lesbian. In both cases, she had no legal recourse, either because of "no evidence" or her most recent one last year, where Virginia's laws provided loopholes for the college to sidestep a discrimination suit. When I was at a Lilly Workshop on the Liberal Arts, the central theme was promoting diversity. Only one session focused on homosexuals, and that was a grassroots effort set up by participants. Several straight people organized a session to do so, and asked if I would participate. I did, despite the fact that my dean was also attending the Lilly Workshop and that was just prior to my going up for tenure and promotion. My friend who had lost one job at that point wanted to participate in the session, but was terrified because her college administrators were there as well.

Now I am tenured and an associate professor. I recently received email from one lesbian who said in response to my sending her my mailing address with that title, "Wow! Associate professor. That must mean there is hope for us!" How does this kind of security impact on my research, my outness, or being political? Did tenure set me free? First I'll address research. When I was in graduate school in the late 70s, Anita Bryant was promoting orange juice and homophobia. I conducted a study tracking the way in which the media advanced this homophobic "agenda" by publishing articles and letters to the editors; my article was published in a minor journal. Because of my fears about being labeled in job searches and in the tenure and promotion process, I omitted that entry from my vita. I included it only for official purposes or for relatively innocuous records purposes. I also avoided gender issues. I have been interested in gay and lesbian issues, but have done no research in those areas for the primary reason of fear. I worry that even with the security of tenure, that I might not be able to achieve promotion to full professor if I became too outspoken as a lesbian. My fear is related to job security, career perceptions—someday I would like to move to a more highly-regarded program in my field, and I remain unconvinced after being part of several search committees that most search committee members are as openminded as they publicly profess.

Another ugly feature of the research process is that grant funding goes to research in many areas, but I suspect little goes to gay and lesbian studies. If my track toward promotion to full professor is measured again by research published and grants funded, then I hesitate to jeopardize that. So, does being an open lesbian limit my career? It has somewhat, and could, but I try not to let it—but my research is in a "safe" area and I have begun to establish a national reputation in my research area, and as we know, it is research that mostly counts. I occasionally foray into gender issues, but never include any attention to sexuality. So fear still sits in residence in my mind and at my research choice doors.

The classroom side is another area that creates dissonance, as is political activism. Facing the status of my "outness" and my degree of politicizing gives me discomfort. When I teach basic communication courses, students make remarks in classroom discussion that show a homophobic bias. I gently admonish them for their intolerance usually without identifying my own sexuality or reminding them of that. Prior to deciding to come out I found myself using the dreaded "we" and "our" pronouns, or even avoiding gender-identifying pronouns of "she" and "her." For the most part, until I received tenure, I did not come out in the classroom, even when it was highly relevant or even awkward not to do so. Even so, I finally confronted my cowardice and fear when an African American friend who had come to talk to my gender and communication class about the intersection of race, class, and gender on communication openly identified herself as lesbian. I was still "passing" in the classroom. Paula's courage pushed me to follow her example.

Because I have some job security, I do not fear that students will run screaming from the classroom, nor to my chair or dean protesting my presence. For the most part, students either react positively, with some curiosity, or with apparent neutrality. I have not had students react negatively to my face. I sense general acceptance from most students because I deal with the sexuality issue in a positive, confident manner rather than apologetically, but there are exceptions.

Since I have been more open I have received death threats at my home and my office based on my being a lesbian, so I have felt more vulnerable. Some of the telephone threats came to my home, and my partner Mary received them, so they also had an impact on her feelings of safety as well. I do not feel safe working alone in my office, especially at night or on weekends when the building or campus is deserted. Just after the threats, I was terrified at home even with the doors and windows locked, as was my partner. We were never able to identify the perpetrator with certainty, but through some of my own detective work, I was convinced that he was an employee on campus who had purchased an old car from me which was titled to me and my partner Mary. After this, I was even more anxious about disclosing sexuality in class, and my secretaries continue to protect my home phone number. One positive note is that both campus security and local town police treated me (and Mary) with respect and did as much as they could. This fear has spilled over to a general soul-searching each time I contemplate coming out in a class, because I had always been afraid that some homophobic student might follow me or wait for me to "bash" me or destroy my property. I have an omnipresent background level of stress and anxiety related to this fear. For the most part, I suppress attention to the fear, the stress, the anxiety—both around potential homophobia and around my relational difficulties. This stress is sometimes not so low-level. That may be one reason why I entertain a fantasy of returning to a straight life. At least I would not be so fearful of being bashed because I am a lesbian. One way some of my gay and lesbian friends have chosen to reduce their fear, or at least counter it somewhat, is to empower themselves through political activism. That small community provides good support.

In the classroom and day-to-day, I believe it is less than ethical to dissemble; my students deserve to know (particularly in classes where my perspective sets agendas or topics) how sexuality impacts that. Furthermore, I would like them to know that gay people are active and can be successful. I have ridden on the backs of my lesbian sisters long enough. When this manuscript is published, I will not exclude it from my vita. I want to publicly thank my partner Mary for being such a source of support to me in my career, and continuing to love me. But I have straight friends who tell me that unless they knew, they would have believed me to be heterosexual. It is time for me to stop passing as a heterosexual when the occasion is important to demonstrate our normalcy, our exemplary accomplishments. It has not been a straight road from a midwestern farm.

Creating
My Own Security

Kathryn H. Larson
Boalsburg, Pennsylvania

16

Two Types of Security

When I was young, and until the writing of this paper, I always felt secure economically. Even my father's death, when I was seven, didn't affect my feeling of material comfort. As the oldest of three daughters, I observed my mother, who never remarried, return to college and work outside the home to support us. I grew up knowing that I would earn my own income, like my mother. My security came from both knowing I could depend on myself to hold a job and a deeply held belief that, as an educated person, I would never have a problem finding a job. I truly had no economic worries.

As a young adult, I came to believe that securing my material needs was independent of my emotional need for an intimate partnership with another person. What I didn't realize until much later was that my ability to produce my economic security was tied to my emotional dependence on the approval of my family and the outside world. My efforts to be independent economically, and interdependent emotionally in a committed relationship with another woman would eventually be threatened by my own unexamined emotional dependency or insecurity.

This chapter explores my personal journey to create the emotional security I would need to be a fully-functioning life partner and to strengthen the foundation of my economic security. Two things were key to maintaining my emotional insecurity: the effect of my father's death on the dynamics within my family and the enormous personal power and status I received by being perceived as heterosexual. Breaking the silence surrounding my father's death in both my family of origin and my extended family and breaking my silence as a lesbian would be essential to my emotional security and eventually, to my long-term economic security.

On Who I Am

As the title of this book would suggest, I am a lesbian and I have spent the majority of my life in the academic world. Defining the term "lesbian" is risky, so I prefer to acknowledge, like Flo Kennedy, that "a lesbian is a woman who says she is." I am both a lesbian economist and an economist who is a lesbian. Both of these fit me, the first because one of the areas in which I specialize is the economics of sexual orientation, and the last because who I am affects the assumptions I make and the professional work I do.

I did not come to accept myself easily as a lesbian. Feeling comfortable about being openly lesbian has taken even longer. While I have always found it easy to secure a job and an income, I was also always in the closet. I have yet to market myself as a lesbian economist. The emotional integrity I would gain by being honest about who I am never seemed as great as the potential loss of employment and income that such honesty could yield. This is why the process of creating emotional security was so long and costly. I had to take great risks, both personally and professionally. It was my long-term life partner and our relationship that was finally the catalyst for my own personal growth and change toward accepting myself as a lesbian. Education and academia, also, played a very important part in the process, simultaneously providing a supportive, accepting environment and an implicit incentive structure to remain in the closet.

On Being a Lesbian in Economics

My undergraduate major was in communicative disorders (otherwise known as speech and language therapy) with a minor in education. My interest in economics grew out of a three-year postbaccalaureate encounter with poverty while working as a Peace Corps volunteer in rural West Africa. I had little formal background in the discipline before I began studying it at the graduate level, and was unprepared for the assumptions which were standard fare in the profession. By the time I entered graduate school, I was also beginning to acknowledge to myself privately that I was a lesbian, which made it even clearer that my future well-being would depend on my own resources.

In 1980, prevailing economic models assumed that market work was a given for men and single women but merely a "choice" for married women. All women were expected to eventually marry. I found that the discipline to which I was newly committed viewed women not as economic agents in their own right but rather in relationship to men. Women were either wives or potential wives and no one, not even other women graduate students except for me, seemed to see that as a problem. Such was the discipline in 1980.

I felt extremely isolated intellectually and emotionally within that program. I began to work at the campus women's center and with the graduate student senate. Within a year of beginning my graduate program, I fell in love and moved in with the coordinator of the campus women's center. This relationship provided me with emotional support, but it also confronted me with the uncomfortable dilemma of balancing three disparate sets of demands on my time: my relationship, my graduate program (and eventual career as an economist), and my family.

They were disparate because neither my partner nor I were open about our relationship. While I considered the relationship primary, I felt uncomfortable acknowledging it to other graduate students, who were (in my view) clearly a heterosexual group. When I did come out privately to one or two officemates, their response was invariably positive. When I came out privately to my major professor, however, his response was more cautionary, suggesting that there were people on campus who might use that information against me. This warning stirred my fears of economic insecurity and, coupled with my own internal discomfort at being in a "different" relationship, kept me in the closet during my graduate school years, and beyond. I discovered that it was not possible to work internationally as an open lesbian. That created another dilemma between the personal and professional.

It was a slightly different story with my family. While they wholeheartedly supported my pursuit of a graduate degree, I did not feel comfortable with my new relationship in their presence. Although by 1980 I had come out to my mother, like most issues involving emotional conflict in our family, no one talked about it. In addition, I felt internal conflict between my need and desire for an intimate partner and fear of the commitment that an intimate partner would involve. The kind of commitment that would give me security in an intimate relationship would also mean limits on my life choices, and disloyalty to my mother, who managed life without a partner to raise us, and seemed freer than most women I knew, lesbian or heterosexual, who were bound by the demands of an intimate relationship.

The stress of balancing three sets of demands was invisible *and* pervasive. From the outside, I appeared successful, passing my courses, maintaining a social presence in the department and visiting my family with my partner. But inside I felt unaccepted and unacceptable. Also, my anger over the male and heterosexual bias within the discipline of economics affected my ability to study and understand fundamental economic relationships apart from the all-too-human assumptions on which models were based.

The personal and the professional are intimately connected. I would discover that I needed to confront my anger over my father's premature death before I could effectively face the gender bias within my economics program and the profession in general. In the meantime, however, I looked for other ways to feel good about myself. For the next decade I found a sense of self-worth through excelling at work, first as a research assistant on a development project in graduate school and then as an assistant professor of economics at a small liberal arts institution. These activities did not dispel my doubts over my ability to conceive and conduct economic research (to "fit in" to my discipline) nor could it make my primary relationship acceptable to the outside world. But they did sustain me economically until I was ready to let go of my anger and bear the cost of being open as a lesbian.

To a great extent my anger toward my father prevented me from developing my intellectual resources in agricultural economics, his own undergraduate college major. Healing my anger toward my father allowed me to love the parts of me I got from him—my business sense, my competitiveness, and my ambition. Developing a linkage with my long-lost father enabled me to claim my identity as the granddaughter of a successful sheep and dairy farmer and the daughter of a successful farm-equipment business manager.

Up until that time my professional identity had been derived primarily through my mother, who worked as a special education teacher and stayed constantly busy with numerous activities. It was in my graduate economics program, where I was called upon to focus intellectually on developing my life's work, that my strategy of coping with life, like my mother's—staying too busy to feel emotional pain—broke down. The long process that followed helped me separate my own limitations from my mother's and learn to love what makes me similar to, and what sets me apart from my parents.

My basic feeling that I don't "fit into" my discipline has never left me. But my attitude toward that feeling has changed and, as a result, my life has changed. I now feel a little more comfortable not fitting in, I take myself seriously when I am uncomfortable over certain propositions or assumptions in my discipline, and I realize I have the tools and the capability to identify the problem and seek a solution for it.

It is important to note that I made significant personal changes within a context of structural change in the discipline of economics. Today, about one-fifth of new economics Ph.D.'s are women. Great strides have been made in the past fifteen years in understanding the role of social and institutional constraints in shaping women's economic behavior. The heterosexual bias of economic models of the household which persists to the present that assumes that men and women will always end up as life partners is no longer a threat but a challenge. The point that I finally grasped was that my perspective and experience of the economy, as the child of a female-headed household, as a woman, and as a lesbian, uniquely positioned me to make a difference in my profession.

Interestingly, the profession became ready for my contribution before I did. A small group of lesbian and gay economists met over lunch at a professional meeting in 1989 and within the space of four months a professional session called "The Economics of Sexual Orientation" had been accepted into the January 1992, American Economic Association annual program. Following that session I was invited to present related papers at two conferences in the coming year. My dissertation still wasn't finished. I was "out" as an economist but I had not yet fully faced my own homophobia. I would discover that I needed to face this internal shame before I could complete my Ph.D. program.

On Coming Out

My overwhelming fear of being open as a lesbian was that I would be treated differently. At a subconscious level, I knew I reaped important benefits, at work and in my family, from the perception that I was heterosexual. Even though the nature of my primary relationship was known in my family and by many at my workplace, the code of silence in which I participated on both fronts extracted a severe personal price. The silence kept me from confronting my homophobia and diminished the value of my partner and our relationship. The silence also reinforced the shame I felt in being homosexual and reduced my ability to be productive. I finally realized it was impossible for me to have any integrity personally or professionally while I felt ashamed of who I was.

It was extremely difficult letting go of this shame. I continued to hide and compartmentalize my life until the emotional costs of remaining in the closet became higher than the economic costs of being open. Over the years, my anger at circumstances which I felt were out of my control was directed regularly at my partner and our relationship suffered serious damage. My mental and physical health suffered. I felt isolated from my family and from my colleagues, both of which at times were targets of my anger. My work suffered. Eventually, my unfinished dissertation would cost me my job. I wanted everyone else to change. I discovered I had to change.

I had thought a Ph.D. in economics would make me acceptable to the world. I finally realized it would never remove my pain and my shame, both of which ate away at my ability to document my voice, even on so neutral a topic as small farm households in Zambia. My voice, my thoughts, and my ideas were too intimately linked to who I was and the shame I felt in being me. Every time I sat down to concentrate on writing my dissertation, feelings of loss and shame rose to the surface and my emotions overflowed. For years even I didn't know why I could never make any progress. Certainly no one in my family or at work could understand.

My process of change has been neither predictable nor easy. Becoming emotionally independent has entailed learning to live with feelings which are often uncomfortable and sometimes extremely painful. There are times when I feel called to act on my feelings and it is not always clear whether the action is the right or wrong thing to do. I chose to live separately from my partner for a period while I struggled with accepting myself as a lesbian and tried to understand what that meant for me professionally. It was during this period that I came out publicly for the first time at a college faculty meeting. It was not an easy decision to make and I was afraid right up until the moment I began speaking, but I felt it was the right decision. After receiving a standing ovation from most of those present and support from across the college community, I felt a great deal of relief. Yet, to the partner who had followed me to this position and emotionally supported me during the most difficult years on the job, my coming out seemed like a betrayal, since I did it alone.

It took me three more years before I could understand that both things were true: It was what I needed to do and it was a betrayal of our relationship. The ambiguity of the process of change makes it very difficult. It entails both loss and gain. I had to lose my job as an academic in order to gain my identity as a lesbian who can choose to work in academia. I had to almost lose my relationship in order to learn that, in a committed, intimate relationship, the personal is always more important than the professional.

Coming out has been a lifelong learning experience for me. As I learn, I try to share what I learn with others. I accepted the responsibility of trying to educate others about homosexuality after I came out. At the college-level, I was comfortable addressing homophobia and gay and lesbian issues in and out of the classroom as situations presented themselves. I had not felt free to do this before coming out. In 1994, I came out to my high school class by sending a three-page letter to the committee chair and requesting that it be available to class members. The letter didn't make it to the reunion because its recipient was "disgusted" by it, but eventually it found its way into the hands of a number of my classmates and a renewed linkage with them has developed. Instead of getting angry that things didn't go the way I had planned, the next time I visited my hometown I made a point to meet the committee chair, introduce myself and thank her for passing the letter on for me. In the past, I would have been too angry to have ever spoken to her. Instead I took the opportunity to seek her out and let her get to know me. This is one example of how I have changed. We ended our conversation that day with her hoping I could make it to the next reunion. I now understand that I can take action, but I can't always control the consequences of my actions. In the process, I have gained a great deal of patience.

Conclusion

This chapter has described my personal experience with emotional and economic security. Both are intricately linked. Silence and shame affect emotional security which, in turn, affects work productivity and long-term economic security. In my case, some of the silence and shame had nothing to do with being a lesbian, per se. Instead, it was related to my specific family circumstances in which I felt a deep need to prove I didn't need anyone to love me. On the other hand, some of the silence and shame were directly related to being a lesbian. Moving away from silence and shame toward voice and acceptance has occurred for me as a process in which there are both losses and gains. I had to become willing to lose what I had materially in order to regain myself spiritually and emotionally.

Note

1. Economists first acknowledged that work inside the home (what is now termed household or domestic production) was work in the mid–1960s. Prior to that time anything other than paid work was couched under the rubric of "leisure." Those who are interested may refer to Becker, Gary S., "A theory of the allocation of time," *Economic Journal*, vol. 75,1965, pp. 493–517.

Being Out in Academia

A Year of My Life in Enid, America

Jan McDonald

School of Education,
Pace University

17

They knew I was a lesbian when they hired me to be the chair of education at Phillips University in the spring of 1992, but I didn't know they knew. I had gone to no lengths to hide it, but neither had I mentioned it during my three-day interview in Enid, Oklahoma. They knew my several trips to Stillwater, Oklahoma, were to see my partner Judy who had been hired at Oklahoma State University the year before, but I didn't know they knew. Since Phillips University is affiliated with the Disciples of Christ, I was not surprised to be asked about how comfortable I would be in a church related institution. But, I must admit that being asked that question by every individual who interviewed me seemed odd.

As I waited back in Upstate New York, negotiations regarding my hiring were bogged down for over a month because of the on-campus debate over my sexual orientation. My references were called a second time and asked if I had ever done or said anything to "embarrass" the institution. The debate continued after my hiring was announced. Several homophobic faculty members (some of whom subsequently left the institution) had laid the groundwork for much concern.

The first day of class I always ask students to tell me a little about themselves in writing. One student wrote: "I'm black, gay, loud, and proud." I was surprised and very pleased to see her pride and openness. I thought, "Maybe Oklahoma is more open than I had thought."

The student began frequenting my office to discuss the course material. Our discussions turned quickly to issues of sexuality and the possibility of starting a gay, lesbian, and bisexual group on campus. Soon more students began arriving in my office and the idea of the club became a reality. I spoke with a few faculty members and administrators. They were encouraging and did not seem very surprised that I was asking. I came out to them. They didn't seem surprised about that either. Five weeks after my arrival, I realized that I didn't have to come out to the campus community. I was already out.

With the help of Oklahoma State University's Gay Lesbian Bisexual Community Association, a group of several Phillips students and Enid residents wrote a constitution and presented it to the Phillips student senate. To our shock, our proposal for a group passed unanimously after extremely limited debate. When the student newspaper announced the group's existence, the local paper, the *Enid News and Eagle* picked up the story and called me for an interview. The next day, the paper's front page headline read, "Gay, Lesbian Support Group Formed at Phillips University."

The article described the purpose of the group (which we called Perspectives) through interviews with me, our club president, and our community liaison. Each of us also confirmed how pleased (though surprised) we were to find the campus to be so open. An associate professor at Phillips Theological Seminary was interviewed and noted the "mixed opinions of church members" on the issue of homosexuality. He added though, that those opinions had no bearing on the formation of the group. He said that "differences of opinion are allowed in the denomination" and that even "though people can radically disagree," the "overriding perspective of the denomination" is to "seek to bring about unity in the face of diversity." He mentioned that there was a gay and lesbian support group "at the denomination's national level" which had the support of "a number of congregations." The director of public relations was also interviewed for the article. He denied a rumor that a member of the board of trustees had threatened to resign because of the new club.

The newspaper coverage outraged a group of faculty, staff, and students who felt that the article portrayed a false perception that the entire university community supported the club. The group quickly organized a meeting on campus called "A Day to Reaffirm Romans I: 24–27." Fliers announced the meeting covered the campus, and the Friday after the article first appeared, we were back on the front page, "Gathering Clears Air on Gays" (October 7, 1992).

The article described the meeting of more than a hundred people who squeezed into a small faculty lounge to hear "several members of the Phillips faculty who wanted to make it clear that they had not sanctioned Perspectives." One organizer noted that their purpose was to "share redemptive powers." Following a heated and extremely emotional exchange on the morality of homosexuality, "a variety of views on the Scriptures, Christian love, and campus responsibilities were discussed." "Supporters of the club challenged everyone to come out to meetings and find out what the club [was] really about."

"Several students broke into tears in explaining that judging fellow human beings seemed completely opposite of Christian love" (*Enid News and Eagle*, October 7, 1992). The campus Chaplain praised the meeting "for creating discussion, bringing people together, and giving people a chance to examine their differences." The university president said that "a university should be a place for free and open inquiry." He "approved of the public forum," and said that the "subject has not been as widely debated as it ought to be."

In the weeks that followed, the *Enid News and Eagle* was filled with letters to the editor from readers who were shocked. They couldn't believe that Phillips could "call themselves a Christian university and yet allow such perverse behavior." They worried about the campus getting a "big epidemic of AIDS," compared homosexuality with "cohabitating with a dog or horse," reminded us that "God made Adam and Eve, not Adam and Steve," and that the "only place [they] had ever read where God wiped out a whole city was because of homosexuality."

In addition to the letters in the press, I received several letters (some anonymous, but most signed) that quoted scripture, reminded me that such behavior was "perverse," and that the writer was "disgusted" about the university's "decision to acknowledge this perversion." Over a period of several weeks, my secretary received harassing phone calls. In December a student wrote a letter to the campus community complaining (among many other things) about my teaching, even though she was not a student in my class. Parents and students visited the dean's office, concerned that I was allowed to teach at Phillips. Colleagues in the School of Education openly worried about the fact that I might "recruit little girls" from school classrooms.

One day I was invited to visit an Enid elementary school for a special reading program they were having. Distraught that the press had not come to cover this special event, one of the teachers said, "Gee, it's too bad that the newspaper wasn't here for this." One of the school counselors responded to the group, "We should have told them Jan was coming!" One fourth of the assembled group laughed hysterically, one fourth laughed nervously. One fourth looked around quickly to see what everyone else was doing. One fourth quickly dropped their heads and eyes to the floor.

In the midst of all of the controversy, I received a wonderful letter of support from a retired Disciples of Christ minister from Enid. He told me of his lesbian daughter and how much he supported her. He said he was "pleased about the formation of a gay and lesbian support group on campus." Letters like his were not nearly as frequent as the others, but they more than made up for the negative ones. Several gay alums living in Enid called to say they wished there had been a group on campus when they were students. Fellow faculty members, the chaplain, and the retired Disciples minister routinely dropped by my office to make sure I was OK, to express support, and to share hugs. One day a student popped her head into my office and said, "Dr. McDonald, you don't know me, but I just wanted you to know that some of us are really sorry to see what you've had to go through."

As the debate persisted, several contributors asked for their money back from the university. "Concerned Christians" questioned the president when he attended community functions. In November of that year, the president wrote a letter to the campus community and reminded them of the mission of the university. He wrote, it is a place "where free and open inquiry takes place" . . . "where each of us is heard, where the opinions of each of us are respected, where our differences are honored, and where our persons are held in the highest regard."

Things seemed to settle down after the New Year. For a while, I thought we were through the storm. The group was meeting twice a month and offered a variety of programs. Our attendance at meetings ranged from ten to twenty-five and included a core group of self-declared heterosexuals (some supportive, some intrigued, some there to "keep an eye on us"). We watched films and videos with gay and lesbian themes, we discussed commitment versus marriage, we had AIDS- and safer-sex-awareness seminars, we shared coming out stories. One night we had a guest speaker from San Francisco who had lived as a transvestite while growing up in Enid and who had recently completed sex change surgery. She wore a gold sequined dress with matching spike heels, spoke bluntly, and announced her HIV-positive status. I recall nervously riding home after her presentation, half expecting to be back on the front page the next morning.

February brought National Condom Week and the Umbrella Coalition on campus planned a week of activities. The activities stimulated controversy and the campus paper and local press descended. The papers, once again, were filled with articles and letters to the editors. Soon after, three churches bought a full page of the Enid paper and filled it with seven full length columns of member names and a letter to the president of the university. They wrote that they were "embarrassed" and "offended" by the "open promotion of the homosexual lifestyle" and "condom activities" on campus. The president's lawn was littered with garbage and an old toilet bowl. More contributors requested that their donations be returned.

The next day, the president and the board of trustees ran their own full page ad. The university seal was set above a bold-lettered banner, "The Purpose of Phillips University." This was followed by the university motto, its mission statement, and its objectives and methods." Appearing at the bottom of the page was a statement signed by the president and the chairman of the board. It read, "There is unanimity on the university campus that gay and lesbian persons are entitled to be treated with all the respect due any student." The university affirmed their commitment to "recognize the profound seriousness of sexually transmitted diseases" and to "increased efforts" to encourage "personal discipline" and "education."

I began my second year at Phillips with no idea of how the year would be for me and the Phillips community. I knew that I felt welcomed and valued. My partner Judy came to the opening campus picnic, something we never would have considered the first year. She was warmly welcomed by those few who had already met her and those who had only known of her. Judy's name was included next to mine in the campus directory.

In the middle of a wall-sized puzzle, showing campus activities and organizations welcoming new students and parents to campus, was a puzzle piece in bold blue that said: Gay, Lesbian, Bisexual Association. The puzzle piece was cut out and removed several times in the first few weeks of school. Each time, though, it was replaced and notes like "this may not be your thing, but this group is a part of our campus community," appeared nearby.

Our group, Perspectives, continued to meet regularly, but with few, if any, self proclaimed heterosexuals. And, when they did come, it was with an announcement of sincere interest or support. We sponsored forums on spirituality and sexuality and forums on the research on sexual orientation, all without catching the eye of the local paper or the rage of the local community. Occasionally a fundamentalist Christian would arrive at our meetings, but our conversations were always sincere exchanges of differences in view.

My office became the place where gay and lesbian students, fearful of attending a meeting, came to talk about problems, or just pass the time of day. The school newspaper occasionally printed editorials condemning the "immoral lifestyle" of homosexuals, but also often printed supportive pieces and releases on important gay and lesbian issues.

In the middle of my second year I was named dean of the School of Education and in the middle of my third year at Phillips, I received tenure as a full professor. The puzzle piece was moved to its "permanent home" at the top left corner of the puzzle on the wall in the Earl Butts residence hall. In similar fashion, our group and my sexuality also moved from the center to the top left corner of the university. We were there, but out of the view of most, and apparently not worth climbing all the way up to bother.

An earlier version of this essay appeared in the October, 1993 issue of *The Herland Voice*, volume 10, number 10, Herland Sister Resources, 2312 N.W. 39, Oklahoma City, Oklahoma 73112. Used with permission.

Transforming "The Master's Tools"

Teaching and Studying Philosophy in Graduate School

Carol J. Moeller

Department of Philosophy,
University of Pittsburgh

18

In my undergraduate years at Oberlin College, I was fortunate to be part of the most stimulating political and intellectual climate I have ever known. In this small private college in rural Ohio, with a progressive history, the women's studies program was phenomenal. Studying with Chandra Mohanty and bell hooks, especially, we challenged ourselves to do the kind of intellectual and activist work which was truly liberating and feminist, confronting the intersections of all forms of oppression simultaneously. We demanded that intellectual work be relevant and responsive to the real crises of our world, enabling us to understand the world and intervene with it. We struggled to challenge ways in which academia reproduces societal oppression but we also aimed to find room to work productively within it, to learn, study, and grow. We saw academia as a vital site for political struggle, a space of contradictions and radical possibilities, one we did not want to leave to the nonfeminist scholars.

Majoring in women's studies and philosophy, I always brought tools of feminist critique to more traditional philosophy classes, challenging those intellectual spaces to be responsive to my concerns, making feminist questions central to philosophical analysis. Even the traditional philosophy professors at Oberlin were open to my critical engagement. In ethics courses, I insisted that ethical theories are flawed if they did not challenge us to confront racism, sexism, and other oppressions. In metaphysics and epistemology (theory of knowledge) classes, I continually brought in feminist work. I wrote and spoke with passion. I listened, argued, and fought my way through philosophical training, developing my philosophical abilities through critical confrontation of disciplinary limitations and assumptions.

I found philosophical tools useful, when critically transformed, but dangerous on their own terms, especially if they are imagined to offer all of the answers to questions of what the world is like and how it ought to be. I accepted Audre Lorde's view on this sort of question, the point she initially made in challenging feminists to deal with difference among women, instead of continuing the "divide and conquer" mindset of the oppressors. Audre Lorde writes, *"Survival is not an academic skill. . . .* It is learning how to take our differences and make them strengths. *For the master's tools will never dismantle the master's house.* They may allow us to temporarily beat him at his own game, but they will never enable us to bring about genuine change."* (Audre Lorde, *Sister Outsider*, Freedom, CA: Crossing Press, 1984.)

As an out lesbian, a feminist theorist, and an activist committed to changing the world and the academy, I anticipated resistance to my voice within philosophy and elsewhere, and I suspected that Pittsburgh's credentials would be helpful to me in being taken seriously. Though I was quite critical of "the master's tools" of traditional philosophy, I came to graduate school with the bold plan of single-handedly forcing male-dominated philosophy to collapse on its own contradictions, so that progressive feminist philosophies might be forged. Having been politically and intellectually nurtured through my undergraduate years, I was ill-prepared to confront a graduate program which was much less hospitable to my no-holds-barred critique of traditional philosophy. I arrived for the very prestigious master's and doctoral program in philosophy at the University of Pittsburgh, a program not famous for being feminist or progressive, being more concerned to *change* philosophy than to *learn* it.

In my physical presence within the Ivory Tower, in my pedagogy, and in my philosophical work, I have done just about anything I could imagine to make my queer feminist presence felt. I have worn t-shirts and jackets with statements like "Queer Girl" and "What Are You Doing About AIDS?" and bright fluorescent Queer Nation stickers saying "Dykes Rule," and so on.

Did this bastion of male-dominated philosophy quake in the face of my combat boots? Not really. They were quite welcoming of me as an out lesbian. The University of Pittsburgh's philosophy graduate department has provided me with fellowship and teaching support for over five years now. My department was fairly queer-sensitive even before I started. Faculty reached out to me, letting me know that other out lesbians and gay men had preceded me. One professor gave me a tape of Bessie Smith, presumably thinking that Bessie Smith and I have lesbianism and jazz in common. For departmental parties, invitations are always addressed to faculty, staff, and students, and their "significant others" or "partners," rather than simply spouses. Each time I brought a girlfriend to a party or other event, the reception was cordial and friendly. Faculty shook hands with a girl-friend at a departmental party; one faculty member's wife made "faculty spouse" smalltalk, saying to the girlfriend, "Let's leave the philosophers to their shoptalk."

My philosophy department seemed to have no trouble with my being an out lesbian with militant views, as long as my views did not impact nega-tively upon my living up to their philosophical standards, "the master's tools." I thought the tools were politically problematic, if not evil, and I had come to graduate school more to be credentialed to do my own revo-lutionary work than to become a "straight philosopher." Whatever trouble I had in dealing with my department was not traceable to overt homopho-bia, sexism, or classism. Rather, criticisms were made (often correctly) of my academic work, since it failed to reflect the standards of the department in which I had enrolled as a student.

At graduate school, I was enrolled in seminars in which men often out-numbered women three to one. The style of philosophy was often ruthlessly combative. Some women in the department came to describe the dominant discussion style as "penis-waving." When we new graduate students dis-cussed our interests, I talked about feminism and rethinking of ethics. One graduate student after another asked incredulously why I had come to phi-losophy to study *that*. One older student made a sweeping judgment that he did not care for any of the work I liked, since he cared about "clarity and rigor." I would later learn that insistence upon "clarity and rigor," the slogan of standards in analytic philosophy, can be used to belittle and dis-credit anything which a traditional philosopher does not understand or does not want to understand.

During graduate philosophy seminars, I often went into extreme panics, as discomfort with narrow intellectualist arguments in seminars gave way to feelings of danger at my visceral experience of male domination. The seminars may have been on philosophical topics, but the mode of argument felt like verbal, sexist violence. The accepted style of engagement was one of verbal attack, and tactics of humiliation were part of this arsenal. Imag-ine the most sneering and sarcastic tone expressing with utter disbelief, when I made a point, "Surely you can't think *that*?" Men and women, but more often men, expressed their ideas in a mode of domination and attack. When this antagonistic mode, along with the potential domination built into the ideas and methods themselves, rose beyond a certain level, I was often triggered into bouts of extreme fearfulness. I would panic with a sudden feeling of danger at the number and style of men in the room. My

experience as a lesbian in these philosophy seminars was extremely difficult. Taking courses in other departments with less combative styles, I had
no difficulties, but in these philosophy seminars, I was plummeted into
feelings of abject terror.

In this academic environment, between my palpable fear and my polit-
ical-intellectual suspicions of traditional philosophy, I failed to thrive. My
own term papers were sometimes weak, one-sided attempts to assert my
own reality, on my own terms. To my professors, I am sure they were quite
incomprehensible. They had no way of knowing that my polemics were
serving to keep me going through a struggle quite invisible to them,
except insofar as they could tell I was unhappy and distressed.

Ultimately, my intellectual crisis manifested in ways that made it clear
that it was interfering with my graduate training. I was brought up short
academically, not for being feminist, queer, or radical, but for lacking clarity
and rigor, for failing to operate within the theoretical paradigm of my graduate program. My academic ideas and methods needed to be constrained, on
my faculty's view, but not my sexuality or politics, per se.

In response to their concerns, I was "grounded" to the philosophy
department for a year, prohibited from taking courses in other departments, especially in women's studies or cultural studies. I was put on a sort
of probation, given a chance to remedy my weaknesses in the sorts of traditional philosophy they valued. They suggested that I prove that I was in
fact "one of them."

I committed myself to studying the traditional work, on its own terms,
with hope that any potential damage to my values and political consciousness would not be irreparable. A few sympathetic professors worked with
me to convey their understanding of the norms and methods of analytic
philosophy. One professor worked with me in using a feminist critique of
logic as a means of access into traditional logic, which had previously
seemed quite impossible to digest. I had seen the methods of formal logic
and heavy intellectualist thinking used against people, to silence and
ridicule the views of those who do not use formal logic, and my concerns
about the abuses of philosophy made me reluctant to learn it, regardless of
whatever productive purposes I might be able to make of it. I wrote an
essay, responding to Andrea Nye's feminist critique of logic, arguing in
logic for Audre Lorde's position that the master's tools can never dismantle
the master's house. When I showed the essay to a professor I had come to
trust, she replied that if I agreed with Audre Lorde, then Pittsburgh's philosophy department was not the place for me. She argued that my struggling through the alienation, disempowerment, and intellectual challenges

of the philosophy program only made sense if I thought their tools had real value and I genuinely wanted to be trained in them.

This confrontation from a friendly philosopher pushed me to really examine whether I thought traditional philosophical methods had value, or whether I just wanted the credentials and privilege that a Ph.D. in philosophy from a top program could offer. I worked my way through this intellectual crisis, writing several drafts of that essay on the master's tools, ultimately developing the view that the master's tools, in and by themselves, could not effect radical change. However, ethical use can be made of those tools, when they are conjoined with tools of radical critique, such as antiracist feminist theory. I came to the conclusion that my strategy of dismissal, fear, and militant confrontation were perhaps less suited to these academic struggles than they had been to my undergraduate activism (such as a takeover of the administration building for three days in an antiracist, antiapartheid action). I overhauled my dismissive strategy to traditional philosophical methods and accepted that I needed to learn the traditional tools, as well as critique them.

I came to believe that it was possible for me to learn traditional philosophical methods without losing myself and my voice. My fears of philosophy—fears of becoming absorbed by the dominant culture, of losing my political consciousness, of becoming someone I did not want to be—somehow transmuted into intellectual energy. My allies helped me learn to write papers and receive comments in which my professors and I did more than speak past each other. I torturously wrote papers which they could recognize, still on matters of interest to me, but more on their turf.

In learning to operate in their mode of philosophy, I often felt completely bereft of voice, purpose, and intelligence. My writing seemed alien, forced, and remote from my genuine concerns. My own work had always been grounded in my experiences as a lesbian and feminist, an activist scholar from a working-class background, committed to politics of liberation. Writing and thinking within the narrow mode of professional philosophy often left me feeling quite lost and out of touch with my own voice.

To my professors, the upshot of all of this stategic "colonizing of the mind" was a vast improvement in my academic work. My grades improved. The next annual review of me was exemplary, and a professor congratulated me, "You really *are* one of us." I cannot begin to explain how this disturbed me, since my greatest fear had been that I *would* become one of them. I had continued with graduate work in philosophy in order to change philosophy, to be part of radical change which would enable voices like my own to be heard, to use the privileges of academic life in the interests of liberation. It seemed that making it through this dominant institution involved working on their terms, which carried a great cost. I only was willing to continue because of my activism and contact with radical friends and professors, who assured me that my friends would keep me from sinking into oblivion within traditional philosophy, so that whatever sense I had of losing myself and my voice would turn out to be temporary.

But I speak too quickly here. These are all the things I cannot go into, until I know who will chance across these words. Being disloyal to oppressive structures serves me well as an activist, but here it might just get me kicked out of graduate school. Having grown up working class, I am all too aware of the risks involved in speaking honestly, when I need my paycheck to continue. Especially when my activism led to some judicial charges against me as an undergraduate, I was continually warned by my late mother that my college would kick me out or cut my financial aid if I did not stop "getting into trouble." Even today, writing this, in my own apartment, with my beloved companion cat basking in the heat of my desk lamp, I am afraid. I can write any of this only by promising myself that it is a draft which I need not show anyone. Even in the relative privacy of my own mind, I find the voices of traditional philosophy, and the particular voices of my professors, chastising me. I lose my train of thought, wondering if I am not just being ridiculous, and exaggerating. After all, I'm told by other women graduate students, they barely speak to women students at Oxford, so what am I complaining about? Hardly any of the women graduate students here claim to experience the difficulties I hesitantly try to raise with them. Sure, none of them are out dykes, but then my department has been supportive of me, have they not? They did not even give me trouble when I wrote "Dyke Power" in huge permanent-ink letters on the bathroom wall in the department. (It was erased in days, met with silence, leaving me feeling even more insignificant when even my rage could be smoothed off the walls.)

A disempowering aspect of oppressive structures is the myriad ways they can reduce us to silence and self-negation, so that even we do not support ourselves through our struggles. The danger is that even we blame ourselves for our trouble fitting into dominant institutions, thus becoming further disempowered. I recall the advice of Clare Dalton, feminist law professor who was denied tenure at Harvard, on working in dominant, oppressive institutions, "Never underestimate the danger you are in" and "don't personalize" your difficulty in dominant institutions. As oppressed people, it is crucial that we not interpret such troubles in overly psychologistic and individual terms, as merely reflecting "insecurities" and so on. To do this obscures the institutional reasons that oppressed people may be more prone to these problems than those who are authorized by race, class, and sex privilege to value their own ideas, to see themselves as the sort of people who should be at the front of classrooms.

During the week of the annual evaluations of graduate students one year at our prestigious philosophy graduate program, one woman graduate student tried to kill herself, and a second was hospitalized as suicidal. Almost as alarming as these facts is how these "incidents" were treated with silence in my department. Some self-avowed feminists found it peculiar when I wondered aloud if these two near-suicides indicated anything about the pressures of our departmental evaluations, or the difficulties women have in our male-dominated department. They attributed the problems to the personalities involved, that the first woman was unreasonable, and the second a reasonable woman made unreasonable by stress and "chemical imbalances in the brain." I wonder how many other women have gone to the verge of collapse in the environment of our department and others like it.

Yet, I have kept going, for five and a half years of rigorous training. I have now only my dissertation to complete, and my department has become very supportive of me since my dramatic turnaround. From the time of that evaluation which declared me to be doing well with "the master's tools," I have gotten nothing but support in using those tools and in fashioning my own. The traditional tools, on their own, will not bring about deep and lasting change, but when appropriated strategically in struggle—and refashioned for radical purposes—can do quite a lot. Not the least of what they can do is to keep me empowered in the face of traditional philosophy, and provide means for critique. Much more, they can be integrated with feminist and other approaches to produce transformative knowledges, oppositional to domination.

In teaching, I get the freedom to practice my own conception of philosophy. In my courses, I taught texts from lesbian writers and other progressive thinkers, in addition to mainstream philosophy. For example, I used Audre Lorde's *Sister Outsider* in an ethics course, as well as Aristotle and Kant. Gloria Anzaldua's anthology, *Making Face, Making Soul: Critical and Creative Perspectives By Women of Color*, was a primary text in my feminist philosophy course. I find that many students want to reject radical writings, especially by those who name themselves as lesbian or feminist or black or Asian. I always insist that they learn to understand the writers on the writers' own terms, in addition to critiquing their views. In this age of a backlash against "political correctness"—a charge which is meant to automatically dismiss and discredit a teacher or text—I have often had to

challenge students to take these texts seriously. I have to struggle, peda-
gogically, to get them to take the philosophical "classics" seriously, but in
very different ways. I am more secure with my institution in the latter
struggle, more ambivalent within myself; the university wants me to teach
the "classics," whereas I most value what Paulo Friere calls "education for
critical consciousness."

Though there have been real challenges in my struggles for change
within and without the academia, my position could not be creative without my asserting all of who I am. I wish I could offer a happy ending, a
redemptive narrative which shows how I have neatly resolved all of my
struggles and questions, once and for all. That would be a mistake, though,
even to hope for. Contradictory positions, with privilege and oppression,
are just the sorts of things that call for constant rethinking and renegotia-
tion. It would be dangerous for me to think I have "arrived" at permanent
resolution, since these concerns are much bigger than me and my particular location. Further, it is part of the arrogance of philosophical method to
pretend that oppression could be transformed by individual intellectual
effort. My work is part of a larger struggle of people learning to live and
think in ways which allow us all to flourish, in the face of forces of domination. Instead, I keep working, writing, and teaching, helping my own
voice grow louder than those which put it down. I try to live my life so that
I am truly part of a collective of people working, across our differences,
toward a world which will be more truly free.

Of African Descent
A Three-fers Story

Akilah Monifa

Law School,
New College of California

19

Three-fers or Myths of Marketability:
I Already Have One of Those, 3-in-1 is Too Much, Thank You

OK, what's a "three-fer?" In employment terms, it's someone who possesses three identities from categories which have historically been underemployed in professional employment. Some would say three minority statuses. But I hate the "m" word, and besides, it is not accurate in my case. I am a woman, certainly not literally in the minority, and I am also a lesbian, arguably in the minority if you believe the 10 percent theory, and I am of African descent, also arguably in the minority if grouped alone and if not coupled with other groups of color, particularly in the state of California.

So, what's the deal with three-fers? I am supposedly guaranteed any job I apply for. I am the person who is replacing heterosexual white men as law professors in the 200-plus law schools in the United States. Merely because of my status schools are soliciting me to teach. Wait, the phone is ringing, perhaps it's Harvard Law School. No, it's just Derrick Bell telling me that Harvard like most law schools and many other institutions, cannot find a "qualified" person of color to teach there.

'57, the Beginning

Let's start from the beginning. Born in 1957 in Manhattan, Kansas, aka the little Apple. Reared in Huntsville, Alabama, the heart of Dixie—Wallace country at that time, although because of the electronic and space-and-rocket industry remarkably like San Jose, California, in the Silicon Valley in its hey day. Left home at seventeen for Atlanta and Emory University, dropped out after my sophomore year, spent some time in Europe and then transferred to Upstate New York, SUNY at Binghampton where I received my undergraduate degree.

Despising the cold and snow, I then headed west for law school. In 1981, during my second year in law school, I fell in love with a woman. That relationship was consummated and we were to remain friends and lovers on and off for the next ten years. I was active in our rather clandestine lesbian and gay men organization on campus. I had a relatively easy time of coming out; I was not in turmoil about my sexual orientation and was surrounded by friends who were for the most part supportive.

I spent the first five years of my legal career not being out in any meaningful way. It did not appear on my resume for I was not affiliated with any lesbian or gay organization. I also did not appear at work functions with any one woman described as a girlfriend or partner. Most folks at work knew that I was a lesbian but because I did not have a steady partner, this seemingly had no effect on them. It was as if they did not see me with a girlfriend, it was easier to take because I was lesbian in theory but not in practice or in reality. Folks did not have to deal with the actuality of my lesbianism in the form of interacting with a partner and all the awkwardness that might present.

Hello Academia

My career in academia began innocently enough in 1990, with a friend, who was then the admissions director at Golden Gate School of Law informing me that there were openings for adjunct professors to teach legal research and writing. With some trepidation I was interviewed by the head of the department, an openly gay man. I felt relieved because he was gay and immediately felt the kinship that folks feel when coming home, so to speak. The interview went well and I taught at Golden Gate for three academic years. During this time I joined a local gay and lesbian bar association, BALIF, (Bay Area Lawyers for Individual Freedom). Because no queer identifying words appeared in the title, only those in the know could out me as a lesbian from my paper trail alone.

Ask Another Queer in the Class But He Won't Tell

During my first year of teaching, in the 1990–91 academic year there was an openly gay student in my class. He came out during orientation as well as during his introduction in my first-year legal research and writing class. He was also instrumental in reviving the defunct Queer Law Students Association. I formed a friendship with this student after the conclusion of the academic year. He accompanied me to the graduation at Davis Law

School where Derrick Bell was the commencement speaker. At that time he revealed to me that every member of our small section of about twenty students had come to him at various times during the academic year and asked if Professor Monifa was a lesbian. The student replied that he didn't know as his gaydar only worked with men. He told me that he never gave my sexual orientation any thought until the other students started asking about it. During my first year of teaching at Golden Gate, no student or professor surreptitiously or otherwise came out to me.

Sight Recognition, Second Year of Teaching

While still an adjunct professor at Golden Gate School of Law and while working at the Public Interest Clearinghouse as project coordinator, I was out at least by sight recognition. While tabling for a public interest event a student walked in and gave that unmistakable double take of recognition of seeing another obviously out lesbian. This student was in her late forties and was very direct when she approached me. She wanted to talk for a couple of reasons. One, she wanted validation that there was someone like her in law school, and also in the legal profession. She merely wanted confirmation of the fact that I was indeed a mirror of her queerness. Another was that she heard that my class was doing a moot court assignment in the courtroom of Judge Donna Hitchens, a open lesbian sitting in Superior Court. The student wanted to accompany me and my class and to meet Judge Hitchens as she wanted to clerk for the judge. (She went on to clerk for the judge and has now graduated and is a practicing attorney.)

Unofficial Mentor to All Queers

The two aforementioned students are among a score of queer students who seemed absolutely thrilled at my mere presence and outness. They gravitated to me for mentorship and solidarity. I must confess that I went through my academic pursuits without having the pleasure of having an out queer as a professor. To my knowledge there were none at the institutions in which I was matriculated. However, many queer students would come to my office to just to chat or to come out.

Out in the Interview and More

In 1991 I began teaching at New College and came out during the interview. Of course I knew that New College was safe because they had several open queers on their faculty and promoted this fact. In fact, in the 1992–93 academic year three of the four second-year professors were out lesbians, and all four were women. In the 1994–95 academic year four out of six professors in the first year class are out queers. We have a very active Queer Caucus and will have our first ever Queer Law Review. Our small school boasted of an entering class of 21 percent out queers. I'm positive the actual percentage is higher.

Students who are struggling with their sexual orientation also come to me on the pretext of discussing something else but usually end up discussing their personal lives in some way. The conversations usually begin innocently enough with some neutralization of pronouns which I am expected to follow up on. I often privately reveal my personal life to students as time progresses and when they are not currently enrolled in my class.

Out in the Classroom, the Third Year

Now I make a conscious effort to be out. I started this in the 1993–94 academic year. I decided to make mention of a partner and specifically refer to this partner with a feminine pronoun. I also make sure queers are present in my lecture, hypotheticals in and outside class, in the course materials, and in examinations. I call students on their heterosexism as well as homophobia. I challenge gender neutral assumptions about the sexual orientation of parties in lawsuits. I also frequently wear a rainbow-triangle gay-pride watch, rainbow rings on a necklace and other queer jewelry.

I am a participant as well as faculty advisor in the Queer Caucus and have even on occasion gone out with a group of queer students. With my queer students, more so than with their straight counterparts, there is a lowering of barriers and there is much more familiarity about my private life.

It's OK, She's from Another School

Still in my third year of teaching I was contacted by a student from Northeastern who was doing an internship in the San Francisco Bay Area. She had seen my bio in a list of mentors for the local gay and lesbian bar association. She was not interested in teaching but contacted me because she was new in town and I was the only lesbian of color in the mentor book. We spoke on the phone and because she lived nearby I invited her over to my home. I had never had a student, straight or queer, in my home. I realized that I was pushing the boundaries of the student-teacher relationship. But I justified her visit by acknowledging that she was not currently enrolled in my class and was in fact attending a school 3,000 miles away. Still I was troubled about what others might think about me associating with a law student. My institution has no written policies on fraternizing with students, other faculty, or staff; this seemed to me more of a moral dilemma, and would not be covered even if there were regulations.

I ended up spending time with the student and even spent a platonic weekend away with her. But I still worried about the impact on other students if I were to be seen with her.

Perception of Straight Students

I wonder what the straight students are thinking about me. Do they perceive a bias in favor of the queer students? Do I treat queer students differently than straight students? Is there an imperceptible smile, delight, joy when a queer student responds well in class? Am I harder on straight students, less frequent with praise? I have received isolated comments on student evaluations indicating that I have a bias towards queer students and students of color. On the other hand I have also received praise from queer students for being there and being out and vocal.

The criticisms were always without examples and seemed to stem more from not being a part of any club/organization that it was perceived that I was in.

Teaching Queer Courses

I initially shied away from teaching queer courses in law school. I did this primarily because I wanted to avoid the ghettoization in pedagogy and research, and fight the notion that my queerness limits my scholarship and teaching. I avoided race theory and feminist theory for the same reasons. I was more interested in bringing my various perspectives to nonqueer substantive courses, to show that they did make a difference in a course. I did this to illustrate the need for true diversity in our institutions, to show that I would teach torts differently than a straight man of European descent. We would both cover the basic so-called black letter law, but I might discuss the reasonable woman theory in torts or the reasonable lesbian theory in addition to the reasonable man (read straight). There were valid reasons to wanting my different perspectives in a classroom environment, and this would benefit everyone regardless of sexual orientation.

In my first three years of teaching I only lectured once in a course on AIDS and the law course. Last year I reluctantly agreed to teach a sexual orientation and the law seminar. I thought, why should I have to teach it just because I'm queer? Then I realized that I in fact wanted to teach such a course, even though I did not want to teach such courses exclusively. I was certainly more interested than I was inititially in teaching either criminal law, torts, or legal research and writing. I felt that I had proved myself, had proved that I was capable of teaching substantive nonqueer courses. Now I was free to branch out and teach a course that I was truly interested in. I would not be subject to the criticisms had I initially started out teaching queer courses and then tried to make the transition to substantive nonqueer courses.

So, I have the privilege of teaching a small seminar course on sexual orientation and the law. But isn't this the natural order of things in academia? First you teach courses where there is an institutional need, then you are rewarded and allowed to put together an elective of your desire. (Ironically my seminar has no men, another dilemma for another article.)

"Hello," or Flirting with Students, or What to do When a Student Has a Crush on You or Vice-Versa.

Somehow this area seems to be more of a problem than for straight professors, even at the graduate school level. As a child growing up in the south, the only time I recall the word "lesbian" being mentioned was in conjunction with a professor at Alabama A&M University who had supposedly seduced an student. The details are not clear: the ages of the folks involved, nor their respective statuses, and so on. But it was clear that the primary reason that folks were shocked was because of the type of sexual activity and not any possible power inequities between the parties. It was as if no one had heard of heterosexual professors having affairs with students.

Appearance of Impropriety

I also see this area as problematic because of the negative stereotyping often accompanying queers, that of the pervert and or the molester. This language is often used in a situation involving adults without determining whether the acts are consensual. As a personal policy I have taken the easy road: Do not get sexually/romantically involved with any student currently attending your institution. This seems to me a good catch-all policy and avoids even the appearance of impropriety.

I extend this policy to usually not going anywhere with an individual student, straight or gay, though I sometimes hang out immediately after school with a group of students. These rules have been violated on occasion but are usually limited to lunch or tea with a student at a public restaurant directly across from the school and meeting with students in a local café on days I am not on campus. However, I do sometimes feel uncomfortable when spotted by other students. Usually it is obvious that it is a student-teacher meeting as the student usually has some writing for me to review. But sometimes I perceive that feeling of disparate treatment from the student not having the appointment with me. Like, why don't I get this length of appointment in a different locale? The reality is that I meet with students if they request it. It's like the Benjamin Franklin adage, "Nothing ventured, nothing gained." If a student requests a lengthy meeting I try to accommodate.

Flirting

I certainly have been attracted to queer students, and to straight students, too. But it has never risen to the point of testing my rules. I'm not sure what period of time needs to elapse after graduation or leaving the school for me to feel comfortable with dating a student; this has not happened yet.

However, I have been at community events in our small school (student population 150) and flirted with someone whom I did not recognize as a student. This person did not know that I was a professor; fortunately before the flirt went on, another queer student intervened and introduced us by name and title of professor and student. Finally, I would be remiss not to discuss a student who had a tremendous crush on me. I cared about this student but stuck to my rules. The situation was certainly awkward for months. When the student came by my office, if I had an appointment with another student, particularly a queer one, I felt as if I were betraying some sacred trust. I finally resolved it somewhat by talking to the student directly and telling her despite my interest that I would not pursue a relationship with her. She remains a friend.

It seems only fitting that queer students would get crushes on queer faculty. Certainly this happens with straight profs and students. I think that some students are predisposed to having crushes on me, just because I am out and visible, almost as if I am validating their sexual orientation.

Conclusion

As might be imagined, my degree of outness has increased over the years of teaching, in proportion to both job security and my own personal growth. I am currently partnered and my partner is taking advantage of the domestic partner educational benefits. Overall, I take my task as a role model seriously and think that my presence benefits both straight and queer students. Perhaps in the future there will be no need for such a book as *Lesbians in Academia*, because it won't be an issue.

This
Is the Place

Sue Morrow

Department of Educational Psychology,
University of Utah

20

"This is the place!" were the words uttered by Brigham Young as he led Latter-day Saints (LDS, or Mormon) pioneers over the Wasatch Mountains into the Great Salt Lake Basin. The Mormon settlers took great risks to find a home in this valley. For the title of this chapter, I have reclaimed Young's words to reflect the risk and hope that are necessary to create a safe home for all of Utah's citizens.

"When I dare to be powerful—to use my strength in the service of my vision, then it becomes less and less important whether I am afraid." So says Audre Lorde in a 1994 calendar.

Some days I cling to these words of Lorde. One of those days occurred last year, when an ultraconservative student organization on campus sponsored as a guest speaker Joseph Nicolosi, a California psychologist who specializes in "reparative" therapy of gay men. ("Given the political climate in Utah," I complained, "was it really necessary to *import* a radical conservative?") Following the adversarial presentation, three of us—a lesbian political science colleague, a gay male graduate student in my program, and I—conducted an informal panel discussion titled, "Healing Homophobia." My heart pounded as I began to speak, authoritatively I hoped, about the statistical evasions that had characterized Nicolosi's speech. With the media in attendance, I had just gone public as a lesbian at the University of Utah!

What brought me to Utah? Arizona was certainly not a hotbed of liberalism, but *Utah?* Periodically, I ask the same question. Most certainly, I came to the University of Utah because the job description seemed written for me: gender issues, multicultural concerns, individual and group counseling, and qualitative research. When one of the search committee members called to tell me I was on the short list, he told me, "Oh, and by the way, we've noticed your interest in alternative lifestyles; and I just wanted to let you know that, should you want to do research in that area, the University Counseling Center is very gay-affirmative and would support your recruiting subjects there." They knew I was a lesbian! And it would be all right! More recently, I learned that my sexual orientation was not an issue among the department faculty, but that my qualitative research orientation was controversial.

The interview process went very well, and at dinner with the department chair, our discussion drifted to music and children. At one point, he asked, "So how do your children—and your significant other, if you have one—feel about your potential move?" Explaining that my children were in college in California and would be largely unaffected, I continued by telling him that my partner was an Arizona psychologist and, although supportive of the move, was concerned about her Utah licensure. He did not bat an eyelash about my use of female pronouns.

My earliest days in Salt Lake City were idyllic. Our lesbian realtor in Tempe had found us a lesbian realtor in Salt Lake City. My program chair and his wife took us into their home when we came to look for a home. The associate vice president of Diversity and Faculty Development insisted Donna send her vita so that his office could assist her in finding a position. At the beginning of the academic year, he invited us to a department party at his home, where he went out of his way to introduce us to other lesbians. I felt invincible, courageous, and supported. Students—not necessarily lesbian or gay—have sought me out, saying how important it is that I am here. I have been encouraged by my chair and program director to develop a course on counseling lesbians, gays, and bisexuals. Serving on the Women's Studies Executive Committee my first year, I met lesbian and heterosexual feminists who have supported me in this transition.

I have found networking with lesbians and feminists to be a very rewarding process. At first, there was our lesbian realtor. In addition, while we were still in Arizona, Donna began calling Salt Lake City therapists listed in our Association for Women in Psychology directory. We found our first friend in the community, a lesbian feminist psychologist, who has become a member of our family in the truest sense. I made my first lesbian academic contact through the AWP directory, as well, when I called the only person listed in Salt Lake City who had named "research" as an interest. I explained to her that I was interviewing for a position and was seeking a feminist contact at the university. It turned out that she was a doctoral student in the counseling psychology program, the very program that was the focus of my attention and hopes! When I asked her what it was like to be an out feminist in the department, she responded that she was also an out lesbian, and that she experienced considerable support. When I came to interview, she was my greatest supporter at my colloquium and student luncheon. Also, because of wonderful lesbian and feminist networking, my partner Donna works parttime at the university's Women's Resource Center, providing training in feminist therapy for doctoral practicum students and facilitating lesbian and women's empowerment groups.

Life as a lesbian feminist in Utah is not always easy. Soon after my arrival I was told, "You just have to get used to the idea that you live in a theocracy." The majority of residents in the state are affiliated with the Church of Jesus Christ of Latter-day Saints (the Mormon, or LDS, church). Church leaders have been known to identify the three enemies of the church as feminists, intellectuals, and homosexuals. The LDS church's official stance against homosexuality is very harsh, varying from condemnation to repulsion. The "walking wounded" here are lesbians and, especially, gay men who grew up Mormon and were unable to resolve the tremendous conflicts between their sexual orientations and their religious beliefs. An LDS young man or woman who admits to being gay or lesbian risks many of the dangers any young lesbian or gay confronts: rejection by family and church, ridicule by peers. However, the believing LDS lesbian or gay man also is confronted with the knowledge that she or he can never, even if celibate, achieve the highest realms of heaven reserved for the most faithful, because she or he will never marry nor, presumably, have children. Marriage and children are central not only to LDS culture, but to its theology. There are also implications for the lesbian or gay person's family: No matter how loving, the family can never hope to be united with their lesbian or gay child in the hereafter. In addition, being Mormon is not just a "church thing"; it involves family, neighbors, persons with whom one does business—in short, one's entire lifestyle. To leave the church may mean losing every support system one has ever had, including one's employment.

So why this digression into Mormonism? The longer I have lived here, the more acutely aware I am of the effects of this culture not only on lesbians and gays who have grown up Mormon, but on every lesbian woman and gay man who lives here. To be lesbian or gay here takes great courage. The people of Salt Lake City are, for the most part, a polite people. But beneath the politeness and neighborliness is an enforced silence about what is euphemistically referred to as "alternative lifestyles." The word "gay" is used infrequently enough; "lesbian," hardly ever (and "queer," never). Although Salt Lake City is approximately half Mormon and the university even less so, silencing is powerful even on campus.

Ignorance is even stronger. Invited to present to a group of student residence hall advisors (R.A.'s) about gender issues, I made a point to include lesbian and gay concerns. When I asked if the R.A.'s had any questions, there was only one, a serious question from a young man: "Just one thing. I don't know, if I'm talking to a gay guy, if I should call him 'he' or 'she.'" Being of the "there are no stupid questions" variety of presenter, I patiently explained the differences among lesbians, gays, bisexuals, transvestites, and transgendered individuals. But I left enraged that any lesbian or gay young people in the group—or in the residence halls—should be subjected to such ignorance. And having believed I had already done "Lesbianism 101," I was disillusioned to know I must begin again, possibly many more times.

The University of Utah includes sexual orientation in its nondiscrimination clause. However, when I signed up for my benefits and asked about the inclusion of unmarried domestic partners, I was told they are not covered. As a result, Donna buys her own health insurance and pays many of her own medical expenses. Between her insurance payments, the deductible, and the copay, we lost $2000 our first year here—essentially $2000 of salary for discrimination. Recently, reacting to Hawaii's upcoming law permitting lesbian and gay marriages, the Utah legislature passed a law stating that same-sex marriages from other states would not be recognized. Shortly thereafter, a faculty committee on campus unanimously voted against domestic partner benefits, lest the university be seen as bucking the legislature.

There is a small movement afoot on campus to address this injustice and to obtain domestic partner benefits for faculty and staff. I have been asked if my tenure would be in jeopardy were I to become a test case. Although I have assurances from my program director and department chair that I am in no danger, I still do not know how those ranking higher in the administration might respond if I were to be publicly identified. So, while I trust the department's tenure process, I do not know what the consequences might be at the university level if I am a test case and if I am publicly identified as a lesbian.

Contradictions abound in my life and work here at the University of Utah. I did not come to Utah to be political or to conduct lesbian or gay research, yet I felt compelled by the environment to do both. Despite the challenges, I continue to be amazed by the unexpected benefits. I received a faculty starter-grant for my proposed research on influences of sexual orientation on the career development of lesbian, gay, and bisexual women and men. I have been able to travel to San Francisco to conduct interviews there, which provide strong contrast to research participants in Salt Lake City. I recently requested an extension for my grant, citing the need to make one more trip to San Francisco. My request was granted. As I enjoyed a chocolate truffle and a glass of sherry at the gay-owned bed and breakfast where I stayed in San Francisco's Castro District, I toasted those individuals in Utah who are open-minded enough to fund my research. One of the participants in my research recently declared, "I'm ready to start being paid for being a lesbian!" While I cannot lay claim to that honor, the fact that my queer research is being funded by the university gives me hope that such a wish is not out of reach for lesbians in academe.

The real joy of this work comes through my relationships with lesbian, gay, and bisexual students. During my own master's program in counseling and, later, my Ph.D. program, I often felt I was single-handedly responsible for raising the consciousness of students and faculty regarding lesbian and gay issues. If not I, then who? Although I received support from faculty (including lesbians), none were overt about their sexual orientations. I promised then that I would never contribute to an environment in which my students felt compelled to come out in order for the issues to be addressed. I made a commitment to myself—and to my future graduate students—that I would take the risks, leaving my students free to make clear choices about how open they would be and how much consciousness-raising they would do. After I asked one of my students—a gay man—to read the first draft of this article, he wrote:

> Coming out in the department has allowed me to do professionally what I intended from the very beginning: queer research. Without a very safe place, I would not have come out in the department. You have single-handedly made this department a safe place. I know that seems like a big burden, and it is; but just you being here and being open and comfortable with who you are is what really makes the difference. I hope that I can pass on your legacy when I "grow up" and become an academic—to be out and making sure the issues are addressed so that my queer students can make the same choice as I did to be out and to come out in a safe place. Thank you! Gaily forward.

Oddly, as I watch my students emerge as lesbian, gay, and bisexual professionals, I feel nurtured. Perhaps I still have within me that "inner lesbian graduate student" who is vicariously enjoying the mentoring she longed for as I now support my own students. As doctoral admission deadlines approach, lesbian, gay, and bisexual applicants, having read in our application materials of my research interest in lesbian and gay issues, call me to test the waters, to learn about what it is like to be queer in Salt Lake City and to find out how I might mentor them in their research interests. This year, we accepted our first openly lesbian or gay student.

My friends from Phoenix often inquire about my well-being as an out lesbian feminist in one of the most repressive spots in the country. Research participants in San Francisco blinked in disbelief as I attempted to explain what it meant to live here. However, a San Francisco "dyke-identified" bisexual woman, one of my research participants, commented after we had talked for some time about the differences between San Francisco and Salt Lake City: "That's why I need to move away. Being a lesbian here is too easy. I need to be somewhere I can make a difference." There have been many times since I made Salt Lake City my home that I have wondered, "What am I doing here?" and "Will I survive?" But for me, as for many lesbian feminists, making a difference is what gives meaning to my life. It may be the very silencing by this environment that compels me to speak out, just as lesbian and gay invisibility motivate me to display symbols— such as pink and black triangles and a pride flag in my office—or hold my lover's hand in public to counter that invisibility. In many parts of the country, it is possible to sit back and let others make changes; not in Utah. There are too few of us yet who feel we can afford the risks of being out of the closet; and there is too much work to be done to leave it to others. So, for now, this is the place.

Skirmishes
in the Borderlands
of Identity
Lesbians in Women's Studies

Sally O'Driscoll

Department of English and Women's Studies,
Fairfield University

21

Recently, a former lover called to tell me that she was planning to take hormones, the first stage of "transitioning," or changing sex. This was not a real surprise, since it was one possible logical extension of the gender presentation she had been developing over the last few years, from butch lesbian to almost passing. But because this lover was the first to make me understand gender violence on a deep level, the news of her transition made me reflect, once again, on the boundaries of gender and the painful and often violent consequences of breaching them. The backlash against gender transgressors isn't usually a big topic of discussion in women's studies programs, where it's tacitly assumed that violence happens on the street, among sissies or dykes or drag queens who don't have much to do with academia. But the experiences of my border-crossing former lover reminded me, if I needed reminding, that violence against gender transgressors is alive and well in such supposedly safe spaces as libraries, restaurants, and universities, and is often perpetrated by nice middle-class women. Let me use "bathroom episodes" as an example—occasions when someone who is culturally identified as female but whose gender presentation breaks rules goes into a public women's room and is screamed at, accosted, insulted, or threatened by women who tell her she doesn't belong there.

Bathroom episodes, however trivial they may sound, crystalize the painfulness of an "inappropriate self" and are a reliable indicator of the perils of gender transgression. They happen a lot, as a quick survey of recent literature and anecdotal evidence attests. I have friends who will never go to public restrooms both because the insults are too predictable and because it's too upsetting to be attacked by women rather than dealing with the more clear-cut violence of men on the street. And academia is hardly immune: Patricia J. Williams describes the harrowing experience of a law student who, after transitioning, was not allowed to use either the men's or the women's rooms—both male and female students united in outrage. Gender, concludes Williams, functions as property in our society, and is thus something to be fought over ("The Obliging Shell," in *The Alchemy of Race and Rights*, Harvard University Press, 1991).

Women who transgress gender boundaries put up with a consistently high level of violent rejection: women with short, "dyke-y" hair, women who wear pants, suits, ties, women who almost pass—but not quite. You'll note that I'm talking as if it were a given that gender transgression is lesbian turf—as if lesbians, particularly butch women, were the only ones who suffered from this. And it is true that in daily life, gender transgression is so frequently associated with transgression of the norms of sexuality that the two seem to be almost synonymous: we assume that these women are attacked because of how they look, *and* that they look the way they do because they're lesbians. The two factors slide into each other and become one, and it is not immediately apparent which—sexuality or gender presentation—causes the hostility. But that confusion of two different oppressions actually obscures the reality of some lesbian lives, and also obscures the root causes of that oppression. In fact, sexual transgression is quite different from gender transgression: the two need to be carefully teased apart. I would argue that of the two, transgressing the norms of sexuality is felt to be less disturbing to the status quo than gender transgression, except where the two merge (when, for example, lesbian sexuality infringes on the "rights" that our culture's gender system gives to men over women's sexuality). The two types of transgression become confused, however, because sexual transgression carries with it the possibility that the transgressor (the lesbian) will then, as a natural consequence, breach the far more important boundaries of gender as well.

The difference between the two oppressions matters to me because separating them helps me to understand one of the most painful forms of betrayal I've encountered in my academic life: the refusal of my women's studies colleagues to accept me or my life. Since I began my first tenure-track job and became immediately involved in building a women's studies program, I have struggled with an isolation and rejection that caught me unawares—I'd expected women's studies to be my haven in an otherwise hostile environment. In these past four years, I've had to come to terms with the complicated dynamic that causes this rejection: My sexual transgression as a lesbian is not an open issue as long as I keep it to myself (there is, after all, a closet to hide it in), but my gender transgression (the hints of a not-"nice lesbian" life, the motorcycle, the leather; the fact that I don't smile "enough," am too argumentative; that I wear too much black) is somehow more visible and makes my colleagues extremely uneasy. What I experience in my gut as flat-out homophobia is, I now think, a complicated mix of the two different oppressions. My colleagues react to me both personally and institutionally: personally, they tolerate a lesbian, but institutionally they find lesbians a problem (they give women's studies programs a bad name); both personally and institutionally they are made very uneasy by my failure to conform to the accepted standards of polite womanhood that prevail at our Catholic institution.

Writing this piece gives me a place to meditate on the continued failure of feminism to deal with someone like me. I should make clear that it's not intended as a wholesale attack: When, in the larger world, I appear as a woman, I benefit greatly from all that feminism and women's studies have achieved, in the sense of job opportunities, legal remedies against discrimination, and the feminist scholarship that has made my own work possible. But inside the enclave of women's studies, a different dynamic is at work: Where the outside world reads my femme self unproblematically as a woman, the women's movement and women's studies see instead all the marks of difference, the factors that separate me from the rigid and narrow concept of a "woman" that still holds sway. In women's studies, there is a refusal of difference that has devastating effects on those who are excluded.

The Wall of Silence

My presence in women's studies is problematic not for the obvious violence of bathroom episodes: My femme appearance precludes that. The violence is the more subtle but equally psychologically damaging refusal to acknowledge my life. My women's studies colleagues diligently avoid any reference to any aspect of my life that involves my sexuality—because, I am convinced, they see my sexuality as necessarily connected to other forms of gender transgression. My own toeing of the "don't ask, don't tell" line makes the avoidance easy: I am not technically out at work—that is, everybody knows I'm a lesbian but I don't publicly announce it. Those people outside my small circle of friends I have specifically told that I'm a lesbian, however, behave no differently in public or private, so it seems clear that most of my colleagues prefer avoidance as a mode.

The essence of what I experience as homophobic violence from my colleagues in women's studies is silence. Not one of my colleagues has ever asked me whether I am married, whether I live with anyone, whether I have a lover, or what I did this past weekend. In four years of friendly conversation at the coffee machine and up and down the department corridors, the only times I've given any information about my life have been at my own instigation. This is an old story, as Paula Bennett's 1982 piece "Dyke in Academe (II)" attests; examining the silence that both our colleagues and sometimes we ourselves as lesbian or gay academics perpetuate, she names that silence an "act of oppression" (in Margaret Cruikshank, ed., *Lesbian Studies, Present and Future*, New York: Feminist Press, 1982).

The refusal to acknowledge the realities of my existence causes a kind of schizophrenia in me. In my home life, with my beloved who gets called "faggot" and "dyke" on the street with equal frequency, I wear leather and ride a motorcycle, and have many friends who, because of their appearance, confront daily violence on the street. But I have another daily life, just as much a part of me: as Professor O'Driscoll, coming up for tenure at a small Catholic university where not one single tenured faculty member is out, though there seem to be a few contenders. What makes the split between my two lives untenable (and untenurable?) is not me: I have no problem seeing my different sides as part of a whole, especially now that my work is becoming more explicitly lesbian. But the ways in which my sexuality seems to suggest to my colleagues a nonconformity in gender triggers a difficult interaction.

Transgressing the Norms: Gender and Sexuality

The assumption that there is such a thing as a "natural woman" (*pace* Carole King) is the ideological sleight of hand that lies at the root of my lesbian self's discomfort in women's studies. Women's studies is predicated on marking gender as the definitive class mark of a group—"women"—who are assumed to have more in common because of gender than they have to keep them apart. Anyone whose life experience challenges that assumption (by designating sexuality, race, ethnicity, class, and so on, as more important markers) is a threat to the discipline of women's studies or the women's movement. Lesbians threaten the concept of "women" on a number of levels: After all, as Monique Wittig has argued, lesbians are *not* women, as "woman" is currently defined. As Wittig says, the concept "woman" "is only an imaginary formation, while 'woman' is the product of a social relationship" ("One Is Not Born a Woman," in *The Straight Mind and Other Essays*, Boston: Beacon Press, 1992). Wittig means that "woman" is not a set of attributes that automatically accompany a particular chromosomal pattern, but rather a set of characteristics that our culture has ascribed to such persons. In our culture, proper womanly behavior includes such characteristics as a certain attitude to male authority, maternal instinct, moral delicacy, a preference for love over sex, and so on. If femininity is determined in relation to masculinity, then a lesbian's refusal of the female role allotted to her disrupts the entire concept of femininity. For a lesbian, sexuality and gender are dissonant: a lesbian cannot be a woman as our culture currently defines "woman." And there is no sign that feminism, outside the ranks of high theory, is willing to rethink the category of "woman."

As a lesbian, then, I enter women's studies with an agenda—which is necessary for my own survival—of disentangling the strands of identity: gender from sexuality, and so on. In theory, women's studies is happy to discuss this. But in practice, theory seems to have made no inroads into real life. My lesbian body entering the women's studies office seems to send theory flying out the window: difference, when encountered in person, makes people uncomfortable. All the recent years of theorizing by women of color, lesbians, and the class-conscious has not made women's studies a comfortable place for any of these people to be. As long as women's studies insists on the primacy of gender and a concomitant consistency of identity, the discipline will continue to inflict violence on those who don't conform to accepted notions of what a woman should be.

A Lesbian in Women's Studies, 1995

When I became a full-time academic in 1991, I was enthusiastically allied with academic feminism, thanks to my dissertation director, who had introduced me to the broad range of feminist theory that fueled my work. In the 1970s, as an undergraduate, I had called myself a feminist without wanting to know other feminists because my self-presentation was not warmly received; I avoided women's studies precisely for fear of the feminist puritanical fervor Joan Nestle describes in the incident where the women's center at her college (also, by coincidence, my undergraduate college) conducted a witch-hunt against her for sexual deviancy:

> That year [1981] marked for me the second McCarthy period in my life. Only this time, many of the holders of truth were women.
>
> They called the organizers of conferences where I was speaking and told them I was a "sexual deviant," labeling me as a dangerous person who betrays the feminist cause. The place where I earn my living, Queens College, was visited by a member of Women Against Pornography who saw it as her duty to warn a group of students and professors about me, "Don't you know she is a Lesbian? Don't you know she practices S&M? Don't you know

she engages in unequal patriarchal power sex?" (Butch and femme is what is meant here, I think.) I was told this when I was called to the Women's Center on campus and asked by the group of women students gathered there whether the accusations were correct. Only those of you who remember the cadence of those McCarthy words—"Are you now or have you ever been. . ."—can know the rage that grew in me at this moment. ("My History With Censorship," in *A Restricted Country*, Firebrand Books, 1987.)

Feminist theory had been for me a tool of liberation in my graduate studies, despite my earlier bad personal experiences, so in my first year as an assistant professor, I threw myself wholeheartedly into setting up a women's studies program: As a newly out lesbian, I couldn't see where else to find support. Our program has been successful; it began in the fall of 1993, and in 1994 we opened a small women's center. Yet after three years of close work among a core group of twelve women, I find those old experiences of judgmental exclusion arising again in the wall of silence.

Ours is a small campus, with only about one hundred and eighty full-time faculty, so close cooperation among those few in women's studies has been key. Yet the women's studies core group has never come to grips with real issues in our lives: no one will discuss what it means to be married, to have children, or how any of this affects their position in the academy. And yet many of my colleagues use their personal lives in the classroom: They mention husbands, or use children as anecdotes; one discussed her upcoming wedding at length in the classroom, and used her own relationship as a model in a course. When the subject of "diversity" comes up, most of my colleagues insist that there is no problem: As one said to me, "I've dealt with a lot in my life—incest, alcoholism, violence: I can handle any 'difference' you might have." Some of my colleagues perceive themselves as being helpful when they tell me not to wear so much black; one gave me a subtle hint about motorcycles when she told me about a former colleague who didn't get tenure partly because he rode one. Those of my women's studies colleagues who know me as friends have told me not to talk about my lesbianism if I wish to get tenure: They're sure it will be the end of me, and they may be right. But there's been no willingness in the women's studies program to confront that issue publicly, to question the status quo. No member of the women's studies faculty will take a stand on defending lesbians in the flesh, or argue that protecting lesbians should be part of our strategy. There was a brief vogue of buttons that said "I'm straight but not narrow," but no one will wear one that says "Queer."

As I write this, I am bitter and frustrated, eager to blame the women I work with for what they do to me every day (a bitterness increased by the strain of approaching tenure, and the fear that no one will stand up for *me* publicly). But I also acknowledge the other roots of that bitterness, which include a failure of the lesbian community outside the institution. The lesbian community itself—if such a thing exists—insofar as it clings to a myth of "woman" perpetuates its own violence. Examples from the past show how lesbians have attacked their own: lesbian-feminists denounced, in the sixties and seventies, butch-femme relationships as "mimicking patriarchy"; Adrienne Rich insisted in 1977 that women's sexuality was not and should not be like men's (see Lillian Faderman, *Odd Girls and Twilight Lovers*, New York: Penguin 1991). And this continues: I think for example of Kate Bornstein, articulate transsexual "gender outlaw," who describes the way some lesbians reject her because she is not a "woman"; this is mirrored by the Michigan Women's Music Festival's decision not to allow male-to-female transsexuals into the festival camp (Bornstein, *Gender Outlaw*, New York: Routledge 1994). It is hard to find a community that affirms one as a lesbian without also imposing a particular and rigid definition of "woman."

The utopian image of women's studies as a safe haven and a place to welcome all women is a fantasy; I long for a safe place that in fact doesn't exist. If I reflect more seriously on history and theory, it is obvious that the discipline of women's studies is, in practice, built on a static concept of identity that cannot be disentangled. When my colleagues offer me helpful advice that I find offensive, they are merely reminding me where the boundaries of gender identity lie, and what will happen to me if I cross them. Taking gender as the primary locus of identity and building a women's movement on that has indeed produced some resounding successes, none of which I would take lightly since I've benefitted from them. But the discipline built on this founding assumption has been unable, in practice, to take that assumption apart: attempts to bring race, ethnicity, sexuality, and class to the forefront as equal or even preeminent loci of identity construction have so far failed. Perhaps that should be no big surprise: I'm not sure how a discipline that seriously questioned identity would be able to reconstruct itself as a coherent academic entity. But the cost of feminism's failure is being paid by everyone who is not straight, white, and middle class.

So those of us who, by choice or not, find ourselves on the margins have to rethink our positions. My identity is painful and provisional: Outside women's studies, I'm a feminist, and I have no reason to deny my strong allies there; but inside women's studies, I'm a misfit—like any lesbian, gender is not my only identity category. Like Gloria Anzaldúa, whose work has been exploring this territory for years, we marginals have to come up with new metaphors: not dancing through the minefields, perhaps, but merengueing in the borderlands. At times, the fact that I don't "belong" in women's studies—let alone anywhere else—paralyzes me: I become numb, depressed, and unable to work as I strive not to let my colleagues' oppressive behavior negate my life. At other times, my position on the margins is energizing; then I feel that my shifting kaleidoscope of identity is a source of power and insight, multiple lenses to understand a pluralist world.

Stray Sheep or Shepherd?

"Out" in the Florida Classroom

Christy M. Ponticelli

Department of Sociology,
University of South Florida

22

Standing in a phone booth on a cold, wet winter night, Rickie, a closeted gay Puerto Rican, listened to Katimski, an English teacher in his high school, tell him that he was worried about him. Though Rickie had called Katimski, whom many students considered odd and eccentric, he was afraid to come right out and ask for help. Instead, he assured Katimski he had a place to stay even though he had been living on the streets since his father had kicked him out the week before.

Tears running down his face, Rickie abruptly ended the call. The camera faded away from Rickie crying and focused on Katimski's silhouette. He was arguing as much with himself as with his male lover, who remained silent for most of the conversation. Katimski finally asked, "Was I supposed to tell him he could stay here? I wanted to, but if word got out, do you know what they'd say? I'd lose my job!" At the close of the show, Katimski embraced Rickie, opening his home to him.

This episode, from the 1994 primetime series *My So-Called Life*, reflects the difficult situations many lesbian, gay and bisexual educators, and students, confront throughout their lives. (To conserve space, I use "gay" when referring to lesbians, gay men, and bisexuals.) Even if gay teachers want to reach out, we often stop ourselves. The fear of heterosexism and homophobia exhibited in the workplace is too real for many. As a result, gay teachers and gay students find ourselves alienated from our peers as well as from one another.

In this chapter I share my awakening at the progressive University of California at Santa Cruz (UCSC) where I was an out graduate student and teaching fellow. My story then moves to a very different world, the University of South Florida (USF), where I currently hold a tenure-track position. By sharing my experiences as a student at a progressive school, and as a job candidate and faculty member at a more mainstream school, I hope that others might find some answers to their own questions and concerns about coming out.

Before arriving in Santa Cruz, I had been out as a student at both Smith College and Harvard Divinity School. At those schools, I was out to a few friends and faculty, but was never in a position of power or leadership. At Santa Cruz, that changed.

I formally began outing myself the day I gave a lecture in the introductory class of 250 in which I was a teaching assistant. I was asked by the faculty member to cover Mills' examination of the difference between "personal troubles" and "public issues." My academic introduction of Mills failed until I applied Mills' sociological imagination to my own experiences as a lesbian. I was relieved at having been a success as an educator, but petrified as a person; I had never come out to so many virtual strangers at one time. At UCSC, my fears proved to be naive, and from that day on, I deliberately worked my lesbianism into course materials. Being out at UCSC, however, was not an onerous burden.

Three years later, I entered the job market. Would my sexuality elicit discriminatory barriers on the job market? This was a question my partner Di and I thought about often, but never discussed. The thought of coming out during a job interview presented a new journey for me, one very different from the many miles we had traveled together over the past nine years.

I received an interview offer from USF, and spent the weekend wondering how I would talk about my research on Fundamentalist Christian ex-gay ministries, designed to "heal" gays, without talking about my own sexuality. Not coming out would go against what I believed as an interpretive scholar. (See my essay "The Spiritual Warfare of Exodus" in *Qualitative Inquiry*, volume 2, no. 2, pp. 198–219).

I rehearsed my formal talk repeatedly in front of Nancy, my dissertation chair, and by the time I left for the interview, I could casually insert without flinching that I was a lesbian. Using humor, I would explain to my potential colleagues during the interview that the Fundamentalist Christians I studied were somewhat suspicious of me and my motives since I was a researcher, scholar, Catholic, and, oh yes, did I mention gay?

The only portion of my USF visit that I remember took place on my first full day. When speaking with a faculty member before my talk, I learned that she had outed me to her graduate class the night before. Carolyn said,

"Have you met with the graduate students yet? I was telling them last night in my seminar about this lesbian who is coming in for a job interview . . . and how interesting your work is."

I might have felt joy, hearing Carolyn talk so eagerly about me and my work, but honestly, I was angry. How could you out me to those students, I thought! What if I wasn't going to come out while I was on campus? I finally interrupted and asked her, "What if I wasn't gay?"

She stopped abruptly. "Oh," she exclaimed. "I just assumed because of your research. . . Oh, no. . . ." Missing or ignoring my point, she tried to comfort me, "This is a fairly open environment. It's OK." Despite this revelation about the openness of USF, she later advised me not to talk about being gay too much, especially about being partnered.

Her advice disturbed me, but I accepted it, and attempted to tone down the "gay-" and "we-" speak. Overall, the three days flew by, and my outing went as smoothly as I could have expected. Several weeks later I was offered the job.

Di and I embarked on our second cross-country move, this time with two birds and a diabetic cat. Periodically on that drive, one of us would blurt out, "Are we crazy? We're going to Florida!" Florida was one of the locations which we had both agreed was not acceptable for us. We wanted a certain level of tolerance around us, and recent reports out of Florida told us this was not an open-minded area. We didn't consider the deliberate burning of a gay woman's home or the setting ablaze of an African American tourist to be signs of tolerance, let alone acceptance. Though not as accepting as UCSC and Santa Cruz, USF and Tampa proved not to be as hostile as expected. USF had its share of gay faculty and administrators, and browsing the shelves of local bookstores revealed gay sections. We even located a gay bookstore and gay film festivals.

My experiences with students, however, were what truly sold me on USF, even if all my experiences have not been easy. There are many students at USF who disapprove of my sexuality and are more than willing to let me know.

James, for example, a member of my qualitative methods seminar, was a frequent visitor during my office hours (I have changed the names of students). We had discussed a wide assortment of issues, from prejudice and discrimination to his own family concerns. Our discussions never focused on me as a person, but on larger social and political issues.

James turned in his final paper and said, "Can I ask you a question?" He claimed the chair farthest from me, in the corner by the door.

"You say you believe in God," he said. "Here." He stiff-armed me with his worn Bible. "Show me where it says being gay is OK."

My heart sank. I sat motionless. I looked at my four different Bibles. No, I would not engage him, though Harvard had prepared me for just such an occasion. I took a deep breath, reminding myself that these discussions were futile and frustrating.

James attempted to prod me into a debate, using Romans and other biblical passages, and I responded by turning the question back to him: "What do *you* think that passage says?"

Each time he gave a blanket response, "Homosexuality is wrong." I explained that the Bible was a historical document and must be translated in its proper historical context. James gave up moments later and quietly went on his way. I followed him to the door, eager to close it. I returned to my desk, wondering whether it had been a good idea to take a job in Florida, to be out in Florida.

The next semester brought with it a more balanced student body, and my first interaction with a gay student. I taught two introductory classes, in which the students and I were continuously challenged by the general conservatism of several students with military backgrounds. One day, however, a young Asian woman came to office-hours late in the semester, and I realized that being out had its rewards.

She said, "I just want to thank you for putting yourself on the line during the semester. Coming out, I mean. It really means a lot to me to be in a class where I know the professor assures a safe environment for me. And I appreciate having a role model. Nobody, none of my friends or family, knows about me, and sometimes it is really hard. My friends in the dorms like to go to Tracks, a cabaret-style dance club that caters primarily to gays, lesbians, bisexuals, and transgendered people and make fun of the gays there," she said, rolling her eyes in frustration. "So, I just wanted to thank you," she said. "The sociological discussions we had about gays helped me accept myself."

I never pushed her to formally place a label on who she was. I remembered how difficult it was for me the first time I called myself a lesbian. I simply explained that I had only done my job, and reminded her that my door was always open.

I had never really thought of myself as a role model before, despite having looked at some of my gay faculty in the same way. Still, I was uncomfortable with the idea, until I realized I was also a resource to my gay students, a role I felt more adequate filling.

In the fall of 1994 I was in my office when I noticed a student walking nervously past my door—one way, then the next, and back again. Joan finally got up the nerve to ask if she could see me. "Sure, come in," I said.

Joan quickly retreated, saying, "If you're busy. . ." "Sit down," I said, pointing to the chair.

Joan came out to me, telling me that her lover left her and that she had been mugged at gunpoint recently. "Do you know any counselors?" she asked abruptly. She continued, as if unable to stop talking once she began. "I've been having these nightmares ever since the attack. I've never felt vulnerable before, and this bothers me. I have always been independent and strong, and now I dream that everyone has a gun. I also want someone who will be sensitive to the other issue [referring to her missing her female lover]."

"I don't know of anyone off hand, but I can certainly make a couple of phone calls for you and get back to you," I said.

"That would be great. I really appreciate it," she said, sounding somewhat relieved. She recently told me that my coming out in class left a big impression on her, and that Di's and my attendance at her athletic events means a lot to her.

At UCSC, the welfare of the gay population was on good footing, relatively speaking of course. My being out simply added to the many visibly out staff, students and faculty. At the University of South Florida, however, not only are there fewer out staff, students and faculty, but the general climate on campus is not nearly as gay-friendly. As a result, my being out affects more aspects of campus life, including students who are simply unaware or uneducated. While I am happy to be contributing to the awakening of the average student, those like Jeff and Barry who confessed that my gender and sexuality class made them more aware of their own sexist and heterosexist behaviors, students like Amy and Joan are the ones I seek to support the most. I cannot deny this. If I can be a role model for these students, in the classroom or outside at their athletic and cultural events, helping to strengthen their sense of self, I will do this.

As an out teacher, will I face the death squad Katimski predicted on primetime television? Only the future holds the answer to that, and the future I have learned is usually unpredictable. All I can do is continue along the path I have chosen. As a sociologist and educator, I strive to unmask the ways in which the status quo is maintained. As a lesbian scholar, I attempt to present alternatives to the status quo. Being out to my students is one way I can accomplish this.

Acknowledgments

I would like to thank Diane Chase, Carolyn Ellis, Laurel Graham and Lynn Stratton for reading earlier drafts of this chapter.

Lesbians in Utah

Behind the Zion Curtain

Patty Reagan
Department of Health Education
and Women's Studies,
University of Utah

23

I usually travel alone. Some say that this is the metaphor of my life. An exception to this general rule, however, was my offer to drive a female colleague to the home of a Brigham Young University professor and her "roommate" in the heart of Mormon-country, Provo, Utah. On the way home we began discussing the day's events and the logical sequitur of homosexuality. I was not close to this colleague, but I admired her intellectual curiosity and seeming openness about the topic at hand. After silently debating the eternal "coming out" question in my mind, I shared with this friend what I had never verbally shared with any other nongay colleague on campus, "I think you should know that I am a lesbian." "Oh Patty," she said, "everyone knows that." That interaction happened eight years ago. I am still stunned by the revelation, that "everyone knows that."

The real question is not how could everyone know, but why was I so insulated and naive to think everyone did not know?

Yes, I am a lesbian associate professor at the University of Utah. Are there really lesbians in Utah is a familiar question. For those who still wonder, there are many, diverse, active, and closeted communities of lesbians and gay men in Utah. We are the movers and shakers, thorns in the sides, teachers, professors, M.D.'s, lawyers, businesspeople, and caretakers of this twilight zone called Salt Lake City. Although no visible or vocal community of gay scholars exists in any organized manner on campus, there are two out lesbian professors, an out gay man, many closeted faculty, staff, and administrators, and I. I grew up a Mormon, painfully obtained two degrees at BYU and found feminism while in my Ph.D. program at the University of Illinois. When my sister graduate students taught me the language of feminism many things happened. There was the epiphany of why I cried so many tears over BYU-patriarchy, oppression, racism, and intellectual demoralizing. Feminism preceded my next personal revelation, my sexual orientation.

I swore I would never return to Utah! I would travel west to California via Canada or Mexico. I would never step foot beyond "the zion curtain" again. Never say never, I have been told. With Ph.D. in hand and jobs scarce, I humbly accepted my first academic job at the University of Utah. I rationalized my decision by saying, at least it wasn't Provo. Who would have thought that Utah, my worst nightmare and fear, would become the stage for my activism, the opportunity for my growth and the vehicle for helping others confront their homophobia?

Two months into my first academic job, the director of the nascent women's studies program dropped by my office. (She now says that she was "cruising" new faculty.) She introduced me to women's studies. She challenged my Mormon, Republican history. She changed my eating habits from Mormon jello to international cuisine and she brought me out. All transformations were exactly what I had been searching for. The metamorphosis to Democrat, nonpracticing Mormon, and lesbian could not have been more natural, or more profoundly important to my role in the Salt Lake City academic and political communities for the next eighteen years.

Clearly I had found home, but I had almost thirty years of Mormon history to transcend. The roots of obedience, deferring to male authority, and respecting institutions are not easily erased even when the mind and heart know differently. Certainly my own internalized homophobia is strong and silences much of my voice. I have chosen not to place my lesbianism at the forefront of my professional persona. It underlies all I do on campus—what and how I teach, the issues I choose to champion, and the professional relationships I nurture. But I have been unable to overcome all my personal homophobia and consequently, hide my lesbianism under the umbrella of feminism. In Utah, Feminism = Lesbian, much like Silence = Death, so the umbrella is rather translucent. The false syllogism that Feminism = Lesbian has been the basis of my "outing" by those who would presume. Despite not being out, I can easily see that I have always been out. I teach human sexuality and I include homosexuals as a part of the natural order of things. There has never been a question in my students' minds that I know something about gay sexuality that is conveyed with a comfort level unfamiliar to heterosexual professors. I am active in women's studies and am certainly "the campus feminist." As a very activist health educator I am in the public eye on issues of AIDS, reproductive rights, school sex education, and mental health issues. Every time I have given a speech, have been interviewed by the press, or I have challenged the status quo, I have surely outed myself in some magical way. It has only been my own homophobia that has prevented me from saying the "L" word. And yet, I have said it over and over again in other words and many deeds. Haven't we all? Oh, my lesbian sisters in academe, "everybody knows that!"

So what does it mean to be out, euphemistically, at the University of Utah? I am a testimonial to an eighteen-year career that has included myth, fear, reality, and wonderful surprises. Before I say anything more I have to "bear my testimony" (Mormon lingo). I believe, given my own experience, that lesbian professors are initially feared, scrutinized, and subject to formal and informal review uncommon to nongay faculty. Lesbian faculty easily survive this attempted pogrom by their own talents, professionalism, initiative, and perseverance. After survival and tenure, which in my case did require a therapist, good friends, submission to the imposter syndrome, and tears, lesbian professors move into a very important and tenure-protected place in the scheme of academic politics and community.

The calling, while not necessarily sought, is one of leadership in university politics. At Utah I believe I am seen as the watchdog of equal rights, of liberation politics, of minority advocacy. I have helped gay students introduce antidiscrimination clauses in student and faculty policy. I have been asked to help clean up language bias in written documents, analyze Title IX (NCAA athletic equity) compliance, do inservice on diversity for faculty and staff, and I am the resource for gay students who think they have no where else to turn. It is both a good-news and bad-news story that I am recognized as and expected to be a leader in all gay "happenings" in our community. I am a hero to those who seek heroes and I am a closeted lesbian's greatest fear. I have been told of my own myths: I have brought out more dykes than anyone else in Salt Lake City; behind closed office doors I do secret lesbian ritual acts. Friends have been asked if they are not afraid to be seen with me for fear of guilt by association.

Despite "everyone knows that," I am still homophobic. It is with the greatest fear of the unknown that I ever find courage to come out to an individual student. Just last quarter a young man in my AIDS Issues class came up after class and said, "You seem comfortable with gay people. I want you to know that I am gay and I have been reluctant to talk about my experience because I was afraid of imposing my life on the class." I assured him that I very much wanted him to add his experience and reality to our class and I thanked him for his courage in coming out to me. I did not do likewise. I went to my office and wallowed in my guilt about not coming out to him. I felt like the coward I often am. He had taken a risk with me and I had not found the courage or words to give him the assurance he could have used: that his professor is a lesbian. On his paper which I graded that evening, I wrote him a note. I told him that I was sorry I had not done this in person, but that I, too, was family, and that I admired his courage. At the end of the next class he smiled at me and thanked me for my note. Nothing more was said. It was a very important interaction for both of us. Mostly for me.

Nongay audiences and social events increase my discomfort-level to a rating off the scale. My own friends never believe me when I tell them that I am not the brave, outspoken lesbian they think they hear. I am just a person who, as Olga Broumas says, "understands the necessity of an impulse whose origin or goal still lie beyond me." But nongay audiences are addressed by someone whom they know is not quite like them. They are given clues in dress, accoutrement, and language. They are free to make the association and hopefully they do. I want people to know I am a lesbian without having to tell them. I want them to make the assumption and see that it does not affect the message.

Salt Lake City has been rich in opportunities to make a difference for lesbians and gay men, people of color, and women. I have been unbelievably lucky to be in this place during these times, post-Stonewall, to have tenure which gives me the freedom of discourse and debate, and to have found my voice. I am not sure there are any other careers that give lesbians more freedom to be themselves and to educate others about reality. Frankly, I rather resent those tenured lesbian colleagues who have yet to risk, to do unto others, and who don't use their privileged status to travel a road of courage. I have had lesbian colleagues thank me for being on the front line and paving the way for them. I wish they would do a little paving themselves. I wish I also had the courage to tell them that.

I want to finish this personal reflection with an example of how impulse and being a lesbian can be part of creating change on campus. Please notice that I am not the brave dyke taking on an important issue, but a conscious dyke who is also part of an academic community. I believe that this combination gives me and others like me a responsibility to contribute our unique knowledge, and to protect our minority rights. This quarter a lesbian student, her partner, and their child were denied student campus housing because they were "not married" (read lesbian). There was some press and community response, but I did not get involved in this battle, explaining that I was busy with my own battle, acquiring domestic partner benefits for gay families on campus. At a faculty senate meeting, an

M.D. from the medical school pointed out a newspaper article about a foreign student who had shot and wounded her ex-boyfriend while at work on campus. What was most upsetting to this M.D. was that living in their *student* housing was the gun wielder, her ex-husband, his parents, and her parents. I could not restrain myself. "I bet there were no lesbians" I blurted out. The silence of the senate was noteworthy. The closeted faculty lesbian had dared to speak the word. After my impulsive outburst I decided a follow-up was in order. I demanded that the administration explain this double standard. How could two unrelated families be living in student housing (planning a murder no less) and yet, one committed lesbian family—a couple who had gone through a union ceremony to try to legitimize their union, not have the same right and opportunity to pursue their education. The administration promised to get back to the senate with the answer to my question.

OK: I didn't make policy change with my outburst, and I didn't raise the consciousness of faculty and administration with my clever denunciation. I didn't come out. Well, I didn't do any of these yet; not yet, but I started the wheels moving. I dared to be an activist lesbian professor fighting for the rights of other lesbians, in this case students. It was just one opportunity among many that come the way of gay people in Utah. What may happen on our campus may be the start of a precedent or at least a point for discussion for similar change in our community.

Although Utah is generally run like a theocracy, it does not resemble the deep South with overt institutionalized bigotry. I always say that Mormons are polite in their bigotry. Amazingly this polite homophobia makes the University of Utah a unique place for lesbians and gay men to teach and study. I have been challenged by the religious right, but the university has always protected my academic freedom and my sexual orientation has never been an issue, at least up front. One day I had to report to the academic vice president's office to respond to a written complaint from the religious right. The vice president asked me to discuss my class lecture and discussion about lesbian health issues in my women's health class. At the end of our very civil discussion the vice president said, "You know, you ought to teach more of that." I have taken her at her suggestion and I now try to "teach more of that" in all my classes. I encourage other lesbian professors to do likewise.

Beyond Silence
Life as Academics
and a Lesbian Couple

Amy L. Reynolds
Counseling Psychology Program,
Fordham University-Lincoln Center

Raechele L. Pope
Department of Organization and Leadership,
Teachers College, Columbia University

24

I have come to believe over and over again that what is most important to
me must be spoken, made verbal and shared, even at the risk of having it
bruised and misunderstood. That the speaking profits me, beyond any
other effect. . . . My silences (will not) protect me. Your silences will not
protect you

—(Audre Lorde, *Sister Outsider*, Freedon, CA:
The Crossing Press, 1984, pp. 40–41).

Being together for the past eight years as lovers, life-partners, and more
recently as sister professors in different disciplines and institutions has
taught us a lot about the importance of honesty, self-preservation, and
learning how to genuinely be ourselves as individuals, as professionals, and
as a couple. The words of Audre Lorde frequently support and remind us of
the importance of moving beyond our silence and entering into dialogues
with each other, our students, and other members of the higher education
community.

While we have been involved in the higher education community for a
number of years (ten for Amy and fifteen for Raechele), we have been college professors for only the past four or five years. Our experiences as faculty
members are limited to what we have learned and observed during these
last few years, however, we believe our perspectives are unique. What we
have learned about ourselves and each other has not always been easy or
comfortable. Each new environment and opportunity seems to offer its
own unique challenges and opportunity to explore our identities, our
values, and our work.

As a lesbian couple we are very unique and from the very beginning of our relationship we have had to address many differences. Amy is a White lesbian who grew up in the middle class. Raechele is an African American bisexual woman who grew up poor. We have been together as a couple for eight years and have recently expanded our family. Amy gave birth in May, 1995, to our daughter, Justice Audre, conceived through alternative insemination. Our second child is expected to be born during late summer, 1997. Clearly ours is not a traditional family. We have taken great pleasure in redefining family and deciding how we want ours to be. Since the beginning of our relationship we have found it important to be ourselves both personally and professionally. Therefore, on some occasions it has been very difficult to not express ourselves or share aspects of our personal life with our professional colleagues.

We are both out, individually and as a couple, professionally to varying degrees in different settings; our last job search, which primarily focused on faculty positions, was done as a dual career lesbian couple. Raechele was very open in her interview process and actually was able to negotiate some part-time faculty work for Amy who did not have a full-time job until the following year. As always, Raechele approached this negotiating task with the perspective that it was what was right and that equitable treatment should be expected. Because of her approach, there was limited opportunity for others to object. Of course, the fact that both of our professions as a whole (student affairs and psychology) have taken more open perspectives toward lesbian, gay, and bisexual individuals and issues certainly has made our decision to be open much easier.

Our approaches to disclosing our relationship have varied over the years and across settings. To us, it has been most important to focus on our *relationship* as central rather than just our sexual orientation. Prior to becoming a college professor, Amy was very out as a lesbian professional in her leadership position in a professional association and her writing. Raechele, while never hiding our relationship or her identity, was less visible as an openly bisexual professional (although anyone who worked with her closely knew about that part of her). At the beginning of our relationship those differences presented some challenges and demanded that we talk with each other about our choices and our feelings. In some ways because she is a White lesbian, Amy's choice to be more out is possible because of some privilege she experiences as a White woman. On the other hand, Raechele's choices have, in some ways, been more complicated and certainly involved needing to consider more communities and identities.

Throughout the years, being a lesbian has been an important part of

Amy's professional identity; however, for Raechele her sexual orientation has been less central to who she is professionally. These differences are probably the result of different life-experiences as well as our other identities. As a woman of color, Raechele is often more focused on that identity and part of her. Where Raechele's sexual orientation becomes central is as a by-product of the importance of our relationship and our family to her life. She is unwilling and unable to make that part of her life invisible regardless of the reactions or issues of others. While our paths of being open about who we are have come from different directions, we are in unison in the importance of being ourselves and not being silent about our love and our life together.

With our most recent job changes and entry into faculty positions, there have been some changes in how we deal with being openly lesbian and bisexual respectively. While some of those changes may be due to now being in an academic context (such as, the uncertainty of the tenure process), Amy has become more cautious professionally in terms of verbally coming out—she works at a Catholic university. She has not changed her research and professional interests which continue to include lesbian, gay, and bisexual issues; however, she is very aware of the values and beliefs of most Catholic institutions regarding lesbian, gay, and bisexual issues. While an adjunct professor at Teachers College, Amy taught a course on counseling lesbian, gay, and bisexual clients. She wanted to continue teaching that course at her current institution, but was advised by some colleagues that it might be better to wait until after she received tenure. Amy recently submitted materials for reappointment and paused to consider the ramifications of submitting this manuscript as part of her file. She decided that she would feel more uncomfortable if she deleted it.

Amy is open with her immediate colleagues and to varying degrees with her students but because she is not sure of the professional ramifications of being out, she is less visible in that environment than she has been in previous work settings. Being less open has been a major adjustment for her and created much discomfort and internal dissonance. The awkwardness and discomfort she has felt was only made more interesting by her pregnancy. While she was concerned about the heterosexist assumptions that would be made about her pregnancies, she actually experienced very little of that. One possible conclusion is that even though she has been more subtle in expressing who she is, others are still getting the message.

In contrast, Raechele is very open about her relationship and her identity with her colleagues and students. She openly discusses her relationship and family with her students. On the other hand, since becoming a faculty member, Amy is much more silent about her relationship in group settings. When in the classroom, if she mentions her relationship, she usually uses the gender-neutral term "partner." In one-on-one interactions she is more open and candid but still at times there is less openness. By contrast, Raechele seems to rarely experience those same pangs of internalized oppression when interacting with her students and colleagues. She openly shares aspects of our family as it relates to the content of the course she is teaching.

One unique difference between our two work settings, which may explain some of why our approaches and opportunities are so different, is that we are more visible as a couple at Raechele's institution. Amy taught there for one year as an adjunct professor and continues to work with students from Raechele's program. While working there, she became familiar with many of the professors and staff members on campus and is currently doing some research and work with several faculty members. In addition, we live in faculty housing provided by Raechele's institution and often work together in Raechele's office. Two years ago when we had a commitment ceremony, it took place at a chapel on Raechele's campus and our reception was in the college courtyard and most of Raechele's students attended. During the first seven months of our daughter's life, she spent significant time in Raechele's office. Justice is well-known throughout the college and our family is consistently supported and affirmed by Raechele's professional colleagues.

These differences in our approaches to being out in our work settings while significant have not had a major effect on our relationship and how we relate to others professionally and personally. While how our professional colleagues and students perceive us is important to us, we try to not let it dominate our lives and our self-perceptions. What is most important to us and what we continually try to learn and relearn is the importance of being true to ourselves and our beliefs. As parents, that conviction has become increasingly important and necessary. We will not have the value for our family and our love for our child be lessened in any way by the homophobia or heterosexism of others. We will treat others with respect and demand the same from them. When others judge us negatively, we will confront such bigotry directly. We want to set an example for our children. Because of these convictions we work just as hard to be ourselves in our professional lives as well.

It's important to acknowledge that these choices are not always simple and our differences not always easily resolved. In fact, even after we had decided to write this essay, Raechele lost interest in completing it. Our dialogue about what to do continued over several weeks and eventually we began to realize that some of it had to do with the content of what we were saying as well as Raechele feeling less identified with issues of her sexual orientation in a professional context. While Raechele typically includes issues of sexual orientation in the multicultural work she does in the classroom and in her writings, emphasizing her own sexual orientation (or her own race) is not an approach she has taken with her formal scholarship. We had a long discussion about whether her reactions were about internalized oppression and eventually Raechele concluded that her priorities were just different. It also became clear as we talked that Raechele saw this essay as having a personal rather than an academic focus which made her less comfortable. On the other hand, Amy felt a commitment because of who we are as a couple and what we have learned about ourselves and each other to share that with others.

In addition to our desire to more fully explore and understand ourselves, we are driven to write about this issue because of our values and beliefs about how the world should be. Our primary professional interests have focused on multicultural issues which for us also includes lesbian, gay, and bisexual concerns. We have not received any negative feedback about our work in this area and our work appears to be accepted and valued by our colleagues. We have struggled individually and as a couple to genuinely be ourselves as professionals and to educate others. We feel strongly about doing this work and have not been afraid to take risks.

We want to integrate our personal and professional lives in ways that are meaningful to us, and have an educational effect on individuals (especially our students), and a transformational effect on institutions (our universities and our professions). We want to be able to do this without being reduced or categorized as a lesbian couple or a professional lesbians. We are committed to creating an inclusive and affirming environment in higher education; being out and working to combat racism, sexism, classism, and heterosexism are some of the major ways we intend to reach that goal.

To us, being in a lesbian relationship is an everyday kind of thing. Loving each other is as simple as breathing. Sharing that love with others is as necessary. Because our love for each other is natural and open, others are easily drawn into our life and rarely question our relationship (at least not to us). Being a lesbian couple in academia is probably a profound and important experience; however, we prefer to just see it as a by-product of our life and our love. On a daily basis, when we interact with others, we refuse to incorporate their heterosexism and homophobia. We believe that by not engaging with the biases of others, we send a message that says bigotry or narrow-mindedness is not welcome. If telling people that we love each other is done as simply and naturally as asking someone at the dinner table to pass the salt, then the awkwardness and dissonance becomes other people's issues and not our own. In that way, our love and our relationship can be transformative. When we were planning our commitment ceremony on the Teachers College campus two years ago, it never occurred to us, until much later, that we were participating in and creating a revolutionary and transformative act for that institution or the people who attended. A colleague later commented to us that the energy and consciousness of that campus environment would be forever changed. In that way our relationship and the power of us as a family has much more opportunity and potential to create change in individuals and institutions than either of us have as individuals.

Maybe the lesson here is that some of our most profound and important transformative moments can come from merely being ourselves. It is amazing what others learn to accept when we automatically expect acceptance from them. Our goal has always been to make the bigotry of others their issue not ours. While such honesty and genuineness certainly requires courage, we are all capable of being courageous in everyday ways. As Audre Lorde said in her closing speech at the I Am a Sister Conference (Boston 1990): "When I dare to be powerful—to use my strength in the service of my vision, it becomes less and less important whether or not I am afraid." These are wise and wonderful words to live by. That is how we want to live our life together, one day at a time. Loving ourselves, each other, and our children, and incorporating that togetherness into our personal and professional lives does not have to be a monumental political act. As long as we do not live in silence and refuse to be defined by others, we can become who we are meant to be . . . two women who love each other and happen to be college professors.

The Perils and Pleasures of Being an Out Lesbian Academic; or Speech from the Scaffold

Jennifer Rycenga

Comparative Religious Studies Program,
San Jose State University

25

If you were on trial for being a lesbian,
would there be enough evidence to convict?

(Slogan on a t-shirt
seen at NWSA conference,
June 1995, Norman, Oklahoma)

To be a philosophic lesbian is to love Sophia, in all her dynamic life-filled contradictions. The lesbian lover of Sophia is immediately mediated, never "natural" yet always intimately in physical nature. Being a lesbian is never stable, solid, or grounded; its status quo is status-less: a free-floating agent of disruptive change and momentous insight.

Publicly claiming one's own intimate life is a lively dialectic, whether as pedagogy, poetry, politics, or pick-up technique. We often speak of the empowerment of the coming-out process, but what might the dangers be? Though I live in an idyllic academic world, free of homophobia, I wondered what could happen if ever I were to be attacked for my philo-politico-lesbo life-thought-style. I contemplated my end at the hands of ruthless author-ity; reflecting on the current political situation, concluded that this was a prudent time to prepare a scaffold speech in advance. I cast it in the form generously suggested to me by some students at Pomona College, who observed in the spring of 1994 that the semester was ending, and it was time for professors to give their "last lecture." Working on the conceit that a professor *was* giving her final lecture ever, I was free to say whatever I wanted.

Last Lecture: Women I Have Loved

Audre Lorde's stirring poetry rings ironic for me today, when she says "it is better to speak/remembering/we were never meant to survive" (Lorde 1978, 32). I will speak, and I will remember, but I will not survive. I've always intuited that something about me would antagonize powerful authorities, so I've been practicing this speech for awhile.

I will do as propriety demands, and give a full confession. It is true, I admit it, I am a lesbian; not just in the bedroom, but everywhere, in my mind as well as in my still-coursing blood. I love women and for women to be free, and I staked my life on it. Even if my life is now at the stake, it was worth it: I regret nothing. But I am assuredly guilty. I am who I am, as one once said, that I cannot deny. And even though my tortures have not been so extreme as to break me, I will name my paramours, and give details of when, where, how, and why.

First there is my Gloriana. Elizabeth the First was *my* first: the first woman on whom I had a crush. Luckily, my love for Elizabeth did not have a lasting influence on my politics: I am no longer an absolutist, a monarchist, an imperialist, or a virgin. In fact, I actively work against those tendencies. But back then I really *wanted* Elizabeth, as well as wanting to *be* her—to have all that power and to refuse to share it with any mere husband! I confess, it was an attractive scenario for an ambitious fourteen-year-old.

Then I found my next love, to whom I have returned often in these times of trial. Her name, I confess: Antigone. The way she combined anger, action, and love created a crush at first blush. Recall the situation: her two brothers, fighting on opposite sides of a civil war, both fall in battle. The new king—her uncle Creon—decrees that Eteocles be buried with honor, but that the brother who commanded the losing side, Polyneices, be left unburied, "his corpse disgraced, a dinner for the birds and for the dogs" (Sophocles, 187). Antigone thinks differently; she maintains that life and meaning depend on the complexities of our lives, and that the contradictions of life do not cancel out human dignity. For this alone I would love her. But the forthright way she could name the truth, right to Creon's face, really lit the fires of my heart.

Antigone has been my lover because she understood that love and anger are not opposites, that together they produce action. She tells Creon that her dead brother is not her enemy, because "I cannot share in hatred, but in love" (Sophocles, 198). Creon's response is swift, caustic and revealing: he tells her to go to hell: "Then go down there, if you *must* love, and love the dead. *No woman rules me while I live*" (Sophocles, 199, emphasis mine).

Always, eventually, the oppressor reveals itself for what it is, reveals that hate rules its ways, and defines its power.

My dear Antigone, if I could have gone with you into that cave . . . and then had us leave together, refreshed for the struggle . . . but it was not to be. Haemon, little twit, wasn't good enough for you, and I always knew that! He's like all those insufferable tenors in opera . . . but I digress. Why must we still be playing out this script? When can I rewrite the ending with Antigone herself?

Isn't it interesting, by the way, that it's the queer Tirisias who manages to teach Creon a thing or two? This demonstrates once again that faculty diversity is simply a pedagogical necessity in all times and places.

But there are others, for example: Joan of Arc. I think I wanted her more for a short-term fling than as a long-term affair. Her rescuing of France for Catholicism always rubbed me the wrong way—I had gone to a Catholic grammar school. If only they had told me that the real reason Joan was executed was for cross-dressing in pants! Then I would have felt a solidarity with her.

Then there was another Tudor woman, Elizabeth's mother, Anne Boleyn. I could have saved her from wasting all of her intelligence and ambition on that man. But "she did not make things as they (were), she (adapted) to things as they (were)" (Wolf, 41). Anne took the heterosexual bedroom route to power, and tried to retain her own voice.

Many people hated her in her own time, and no doubt she was ruthless. But her sad end pointed me in the direction of something so important that I spent two years writing and producing an opera about her final days. What I needed to know, in music, in sound, on stage, was what it meant to be entrapped by a single authority that had everything in its hands: religion, the state, the law, and the family in the person of her husband. The growing terror of being at the mercy of an autocratic, mono-interpretive world was Anne Boleyn's fate.

Anne discovered, as the Amazons knew, that her own voice could vanish. All that would be left would be the dramatic narrative, not the fabric, the feelings of being alive, of having subjectivity. I was in love with Anne not because she was blameless, but because she gambled everything on outfoxing the patriarchy's systemic vise. Even though she lost, she got the last laugh, via Elizabeth.

But my next lover had no chance for a final speech, and I fell for her so hard that I changed everything in my life to be more interesting to her. It was my love for Hypatia that led me to study philosophy and religion, and so led me to my teaching, and thus my doom. Hypatia was a neo-Platonist philosopher, a mathematician, and curator of the library at Alexandria in the early fifth century. But above all she was a teacher. The most endearing memoirs we have of her are testimonies from her diverse students: Pagans, Christians, and Jews. Diversity is not new: exclusion and oppression are the fragile innovations.

Alexandria had its narrow-minded enforcer in its bishop, who is now honored as St. Cyril (which speaks volumes about how history is written). He is best known theologically for the elevation—it is better termed fetishization—of Mary to the title of Mother of God. Cyril, like a modern televangelist, felt he had a direct pipeline to God's blueprint for Alexandria. The first thing he did was to drive the Jews out of town, thus challenging the authority of the prefect, and when that public official was attacked by some monks, Cyril honored the attackers as soldiers for Christ. Having beaten back Judaism and secularism, the bishop turned his attention to the pagan woman philosopher: oppressions have been linked before our time. He took the opportunity of a sermon to speak against bad influences in the community: pagan women, loose women, women who dared to instruct men (contrary to the epistles of Paul). The monks, fresh from meditation in the desert, got the message. They encountered Hypatia in the streets, grabbed her from her chariot, dragged her to their church, and literally dismembered her—they tore her body into pieces with oyster shells, and burnt her remains.

I do not love Hypatia for her martyrdom; I love her for her life. I want to remember her, in my heart, in my arms, under my hands, with my mind, in my work, in my life. By naming a journal of feminist philosophy *Hypatia*, contemporary women thinkers are revitalizing this harshly decapitated tradition. I wish I did not have to join the decapitated line, but at least I am in excellent company.

Another such martyr was Rosa Luxemburg, a more recent lover of mine. In pre-World War I Germany, her socialist allies were assimilating, compromising with the power structures, but Rosa kept hewing to her radical Marxist line, insisting on totally uprooting unjust social systems. Her male comrades called her sexist names behind her back: "poisonous bitch," "monkey," and "wretched female" (Dunayevskaya, 27), while her enemies misunderstood her humanism and called her "Bloody Rosa." But listen to what she writes from prison where she languished for opposing the imperialist, useless bloodshed of World War I:

See to it that you stay *human*. . . . Being human means joyfully throwing your whole life "on the scales of destiny" when need be, but all the while

rejoicing in every sunny day and every beautiful cloud. Ach, I know of no
formula to write you for being human. (Dunayevskaya, 83)

It is ironic that Luxemburg, who valued the joy and ecstasy that make us
strive for freedom, should be remembered for her death. Rosa was mar-
tyred, though, not by the Kaiser's forces, who had imprisoned her during
the war, nor by the impending Nazis. She met her death at the hands of her
former allies. When the war ended, the assimilationist socialists were asked
to form the new German government. But Rosa and her friends who had
stood against the war were not ready to capitulate to a new form of power,
and were not fooled by what was socialism in name only. While this coun-
terrevolutionary state pleaded for order, calm and unity in *its* name, Luxemburg's last written work states:

> Your "order" is built on sand. Tomorrow the revolution will rear its head
> once again, and, to your horror, will proclaim, with trumpets blazing: *I was,
> I am, I will be!* (Dunayevskaya, 75)

Her brutal murder was carried out the next day, January 15, 1919, by
agents of the Social-Democratic Party of which she had been a leading
member for over a dozen years. Some things haven't changed; voices for
change are repugnant to more than just the conservatives: we kill each
other in the name of safety and order, prestige and process. What would it
mean to be human? What are the glimpses of life you've had that tell you
there is more to it than profit and loss, more to it than position and ambition, more to it than surface and effects? That is why I confess to my loves,
because it is being a lesbian, living my life on the terms that matter to me,
and, if need be, dying by them, knowing those moments of ecstasy—
ecstasy of the mind, of the body, of the emotions, of the music of life—and
knowing them *in relation* to others, not alone, but *making* love, *creating*
life—all this assures and reassures me that we were, we are, we will be!

Rosa Luxemburg saw herself as an Amazon; I imagine the Amazons live
free of statist bureaucracy, and that their idea of organization on the bat-
tlefield is rather fluid. I learned this from one of my most intense lovers:
Penthesilea, the great Amazon queen who fought at Troy. Fighting along-
side her has not been easy, and I know now why she can be so moody. The
battle never ends for an Amazon: no matter how fiercely you love life, it is
difficult to get to live it when there are always patriarchally-created emer-
gencies to face.

The basic Trojan storyline has Penthesilea and twelve of her finest fighters arriving to assist the Trojans after the death of Hector. But that's about all that is clear, I found after I started to examine the mythology around this most controversial of Amazon warriors. Some accounts have the Greek (so-called) hero Achilles slaying her with ease. Others have him defeating her in a very difficult battle. Some ascribe her death to other Greek fighters. Most of the accounts say that Achilles raped her corpse. This was, for me, as a lover, too much to take, too much to believe: it couldn't be so, it mustn't be thus! And, it turns out, there is a version of the story which rings true. In this one, Penthesilea defeats Achilles in battle and kills him. At this reversal of the given order, the Olympian gods are aghast, and Achilles' mother, Thetis, restores her son to life. In his resurrected form, Achilles now slays Penthesilea, with further divine help. Yes, *this* is what happens to women-who-love-women, and women who fight for their own lives. We are forced to fight the same battles, over and over, until we are worn down and unable to fend off the multiple attacks. Dear Penthesilea, my love for you is so intense that I can deny nothing—I must confess all: The touch of woman to woman, our freedom *to* love, our freedom *in* love, is worth the struggle; yes, I have loved and feared your power. The way you faced the contradictions with your double-edged battle axe is why I wear a representation of that same labyris on my hand.

When Audre Lorde speaks of her Amazon lovers from Dahomey, the words resound lesbianically. In "The Women of Dan Dance with Swords in their Hands to Mark the Time when They Were Warriors" Lorde rejects simplistic symbols and compromised silences: "I do not come like rain/as a tribute or symbol for earth's becoming. . . / I do not come like a secret warrior/slicing my throat to ribbons/of service with a smile" (Lorde 1978, 14–15). She graphically manifests as a power of destruction which is also regenerating: "some times I fall like night/softly/and terrible/only when I must die/in order to rise again"; "consuming/only/what is already dead" (Lorde 1978, 14–15). Our being alive is every moment precious, contextual, and contingent. "I come like a woman/who I am" is why I am out, even at my peril. It is a way of "spreading out" and "warming whatever I touch" to be "who I am"—"*that* is living" (Lorde 1978, 14–15, emphasis mine).

Two women I have loved from India are warriors and goddesses from the great South Indian epic *Shilappadikaram*. The Eiynars worship a young woman who is most literally an embodiment of the goddess. Shalini sees and recognizes the epic's heroine Kannaki as "the flower of virtue, a matchless jewel crowning the earth" (Ilango Adigal, 78). Shalini then proceeds to dance. I love her so because as the goddess she is simultaneously all things, and all power in all things, with no deference in her. She is black, she is white, she is blue, she is the warrior, she is the richness, she is knowledge ... Ach, I know of no formula to write you for being a goddess! But here's what some of her admirers describe:

> Shalini ... came nearer. ... She held the bow of the northern mountain. The skin of the venomous snake covered her breasts. An elephant's hide hung from her shoulders, that of a lion formed her skirt. She brandished a blazing trident in her hand. A heavy circlet adorned her left ankle. Small bells tied to her foot seemed to foretell a victory. Deft in swordplay. (v)ictorious in all battles, bearing high her fearful axe, she was truly Durga, the goddess beyond reach. ... All who saw her could attest that the form and appearance of Shalini, possessed by the goddess, was prodigious. Her pubis is like a cobra's hood. (Ilango Adigal, 78–80)

I love Shalini, because there is no chance that we will lose with her! She is no martyr, and no empty vessel for men. Note that she assumes her goddess-form precisely when another woman—Kannaki—appears. Shalini's strength is unabashedly in her female sexuality, in her wild art, and in her death-dealing abilities as a warrior. This is why our enemies fear multiculturalism: They know we will find succor everywhere we look!

Perhaps scaffold speeches shouldn't include such a sense of victory, but when it comes to *Shilappadikaram*, I feel empowered. The denouement of the story occurs when the king of Madurai has made a mistake. He accuses Kovalan, Kannaki's husband, of having stolen the queen's ankle bracelet, and has him executed. When Kannaki finds out, she's furious. First she proves to the king that his decision was wrong, and, in honor, he takes his own life. But Kannaki is not done yet, because the very site of such injustice is forever sullied. Cursing the city, she quite literally tears off her left breast. From her discarded breast springs the Fire deity, and the city of Madurai is set ablaze (Ilango Adigal, 132). Eventually, the goddess of Madurai convinces Kannaki that she has fulfilled her duty by releasing her righteous anger, and informs her that she can now be elevated to the status of a goddess in perpetuity.

How could I help but love Kannaki? She wins, her protest is a complete success (without having to call a lot of boring meetings), she is rewarded for bringing the revolution, and she survives. Go, girl! I don't know if she'd have me, and there are obviously risks in flirting with someone so incendiary, but my crimes in league with nature seemingly propel me into such situations.

Thinking about Kannaki leads me to Virginia Woolf's *Three Guineas*. Woolf ponders how the education of women can also be an education that will prevent war. She pointedly asks "what is the *aim* of education, what kind of *society*, what *kind of human being* should (it) seek to produce?" (Woolf, 33, emphasis mine). Woolf sees that the inhumanity of war is linked with the inhumanity of social constructions of power, that the very structure of the university echoes, mirrors, and supports war. But her plan for a financially poor college runs into reality: "students must be taught to earn their livings" (Woolf, 35). Her depressing conclusion is that the colleges of the daughters of learned men will eventually reproduce the same structural problems: "bequests and donations from rich men . . . competition . . . degrees and colored hoods . . . [it] must accumulate great wealth; it must exclude other people from a share of its wealth" (Woolf, 35). She predicted this a bit too clearly, except she guessed it would take 500 years, and it's taken less than sixty! But Woolf gave us another option: the way of rejection and creativity, starting from a clean slate, naming the crimes and not imitating the oppressor. Woolf says, in her best Kannaki voice:

> Take this [money] and with it burn the college to the ground. Set fire to the old hypocrisies. . . . And let the daughters of educated men dance round the fire and heap armful upon armful of dead leaves upon the flames. And let their mothers lean from the upper windows and cry, "Let it blaze! Let it blaze! "For we have done with this "education!" (Woolf, 36)

This is, of course, why I am here, on this scaffold, on this day: because I corrupt the youth with passages like this! I tell you to be brave, to be courageous, to be true to yourself and to work for integrity and ecstasy; but, you ask, how can I say that when I see what has happened, and I am giving my last lecture, and the axe has fallen? Am I optimistic and idealistic to a fault, like a chipper chicken with its head chopped off?

The fact is, I am still in love, holding all these lovers in my head, my heart, my body, and my soul. Every time we create love, it is a victory, it gives the lie to the hypocrisies. As Adrienne Rich asks, "Why should feelings of love appear politically ridiculous, why would we ever assume that private love can have no public meaning? . . . [What] ways of being . . . might make love—in all its dimensions—more possible?" (Rich, x–xi). Let something mark that we were here, that we loved deeply, that being human has meaning, and that life itself feeds wisdom to its youth, that constant craving has always been (lang), the craving to touch our mutual and separate powers, which is queer no matter what gender/sex/body you are.

Always re-vital-eyes, recreate anew. I go to my end, unrepentant and full of It, that is, Life herSelf, the finest and steadiest of lovers (Daly, passim).

References

Daly, Mary. *Pure Lust: Elemental Feminist Philosophy.* Boston: Beacon Press, 1984.

Dunayevskaya, Raya. *Rosa Luxemburg, Women's Liberation, and Marx's Philosophy of Revolution.* Second edition. Urbana IL: University of Illinois Press, 1991.

Ilango Adigal, *Shilappadikaram (The Ankle Bracelet)* (translated by Alain Daniélou). New York: New Directions, 1965.

lang, k.d., "Constant Craving" on *Ingenue,* Sire 9 26840–4, 1992.

Lorde, Audre. *The Black Unicorn.* New York: Norton, 1978.

Rich, Adrienne. "Foreword" to June Jordan, *Haruko/Love Poems* (New York: High Risk Books, 1994), p. x–xi.

Sophocles, *Antigone* (translated by Elizabeth Wyckoff), in *Greek Tragedies, Volume 1*, ed. David Grene and Richmond Lattimore, Chicago: University of Chicago Press, 1960.

Wolf, Christa. *Cassandra Four Essays and a Novel.* (translated by Jan van Heurck). New York: Farrar, Straus, Giroux, 1988.

Woolf, Virginia. *Three Guineas.* New York: Harcourt Brace Jovanovich, 1966.

Reading, Writing, and Talking to People

Bonnie R. Strickland

Department of Psychology,
University of Massachusetts at Amherst

26

As I write this essay and occasionally look across a snow covered lake, I have more questions than answers about my life as a lesbian and academic. How did I come to be a half century, two thousand miles, and at least thirty degrees from home? Raised in Birmingham, Alabama, distinguished by the vehemence of its violence, and the "redneck riviera" of the panhandle of Florida, how did I find my way to the gentle, sophisticated Pioneer Valley of western Massachusetts? The first of my family to go to college, how did I become a university professor and live among the Yankees of whom I had always been suspicious? How did the dark secret of feeling different evolve into an integration of my private and public lives and lead me to do research on gender and teach lesbian psychology?

My mother and father's fore families were predominantly English—not the royalty of the courts nor the dons of the universities but debtors and prisoners who sailed to the "new world" on the condition that they would never return to the old. Early immigrants seized the great southeastern frontier, made their own laws, if any, and eventually mobilized an army to defend their independence. I was raised in a land still bitter at losing the "War of Northern Aggression." My prejudices toward Yankees and Republicans, none of whom I'd ever met, were such that all other groups, including Blacks, seemed paragons of tolerance and trust.

My mother was the twelfth of thirteen children. Her mother was a postmistress and her father worked on the Appalachicola river with my uncles farming, cutting cypress logs, cultivating Tupelo honey, and making illegal whiskey. Any law in those swamps was enforced by my grandfather, an undertaking that eventually led to his being jailed for murder along with one of his sons.

My father, the second of three sons, lived in the community eventually made famous in *Fried Green Tomatoes*. Being a typical railroad family, my father's father worked on the trains and his sons were expected to do the same. Typical, as well, were the "nervous breakdowns" my father's mother suffered. Tearing off her clothes, she would run through the neighborhood in a frenzy. Southerners seldom ask which side of the family is mentally ill; we simply wonder who is the most crazy. My father's family easily won.

In 1934, during the depths of the Great Depression, my eighteen-year-old mother met my twenty-four-year-old father at a party in Birmingham. It was love at first sight and they married within three weeks. A second look, however, raised considerable questions about their marriage which lasted until I was seven and my brother three. During the frequent separations and after the divorce, I moved regularly between the Florida swamps and the streets of Birmingham.

I knew every stream and slough of the river and could handle a boat and rifle as well as any of my countless cousins. I fantasized the cypress trees and tupelo trees to be ornamental hedges on the liquid lawn of the house that I would eventually build. My uncles and cousins built homes near the river and I assumed that I would do the same. Like them, I would live off the land—well, at least the water. In Birmingham, my father and his brothers took me on long walks, to baseball games to watch them play, and hoisted me onto the trains to let me blow the whistle. My father's oldest brother, John, read important books to me and let me read to him. Although the men had only finished high school, they had books at home and a sense of wonder about the world—perhaps their attempt to escape the trains that they rode, back and forth, between the railroad yards of Birmingham and the small-town stations of Alabama.

My life as an academic lesbian began in earnest at age six when I started school and promptly fell in love with my first grade teacher—a woman. For over fifty years, I have enthusiastically returned to school every September, secure in my assumptions that the easiest way to spend one's life reading, writing, talking to people, and occasionally falling in love, is to be a school teacher. I never considered another career.

The fall I entered the third grade (I skipped the second and have always wondered about that teacher), my mother bought a home across from a public park with tennis courts and a library. I was usually on the courts or in the stacks. I also attended a Southern Baptist Church, which was devoutly devoted to keeping me from sin. In spite of their best efforts, however, I cheated on Bible drills, beat up my little brother, and lusted in my heart after girls.

Most of my playtime was spent with boys—my colleagues in adventure and best friends. My mother tried in vain to dress me in frilly clothes, a struggle that succeeded only for some best forgotten piano recitals. I learned to box, played center on a boys' football team, and was eventually nationally ranked in tennis. In school, I competed through spelling bees, drama, or poetry reading. At home, I built crystal radios, mixed explosive concoctions with my chemistry set, and dreamed of becoming a scientist, maybe exploring the stars. School and books gave me a potential avenue of escape from what I perceived as the dreary lives of my hard-working neighbors and parents (my mother was a cocktail waitress, my father a brakeman on the trains). Although unrevealed to me as yet, I knew there must be life beyond the soot of the steel mills and the sludge of the swamps. I thought about joining the military, a way out for my cousins and other poor southerners (Black and White); I never considered college, a completely foreign concept to me.

My Uncle John seemed one who was able to cross boundaries and bring diverse worlds together, although he did so at some cost. Drafted into World War II, he took his rifle apart in basic training and refused to put it together again. He further refused to talk to anyone, a dilemma resolved only when the army pronounced him paranoid schizophrenic and sent him home to a V.A. hospital. On one of his visits to my grandfather's home, my mother invited him to come over and see us sometime. The next day, he packed an old metal suitcase, walked across town, and moved in with us. This is not exactly what my mother had in mind although she was always inviting people to live with us. Uncle John simply joined the long parade of housekeepers, cousins, aunts, uncles, friends, and neighbors who were my immediate family from time to time.

Uncle John was with us for a few glorious weeks. He gave me his baseball shoes (that I still have), showed me how to clean the cleats and various other baseball intricacies known only to the initiated. He believed himself to be the manager of the New York Yankees (they were always winning then) and considered me another budding baseball star, conveniently ignoring the fact that I was a girl. He also sat at a card table on the front porch and wrote long letters to the president of the United States. If Uncle John could direct the president on how to run the world, I had no doubt that he could turn me into a major sports figure. This happy state of affairs lasted until one evening when my cousin Charles, who was also living with us, didn't come home for supper. Close to midnight, my mother found Charles who explained that Uncle John has threatened to bash his brains in and boil them in a dish pan for supper. Charles had wisely decided to avoid the evening meal and mother decided that Uncle John needed to go back to the hospital.

Losing Uncle John not only interrupted my baseball training but about that time my mother abruptly announced that I was too old to play with boys; she refused to let me go to the park for our innumerable pick up games. I remember that I sat on the steps of our front porch looking toward the park. Hurt, helpless, and confused, I dropped my face into my hands and sobbed like the sissy girl my mother wanted me to be.

Since I could no longer play with boys, unbeknownst to my mother, I found a softball team of grown-up women, most of whom worked in the mills, cross-dressed, and were as good at brawling as they were at softball. My new set of mentors launched me into an additional athletic career—fighting. Already skilled at boxing, I now learned more specific techniques of face to face combat—keys between my fingers, well placed knees, and so on. Physical competition was clear to me and I came to understand the dictates of brute strength and gauge the caliber of my opponents, including the police who were often called to break up our softball fights. Indeed, the long term physical abuse that I visited on my little brother abruptly ended one day when he flexed his muscles and slammed me through a door. No parental interference, no psychotherapy and/or mediation—just immediate conflict resolution and simple justice through one well-placed punch.

In high school, I continued to be torn between sports and academics, taking Latin and physics while I played on the boy's tennis team. I set my sights on professional tennis but my gym teacher not only sent me to her college but arranged an athletic scholarship. I was amazed that someone would pay me for going to school and ecstatic to learn that I could major in physical education and become a school teacher.

Being in a women's college was like coming home to a loving family. We ran our student government (I was the recreational director), wrote and produced our own plays, dissected cadavers, learned opera, and generally completed the usual academic requirements and extracurricular activities with a sense of self-sufficiency and pride. Men seemed neither necessary nor useful in the life of the college and I was devastated to learn during my sophomore year that we would become coeducational to increase enrollments and avoid financial disaster. I preferred bankruptcy.

Physical education classes were great fun but I was still intrigued with science and now just as curious about people as the planets. Camp craft gave me no clues as to why my uncle John would not fight in the war but threatened people around him, fly casting no hints as to whether families really needed fathers. Friendly faculty encouraged me to pursue clinical psychology and apply to graduate school. I was accepted at Ohio State no doubt because a kid named Bonnie Ruth from Alabama College gave a major boost to their Affirmative Action efforts.

Few positions were open to women when I received my Ph.D.in 1962 but Jules Rotter found me a job at Emory University in Atlanta. I welcomed the chance to return south, to revert to my first language, and to happily teach psychology. Perhaps I could finally learn why my grandmother and Uncle John became psychotic and whether I would as well. I already knew that being lesbian marked me as mentally ill (and female as emotionally unstable) but I kept wondering just which specific and unique differences condemned one to craziness. Could it really be that *any* deviations from majority norms were *always* deficits and disorders?

My public and private lives were distinct and disconnected most of my time in Atlanta. The suburban manicured elegance of Emory and the well-mannered students were a far cry from the noisy downtown streets of the civil rights demonstrations. My life of teaching, research, and clinical practice never overlapped with my private world of playing on yet another women's softball team and partying with lesbian friends and lovers. With few exceptions, my work colleagues and close women friends never met. My partner's picture was *not* on my office desk and my friends preferred the sports pages over my research articles. I attended faculty social events with handsome, charming gay men who were judged by my colleagues to be high quality husband potential. My faculty, like my family, were happily match-making and benignly indifferent to the fact that I would rather have a wife than be one.

At times, magic moments of integration merged the lessons of the classroom and the streets. My first research project in Atlanta, which would eventually become a citation classic (an article most heavily cited in its area of research), was a prediction of Black social action in relation to internal locus of control. Later, my women friends, while not altogether sympathetic to psychology, became a part of the largest sample of lesbians ever involved in research to that date. Although the psychological and medical worlds still proclaimed homosexuality an illness, working with graduate students Norm Thompson and David Schwartz, we found no differences between socially functioning gay men and lesbians in relation to their heterosexual counterparts. In fact, lesbians were more self-confident and gay men less defensive. This in spite of the fact that I hadn't been at all certain that my lesbian friends, or I, for that matter, were models of mental health.

Although the administration at Emory didn't know quite what to make of me, I will always be grateful that they hired a woman and even asked me to be dean of women for a time. For many women students, I was their first and only female university administrator and/or professor. I naturally assumed that they wanted the option of a professional or scholarly career and sent a number off to graduate school whether they planned to go or not. Many became distinguished in their own right; I treasure our continued contact.

After a decade at Emory, I took a sabbatical to Hawaii, a course in scuba diving, and, for the first time, seriously considered seeking another position. Promotion and tenure had been hard to come by at Emory and I chaffed under a set of parochial and conservative attitudes that limited an openness to social change. White southerners did not welcome integration or the women's movement; Emory students *affirmed* the war in Vietnam.

In 1973, I moved to the University of Massachusetts at Amherst, a community that had held a nine-year weekly vigil against the war. UMass was and is a "people's university," with most of the students, like me, first-generation college. I joined a psychology department comprised of more women and minority faculty than had ever been hired in the history of Emory. My long-term partner (a school teacher) and I moved to the Pioneer Valley; we were another faculty couple, warmly welcomed by my colleagues and dean. A new family of faculty and friends allowed and encouraged a true blending of my public, professional, private, and personal lives. I taught the psychology of women, conducted research in women's health, and served as department chair (and recreation director). I organized intramural sports teams, including a women's touch-football team and departmental socials (one of which was closed down by the police because of noise).

In the community, I played on a softball team in a feminist league characterized predominantly by our definitions and deconstructions of politically correct competition. Although we kept score and liked to win, we never came close to fighting. Rather, we held homecoming celebrations with our arch rivals, the Hot Flashes, complete with lesbian queens and majorettes. As best I can recall, through a dozen seasons, State Troopers were only called once when a woman's team held a sit-in on second base as two men's teams played each other thinking they had scheduled the field.

Three years ago, I hitched a ride toward the Cape with some department colleagues who asked if I would consider teaching a new course on health psychology. Feeling rather generous of spirit, as I was on my way to Provincetown, I offered to teach lesbian psychology instead. You would have thought I had endowed a building. The course sailed through the Faculty Senate and the provost unexpectedly found funds for a teaching assistant. "The Psychology of Differences: The Lesbian Experience" (affectionately called Dyke Psych), includes every part of psychology, guest speakers, films, and considerable interdisciplinary readings. We discuss our differences but talk even more about our similarities. Class members keep personal journals and complete groups projects of their choosing, including videos, a "Gay Awareness Day," and a psychedelic poster (decorated with the multicolors of the gay flag) presented at a national psychology convention.

My professional and social lives as a lesbian and academic have come together in a full and happy way. I live in a small town on a lake and after a lapse of forty-two years attend the Congregational Church which has a lesbian minister. But, having always wanted to be a southern gentleman, I have sometimes envied my successful brother his story book life. He has a lovely wife of thirty years, the joy of daughters, is nationally ranked in Master's tennis, and seems to have fully recovered from the childhood physical abuse I perpetuated. I have wondered if I would exchange my life as a lesbian and an academic for his. The answer is always the same: Among the lessons I've learned from reading, writing, and talking to people is a sense that sometimes being strange is more of a blessing than a burden.

Subversive Education

Lynn A. Walkiewicz

Center for Humanities and Education,
Cazenovia College

27

I am a Feminist, a lesbian, and a philosopher.

I am also a subversive.

I don't try to hide the fact that I am a lesbian. I wear my labyris every day; I often wear freedom rings or lavender triangle pins or earrings. The dyke look is complete with the butch haircut and the tweedy blazer or suspendered khakis. The pink triangle is prominently displayed on my bookbag, along with the "Uppity Women Unite" button. I'm a Faculty coadvisor to the gay and lesbian student group on campus. There's a poster of Gertrude and Alice on one office wall and titles on my office bookshelves such tomes as *Lesbian Ethics.* How much more obvious can you get? Still, I am always amazed at how many of my student don't realize that I'm a dyke.

This shows just how much people can ignore when they don't want to see the truth. Just because I don't explicitly state my sexual identity in front of every class of every term, people assume that I'm heterosexual. This puts me in a wonderful position to enjoy my subversive strategies, because I can give my students enough rope to hang themselves on their homophobic beliefs, all the while gently attempting to drag them into open-mindedness. They come kicking and screaming, but sometimes they actually make it.

I make sure that I include lesbian and gay rights in every ethics or values class that I teach. Many of the straight professionals that I know won't touch the subject in a classroom situation. I want the students to start think about issues surrounding homosexuality in a controlled situation where things won't get out of hand and people won't get bashed. Finally, as a lesbian, I feel honor-bound to discuss this issue. After all, if I won't talk about myself and my culture, who will?

Rather than teach through the sole use of lectures, I enter into all classroom discussions as a Socratic devil's advocate: ask questions from any point of view and grill the students for further details no matter what their answers. This allows me to be subversive because I can phrase the questions in such a way that guarantees the issues that I want to highlight will be aired and ensures that conventional thinking will be challenged.

Within discussions, I attempt to direct issues in particular ways: I inevitably hear student arguments about the abomination of homosexuality in the Bible and references to God's plan for the universe. Sometimes I have the class go directly to the primary source and *read* critically. Students are generally puzzled when we actually read the story of Sodom and Gomorrah. Funny, it doesn't say anything about queers. One interpretation would allow Lot to be seen as a pimp, offering his daughters to the crowd instead of his guests (this suggestion usually sends at least one student into orbit). Not that I think that Lot was a pimp, mind you, but it becomes a point of comparison. We can then enter into discussions of *how* things are interpreted by the reader and about language translatability and the problems associated with these interpretations.

Homosexuality as an illness is another student argument that always surfaces. This leads us to talk about what constitutes "illness" and "normalcy." I try to point out to my students that sometimes these determinations seem to be a matter of situation and circumstance. During classroom interaction students begin to consider their standards and how these standards may be influenced by "experts" who have their own agendas.

These discussions can become quite amusing (to me, at least). I often count the people in the room and announce that (for example) there are thirty of us. Statistically, I said, it's likely that three of us are gays or lesbians (notice the emphasis on the plural; they usually don't!). These students follow a pattern that I have come to see as predictable. They sit quietly in their desks for a moment. Then they start surreptitiously looking at their neighbors. You can almost see their thoughts. "I'm not queer. What about her? What about him? Is it you sitting next to me? Or you on the other side?" While they are sneaking peeks and looking, their body posture closes in on itself. They draw their arms closer to their sides and sometimes even cross their arms in front of their bodies. Their torsos hunch over to protect themselves as they scan the faces of their classmates. I let them go on this way for a minute or two, and then I point out to them what I have seen. We talk about how they reacted to my offering and why they tried to identify the gays and lesbians in class. We explore the types of clues that they looked for in this identification process; this discussion includes both why they choose these clues and what happens when these clues are inappropriately applied.

I've always found that asking students to delineate their positions is effective. Asking students why lesbians and gays should be considered different from heterosexuals is very different from asking them why people think gays and lesbians are bad, evil, or sick. When students try to say why we are different, we often end up sounding much the same. This is very enlightening to them.

Sometimes when I teach these sections nothing happens. I always have a few students who are determined not to think critically, but there are always some that do. It's hard for them. They're questioning their values and worldview in a way that they've never done before. Sometimes they become hostile. I had one student who was so homophobic that I could almost see it as a cloud around him. We argued back and forth for several class periods. Then he wrote his paper on homosexuality—and I found out that not only was he was grappling with the fact that his favorite uncle had just come out, but to take the issue even more emotional, the uncle came out because he was dying of AIDS. My student's arguments with me were, in fact, arguments with himself so that he could come to the point where he could still accept his beloved uncle.

Students usually have the option to write one of their class papers on homosexuality. They have no idea how much some of their papers pain me. This is where I pay the price for teaching these issues in class. Sometimes the papers are so blatantly homophobic that I find it impossible to grade them. It's difficult to be objective on the structure of their argument and how well they express their views when those views would condemn me to life on an island (at best) or immediate death (at worst). Sometimes their papers are very well written. I can't fail them because they are homophobic bigots, although this has crossed my mind.

These are the times when I wonder why I teach. Why subject myself to such hatred and narrow-mindedness? But I know that it's something that needs to be done. And for every student who clings to the bigotry, I find one or two who use this opportunity to voice their thoughts for the first time.

It's also important to me to be faculty coadvisor to the gay and lesbian student group. When I was their age, I was so frightened of myself that I refused to believe that I could be a lesbian—even though I was sleeping with women, I married and then disastrously divorced, and then spent several more years before I came out even to myself. Some students are amazed that I have not always been out. Some desperately need to hear from me that it has been difficult for me and others to make our decisions. They all need to know that I respect the courage of their decisions.

My interaction with the students is not limited to an on-campus setting—and it's not limited to me interacting with students alone. My partner and I went as chaperones on an overnight student trip to the Holocaust Museum recently: two dykes and seventeen students of assorted sexual preferences in two college vehicles for a long weekend! Not only were the students excited that we were going, some of them signed up for the trip expressly because we were the chaperones. My partner is beginning to think that this faculty wife thing is OK!

And that's how we are treated by all of the constituencies on campus— I'm faculty, and she's my other half. We come as a matched set. People don't expect me to go alone to any function unless other faculty and staff must also. Our partnership is treated the same way as any other partnership on campus, either married or cohabitating. We've never assumed that it should be otherwise, and we've never been treated any other way. My colleagues seem to take it well. I can only assume that the ones who don't like queers avoid me. And that's OK with me, because then I don't have to deal with their attitudes. People don't have to like me because I'm a lesbian, but they do have to respect the work that I do.

Education doesn't occur just in a classroom. My partner and I live openly in a very white, very conservative Republican town in central New York where my college is located. Only one person that I can think of ever showed outright hostility—the bank teller who took our initial deposit for our joint checking account. Now I make sure I go to her window at every opportunity. It is an educational opportunity for her to wait on a polite, smiling lesbian every chance she gets.

I can educate through subversion and humor, and I have found that I can do it in almost any situation. I have to admit that I take great delight in baiting the straight women—especially the ones who pride themselves on being "open-minded." My partner teases me about it constantly. I keep telling her that I need to have *some* kind of hobby.

I don't mean to sound like I live an in-your-face lifestyle. It's not as though I have women's symbols carved into my hair or wear Queer Nation t-shirts to school. What I do is *live.* I am out as a lesbian as I am out as a human being. I work, I play, I eat, I love, and it's all as a lesbian. It's not that I'm constantly rubbing people's noses in it; I simply refuse to hide it. If everyone else is talking about their partner, I talk about mine. I ignore the fact that the gender combinations fall in different ways, and I expect everyone else to ignore it too. The more comfortable I am with myself, the more comfortable people are with me; the more I expect to be treated equally, the more I am.

I think that I can be more useful to my college community by being out and about than by hiding. From lending books to being interviewed, I am an information source for the students. I have also found that the reason many of my students continue to hold homophobic views is that they don't know any lesbians or gay men—or at least they think that they don't know any. Allowing people to know I'm a lesbian can be a valuable experience for them. I'm not saying that people won't be homophobes just because they know me. But at least I can at give a face to the word "lesbian" and help make responses to the word more thoughtful.

I'm lucky that I work for a dean who's also an open lesbian. The first time I actually came out to a straight, homophobic student I was a little nervous. Then I thought, "Well, what is he going to do—I complain to my boss?" This gives me great freedom to be myself without worry. I have a sense of security that many on other campuses may not have.

I treasure a quote from Audre Lorde, from "Age, Race, Class, and Sex" in *Sister Outsider* that is posted on my bulletin board both at home and at work. These words seem to reach the root of my feelings and beliefs:

> My fullest concentration of energy is available to me only when I integrate all the parts of who I am, openly, allowing power from particular sources of my living to flow back and forth freely through all my different selves, without the restrictions of externally imposed definition. Only then can I bring myself and my energies as a whole to the service of those struggles which I embrace as part of my living.

I cannot be what I want to be, who I *am*, without being a lesbian. It takes more energy to try to hide it than to try to live with it. The further I get out of the closet, the harder it would be to go back in. Not that it's always easy, but I know that it has to be done. And it has to be done not only for me, but for all of those women (and gay men) who can now see an active, alive, happy, and honorable lesbian teaching their class or strolling on their campus. Some parts are good; some parts are bad. But I am able to be myself, and that is worth more than anything else.

Consenting to Relations

The Personal Pleasures of "Power Disparity" in Lesbian Student-Teacher Partnerships

Stacy Wolf
Departments of Theatre/Dance and English,
George Washington University

Jill Dolan
Theatre Program and Center for Lesbian and Gay Studies,
City University of New York

28

"Common" sense, most brands of feminist politics, and virtually all university policy statements on consensual relationships between professors and students advise, moralize, or legislate against them. Even most lesbian academics would agree with Michele Aina Barale, who contends, "I do not think we should ever sleep with our students—even when both parties, sober, thoughtful, and still clothed, find it a pretty nifty idea" (p. 17). Barale describes the sexual as "the primary boundary that cannot be breached" (p. 22). Similarly, other lesbian professors who say they perform their sexuality and their politics with panache in the classroom employ such rules as extracurricular comfort zones. As Wendy Chapkis writes, "[D]espite my flamboyant style—or better yet, because of it—I appreciate the prohibitions against sexual intimacy between the ranks in the context of gross institutional inequality" (p. 14).

Given that the field of gay and lesbian studies has long been influenced by Foucauldian theory, we find it surprising that lesbian academics should rely on idealist notions of sexual practice and power. Barale and Chapkis presume that sex draws a mystical boundary between students and teachers that cannot be brooked. Such an attitude makes of sex a secret (once again) and reempowers it as an ultimate determinant of identity. We don't want to suggest (necessarily) that every lesbian professor should sleep with a (or some) student(s), but we would like to use our own relationship as a jumping-off point to discuss the positive and useful aspects of such a relationship—and we mean positive and useful for both parties.

Our sexual and emotional relationship started six months after Stacy enrolled as a Ph.D. student in feminist theatre studies at the University of

Wisconsin-Madison, where she came expressly to study with Jill in 1989. Jill was an out assistant professor who had been on the faculty for a year; Stacy was the first student who applied to work with her.

In those early months, Stacy looked to Jill as a role model as well as a teacher. She knew Jill only through her writing, and admired the thorough intertwining of personal, theoretical, critical, and political styles in her work. On the other hand, Stacy was at pains not to ask too much of Jill, not to assume that we would even be friends. She went to Madison intending to engage in a completely professional, productive, congenial relationship.

Meanwhile, Jill was negotiating the boundary issues many new female assistant professors confront, and appreciated that Stacy kept her very organized, reasonable requests of Jill strictly professional. Jill admired Stacy's clear, strong sense of herself as a graduate student who would take initiative with her work, and who saw herself as someone with something to give as well as to learn.

That first semester together at Madison also established what would become a mutually productive intellectual relationship. Jill's pedagogical model presumed that she had something to learn from students, and Stacy offered intellectual stimulation with her clear, contentious engagements with the course material. Our written dialogue on the margins of Stacy's course journal set a pattern in which each of us learned to critique constructively the other's work. Jill soon began sharing her writing with Stacy, and continued to read her seminar papers, regardless of the course for which they were written. We became each other's most productive critics and inspired each other to think in different ways. Jill encouraged Stacy (and all graduate students) to publish her work, and Stacy read and edited everything Jill wrote for publication. As we gradually got to know each other better, the similarity of our backgrounds—both Jewish, both from the East Coast, both eldest daughters, four years apart in age—sealed our developing bond.

Our decision to embark on a personal relationship had to be made in the context of a loud discussion about the recently approved sexual harassment policy at UW-Madison. The policy includes a statement on consensual relationships between people of unequal institutional power that explicitly warns against such relationships, and states that the person with power will not be protected by the university should the person without decide to bring future legal action. The UW systemwide policy states that:

> the respect and trust accorded the instructor by the student, as well as the
> power exercised by the instructor . . . , greatly diminish the student's actual
> freedom of choice concerning an amorous or sexual relationship. . . . All

instructors . . . should understand that there are substantial risks in even an apparently consenting relationship where a power differential exists.

Under this scenario, Stacy could only *believe* her choice to enter an amorous, sexual relationship with Jill was consensual, since real agency, according to the policy statement, was beyond the situation's pale. We could both understand how such a policy might, in certain circumstances, protect some students from questionable advances by professors, but we felt that the policy tended to write only one scenario for consensual student-teacher relationships, and not to consider the benefits that might accrue emotionally and intellectually in such a relationship. In its conservative understanding of power, the policy refuses to acknowledge that some of these relationships work and last.

Although the policy left Jill most vulnerable institutionally, we soon found that both of us became subjects of the regulatory system when, as the policy instructed, we declared our relationship to the department chair. Our acquiescence to the policy created a paper trail that documented our relationship in both of our institutional files.

But in spite of the local interdictions that circulated around student-teacher relationships, which very much provided a discursive caution to our nascent relationship, we found in Teresa de Lauretis's theorizing about Italian feminist strategies a different language with which to view our desires. Her notion of "entrustment" describes a relationship between women that relies on "coming to terms with the power and the disparity—the social and personal inequality inherent in them" (p. 21) as a positive possibility rather than a negative consequence. De Lauretis is worth quoting at length here:

> [T]he relationship of entrustment is one in which one woman gives her trust or entrusts herself symbolically to another woman, who thus becomes her guide, mentor, or point of reference—in short, the figure of the symbolic mediation between her and the world. Both women engage in the relationship . . . not in spite, but rather because and in full recognition of the disparity that may exist between them in class or social position, age, level of education, professional status, income, etc. . . . Female symbolic mediation . . . is achieved . . . because of the power differential between them, contrary to the egalitarian feminist belief that women's mutual trust is incompatible with unequal power. (p. 22)

This notion became crucial to us. We knew there was a power differential between us, but other language implied judgmentally that Stacy would always be the victim in this distribution of power, and seemed to deny her the right to choose how she might benefit from intimacy with Jill.

One way in which power was perceived to reside with Stacy was through the gaze of other students, who implicitly felt that she would benefit professionally from her emotional proximity to Jill. Jill tried very hard to make professional access a hallmark of the graduate program in general, and not limit it to any one student. In addition, we find that there is a naive notion of "fairness" in many discussions of relationships between students and teachers generally. The presumption is that teachers should be liberal and democratic in their accessibility to all students. But not all students warrant or require equal time and attention, even from the most caring of teachers, for various and appropriate reasons.

De Lauretis's concept of "entrustment" also allowed our relationship to work on other, extra-institutional levels. The operative assumption in currently conventional languages around student-teacher consensual relationships presumes that the benefits of intimacy are only intellectual and institutional, only derive from the professor toward the student, and never *change*. Much of the literature also implies that the institutional relationship is primary and determining. In our case, the institution predominated, but we related at many other levels in which power was distributed differently. For instance, Jill learned quite a lot from Stacy emotionally, as we worked openly, honestly, and consistently on our partnership in the context of intense and continued institutional surveillance. We learned from each other socially, as we found our temperaments complemented each other. And now that Stacy is an assistant professor, the ways in which we assist each other continue to change.

But most insidiously, the language prevalent in current descriptions of consensual relationships between students and professors discounts the possibility of agency, at any historical moment, for the person with less institutional (or social) power. As Jane Gallop writes in her own retheorizing of such languages,

> As a feminist, I recognize that women are at a disadvantage, but believe that denying women the right to consent further infantilizes us, denies us our full humanity. Prohibition of consensual relations is based in the assumption that when a women says yes, she really means no. . . . Common to both is the assumption that women do not know what we want, that someone else, in a position of greater knowledge and power, knows better. (p. 22)

(We have to mark here our own ambivalences about quoting Gallop approvingly in the context of our article on lesbians and the academy, because of our mixed reactions to the press's documentation of her own sexual harassment case [see especially Talbot]. For example, the *Lingua Franca* article that describes the sexual harassment charges two lesbian graduate students brought against Gallop infantilizes them, and makes them appear naive and idealist, as though they're interpreting Gallop's erotic pedagogy too literally as sexual provocation, as though lesbians can't read the subtle differences between "performance" and the "real." Although the press coverage of Gallop's case at UWM has been problematic, we appreciate her willingness to treat the issue of sexual harassment differently from the standard-issue feminist line).

Barale assumes that not only can the student not choose freely, but that because of inherent power and social disparities, the student has nothing to give back to the professor. She clearly implies that the direction of emotional need comes from students and intellectual empowerment comes from the teacher, and should never be more dialectical or mutual. Barale suggests that because classrooms that address "queer" material are infused with students' emotional responses, for a teacher to bring her own needs to the same space is to court mutual disappointment, and to compromise the rigor of the classroom by corrupting it with the teacher's desires, emotional or intellectual. She writes that such a dynamic "feels better than it teaches" (p. 17).

Both of us have become increasingly aware that, following Barale's and similar prohibitions, lesbian (and feminist) faculty are supposed to teach the blurring of boundaries between the public and private in the social sphere, while keeping them absolutely distinct in our own lives. Gallop also points out the risks incurred in policing too closely the "line separating the professional from the personal in the institution of knowledge" (p. 19). She notes with irony that feminism brought the personal to the professional as a political strategy in the academy, and now, many feminists are vociferous advocates of sexual harassment policies that would keep the personal resolutely disentangled from the professional in their own locations. Gallop argues that regulating such a divide clamps down on teaching that admits an erotic, personal, political dimension that can be empowering for students and professors alike. She says, "While desire can indeed be demeaning and dehumanizing, it can also be the mark of profound esteem" (p. 23).

Barale also advocates an erotic style of pedagogy, but she insists that such a performance of desire in the classroom is only made possible by the enabling prohibition on entering students' beds. She writes, "Since neither the material of the classroom nor pedagogy itself ever can or should be made off limits for erotic pleasure, the students must be" (p. 22). In such cases, hard-working lesbian professors can use the power of erotics in their classroom performances, but must disavow any notion of "real" practice with the very spectators for whom they perform. This reading also implicitly moralizes against professors who admit to needing things—emotional, intellectual, or otherwise—from the students with whom they often have their most intense daily contacts.

While our institutions often forbid personal expressions and commitments in professional relationships, the time and energy they require of women academics forces us to invest heavily and often prevents us from having the energy or the ability to form deep emotional attachments outside the academic environment that structures so much of our lives. When policy statements like UW-Madison's on consensual relationships discourage the kind of relationship that we formed, they institutionalize a short-sightedness about how much of women (and probably especially lesbian) academics' lives are wrapped up in our work.

Stacy is now an assistant professor and Jill is a full professor, both at different locations, suffering the commuting relationship of many academic couples. We continually negotiate the ways in which our work is similar and different, complementary and contentious, divergent and convergent. Some pragmatic frustrations remain; we can't write recommendations for each other, and our relationship will always limit the ways we can help each other professionally because of presumptions about "conflict of interest." This seems small, however, compared to the ways in which we have enabled each other intellectually and emotionally, financially and logistically, over the last seven years. We have learned quite a lot from each other, about how to be teachers, writers, and scholars, as well as how to be good, compassionate people in a profession that breeds cold competition. Disparities still exist between us, institutionally and professionally, but we expect them always to shift and move and change over time, as they have since we met in 1989.

All relationships are about power, institutional or otherwise, *even* those between lesbians, whether or not they are students and teachers first, friends, lovers, or partners later (if at all). Academic institutions provide another site at which to negotiate these relations of power. We find it enormously pleasurable to engage the eroticism of teaching and learning, between ourselves, with our current students, and with our colleagues. To deny the mutuality of eroticism and the complexities of desire's circulation through our classrooms, research, and lives would indeed make us prisoners of a dusty, truly *academic* ivory tower.

References

Anon. University of Wisconsin-Madison Statement on Consensual Relationships. September 1987. Adopted by the UW Board of Regents July 12, 1991. 2818a; 5513h. Document #4.

Barale, Michele Aina. "The Romance of Class and Queers: Academic Erotic Zones." In *Tilting the Tower: Lesbians Teaching Queer Subjects*, ed. Linda Garber. New York: Routledge, 1994. 16–24.

Chapkis, Wendy. "Explicit Instruction: Talking Sex in the Classroom." In *Tilting the Tower*. ed. Linda Garber, 11–15.

Foucault, Michel. *The History of Sexuality: Vol. 1*. New York: Vintage, 1980.

Gallop, Jane. "Feminism and Harassment Policy." *Academe*. September–October 1994. 16–23.

De Lauretis, Teresa. "The Essence of the Triangle or, Taking the Risk of Essentialism Seriously: Feminist Theory in Italy, the United States, and Britain." *differences* 1:2. 3–37.

Talbot, Margaret. "A Most Dangerous Method: The Pedagogical Problem of Jane Gallop." *Lingua Franca*. January/February 1994. 24–40.

My, How Times Have Changed ... Or Have They?
A Quarter Century as a Lesbian Academic

Anonymous **29**

How it Began

While in graduate school in 1969, having been "women identified" since at least the age of eight, I decided to act on my feelings for a woman. My first long-term partner was a nonacademic. We lived on her family farm, thirty miles south of my graduate campus. I finished my master's degree in a year and began work on my doctorate. My major concern, in this blissful, youthful relationship, was that I would never get an academic job in a small rural community.

Amazingly, the following August, a faculty member at the only college in that town resigned, leaving a vacancy in my field. I serendipitously became a college instructor in the town I wanted to make my home, at twenty-five years of age, holding a newly minted master's degree, no college teaching experience, and about a year of identity as a lesbian.

Leading Two Lives

I was very closeted and lonely at the college, petrified of being denied tenure and *not knowing why*. Since we lived on a farm, I was also aware that I might reek of manure. I hid from my colleagues information about where I lived (a tiny tenant house), and anything else personal. I knew no one at the college who was gay or lesbian.

A sad experience occurred while I was serving on our faculty senate in the early 70s. The campus had an active body of gay students who had proposed a gay and lesbian students' organization. The issue was brought to the faculty senate and a faculty member circulated an inflammatory document comparing a student organization for gay and lesbian students to a hypothetical one which would condone illegal acts (e.g., a student organization for murderers). This document, sadly, was found hilarious by many colleagues. I did not feel secure enough to speak out against it publicly, though I was strong enough to vote my conscience.

Breaking Up is Hard to Do

In the mid-70s, my partner and I encountered difficulties in our relationship. We parted in 1976, but have remained friends since. Her mother considers me her "other daughter" and my parents (aged 89 and 94) ask about her whenever we talk.

At the time of the break-up, however, I knew I would be in a difficult emotional state (I was finishing my Ph.D., seeking tenure, and losing nearly everything that meant much to me personally). I decided to come out to my parents, so they would know what was wrong. My mother's first comment was "I'm sorry," because she believed that she might have caused "it." Later, she read voraciously on the subject so she could "understand" and became one of the few people in my life with whom I could discuss almost anything. My father was at first somewhat closed-minded on the subject, but later became one of my greatest champions. Their support over the past twenty years has been immensely important to me.

In 1976, I was approaching my tenure decision. I had done everything I was supposed to do and I knew it, however the thought that I might be denied tenure for something unknown haunted me. I was out to my mother, so I could say to her one day, "If I have any trouble getting tenure, I will pursue it, even *legally* if necessary." She was horrified; a quiet person, for her the thought of a public fight over something like this frightened her. She did say she would support me in whatever I chose to do. Fortunately, the problem never came up.

That Was Then, This is Now

Currently, the college has policy statements which affirm the rights of students and faculty in areas including affectional orientation. Our definition of "diversity" is also broad enough to include lesbians and bisexuals. In a recent term on faculty senate, I was able (now a tenured and fairly secure faculty member) to work publicly to clarify the wording of that diversity statement without fear of retribution or labeling.

Am I out as an academic? I would not deny my affectional orientation to anyone, and a wise person reading cartoons on my door, posters, and pictures on my desk would know. I do not announce my lesbianism on the first day of class or in public settings. I feel that, if I come out, I may inhibit some students. I would rather know what they are thinking.

Living with Invisibility

Recently, teaching a course in gender issues in education, we spent an evening on intersections of oppression. During that class, I had students randomly draw the name of an oppressed group. In small groups, they were to identify with the chosen group and answer some guided questions. One young man in the group which drew "gay and lesbian people" announced that he could not do the task, because he did not know any gay or lesbian people. The class found this amusing, as many (I think) knew that I was a lesbian. However the class would never have dealt with the issues which emerged, had he already known my identity. He learned more as the students helped him realize that he probably did know gay or lesbian people, but that they were often forced to be invisible.

I often come out to specific students (in marginal notes in their journals) if I feel they need to know. I conduct research and write in areas related to gay and lesbian issues, but edit my vita, depending on where I am applying.

As an elected member of my local school board, I often speak at gay and lesbian forums about such issues as "the school board's view of gay and lesbian teachers," or "gay and lesbian teachers," but I do not come out in those sessions. I am sure that gay and lesbian attendees know, but I do not make a public announcement. I also recently participated in our school district's decision regarding the right of a gay high school student to bring his lover to the prom. Sitting in that discussion (and not coming out) was difficult to say the least.

Sociologists often discuss the "costs" to individual and society of various oppressions. In terms of invisibility (which, I realize, I contribute to) there are serious costs—not so much to me as a person, I feel, but to the gay and lesbian young people who need role models. Had I known at nineteen that there were lesbian academics, lesbian school board members, lesbian college presidents, it would have made my life much more peaceful. By choosing not to be totally out am I denying young people the role model of a strong, successful lesbian academic? What are the costs to me if I come out (in terms of the perception of a "one-issue" person; in terms of not being listened to and respected, simply because of a label)? These are questions I ponder every day.

The Love of My Life

I am, and have been partnered, to another lesbian academic for seventeen years. We met through a mutual friend, corresponded for years, and finally got together, in the late 1970s. She began her doctorate and moved to my home in 1980. We bought a home together in 1983, and she received her doctorate two years later. We work, write, and travel together, but have not been able to find a job at the same college. We work eighty-two miles apart and live together on weekends. Due to the winter weather patterns in our part of the country, we did not choose to live somewhere between and each face a forty-mile commute daily.

She is a sociologist, trained in qualitative methodology. I am an educator, trained quantitatively, and also very much (by philosophy and temperament) a generalist. Living with my partner, talking, team teaching, and collaborating with her, has enriched my academic and personal life over these years.

We are very different; while I have very strong self-esteem, her ego is easily crushed and bruised, which makes collaboration interesting. We do, however, have a good working relationship, having coauthored published works; I prepared the index for one of her books; and we have copresented in her field and mine over the past ten years. We provide a contrast—she can be strident and what seems to me to be overly passionate about her beliefs, giving people very little slack. I feel that you "get more flies with honey than vinegar," especially in diversity work, so I try hard to understand where people are coming from, listen to them (even if I don't like the message) and try slowly to help them see another point of view. Evaluations when we do collaborative work would indicate that we complement each other.

I feel I am accepted on campus most of the time. For years I urged our college president (now retired) to be more inclusive on invitations. Finally, he began to invite any faculty to bring "a guest" (as opposed to "spouse") to official functions. I have taken my partner to such functions for fifteen years and I attend events at her college as her "significant other." We have a holiday party at our home each year and invite numerous officials and faculty from the college. At that time, we neither take down nor obscure the many pictures (or even our domestic partnership agreement) which reveal the longevity of our relationship. People come year after year—so either they don't realize where they are or they don't care.

Where I Am Now

On campus I have worked hard not to be viewed as a "one issue candidate" (about women's issues, or gay/lesbian issues). I pride myself in being able to listen to others and have them listen to me. Perhaps I could do more for the gay/lesbian cause were I more out; however I chose this path long ago and have continued to follow it. It has been a rewarding quarter of a century, both from the perspective of being a respected faculty member at my academic institution, and from the perspective of growing in a stable relationship with my partner over much of that period.

The Lesbian Experience

An Analysis

Degrees
of Freedom

Penelope Dugan

The Writing Program,
The Richard Stockton College of New Jersey **30**

When the editors of *Lesbians in Academia* asked me to respond to the narratives comprising this volume, I thought it would be a relatively easy task. My plan, before I saw any of the narratives, was to read them against Nadya Aisenberg and Mona Harrington's *Women of Academe* (1988). In their preface, Aisenberg and Harrington state that among the sixty-two women they interviewed: "We know that our interviewees in both deflected and tenured groups included lesbians, *but none identified herself as such.* Thus we have stories from these women that correspond in many aspects to those of heterosexual women, but we cannot draw explicit parallels or distinctions because the lesbian women themselves did not do so" (xii, emphasis mine). I thought I would focus on those aspects of life experience and career plots as rendered in *Lesbians in Academia* that do and do not correspond with those reported in *Women of Academe*.

But once I started to read the narratives in all their unmediated, first person glory, I realized that the texts they should be read against and with are other narratives—exploration narratives, spiritual autobiographies, captivity narratives, and slave narratives. Unlike the unidentified lesbian interviewees of Aisenberg and Harrington's *Women of Academe*, these narrators claim and proclaim their lesbian identity. For these narrators, like Frederick Douglass in his *Narrative of the Life of Frederick Douglass, An American Slave* (1845), telling their stories in the context of this volume is a further act of self-emancipation.

At the end of his narrative, Douglass writes about the first time he spoke at a Nantucket antislavery convention three years after escaping from slavery. "I felt strongly moved to speak. . . . The truth was, I felt myself a slave, and the idea of speaking to white people weighed me down. I spoke but a few moments, when I felt *a degree of freedom*, and said what I desired with considerable ease. From that time until now I have been engaged in pleading the cause of my brethren" (326, emphasis mine).

Like Douglass, the narrators of *Lesbians in Academia*, must, in order to write for this volume, overcome their internalized oppression and fear of how their stories will be received by their potential audience. As Valerie Miner writes in *Lesbian Texts and Contexts* (1990), "Although I have 'come out' many times in print and in person it still feels dangerous" (13). Some of the very real dangers detailed by the narrators in this volume include, harassment, loss of jobs, loss of health, loss of partners, loss of family, and death threats. Still, they feel compelled to tell their stories under their own names (only one of the narrators uses a pseudonym). Their desire for wholeness outweighs their need for safety: "I have come to believe that a lesbian cannot achieve a sense of wholeness until she embraces herself completely. Every step out of the closet is a step into self-integration, toward wholeness" (Charlotte L. Goedsche). To claim and proclaim lesbian identity is to withdraw from a "conspiracy of silence, a tacit contract between oppressor and oppressed never to name or manifest the secret state of being gay" (Mildred Dickemann).

Ten of the narrators quote Audre Lorde—poet, Black woman, lesbian, feminist, mother, teacher, political activist, and cancer fighter—who named and claimed every portion of her identity, every marker of her difference in her writing. Five of the narrators signal their recognition of danger and desire to overcome fear by quoting Audre Lorde's statement, "When I dare to be powerful—to use my strength in the service of my vision, it becomes less and less important whether or not I am afraid." In many ways, Lorde's collection of essays, *Sister Outsider* (1984), is the embedded or prompting text of this volume.

This is most apparent in Carol J. Moeller's narrative, "Working With 'The Master's Tools': Studying Philosophy in Graduate School." Moeller's title refers to one of Lorde's essays in *Sister Outsider*, "The Master's Tools Will Never Dismantle the Master's House." And Moeller is the narrator who most explicitly addresses the constraints of audience:

Writing for this volume on lesbians in academia . . . I fear that my words and my outness could be used against me. Who will read this volume, or know of my article's existence? Will I ultimately name this essay on my cv (the academic equivalent of a resume)? If I write an essay with which my academic department would be comfortable, would it still be *my* article? Would it be honest? Would it be worth writing? In whose voice would it be written? (Moeller)

Voice, of course, is the key issue in narratives. To trust the tale, we have to trust the teller. William Andrews (1990) details the problems of formerly enslaved narrators. To assume the status of authors, to have authority, they "would have to write self-authoring, that is, self-authenticating narrative. . . .[T]he narrating itself, the voice that embodies the 'producing narrative action,' the storytelling, would have to sound truthful" (23). But telling the truth in the master's house can be dangerous, and *how* one tells can undermine or diminish what is told.

The academic voice, principal among the master's tools, projects the objective, impersonal, detached scholarly stance. Academics are rewarded for their "mastery" of it. Kathryn M. Feltey in her narrative, "Living Outside the Center," addresses the issue of academic voice. Analyzing interview data with women jailed for killing their abusive partners, she sees them trying to reveal what their experiences were in these relationships and meeting resistance to their efforts "to voice their truths." Unheard, they resorted to violence. She writes of her own reaction:

> Trying to make sense of all this, I felt violent. I could not find my voice. . . .I wrote in an academic voice, separate from the data I had collected, separate from the analysis I was conducting. I was promoted and received tenure. (Feltey)

Is narrative—which by its very nature is subjective and which derives its power from the personal, engaged voice of the narrator—even appropriate for an academic audience? Central to the process of asserting a gay or lesbian identity and claiming membership within a lesbian and gay community is narrating a personal coming out story. The audience for that story is other gays and lesbians who, recognizing their own stories within the narrator's story, will acknowledge the narrator's claim to be part of the community. The purpose of the coming out story, within this context, is not to educate the audience but to show oneness with it. The same is true for the "bottoming out" or "hitting bottom" story narrated within twelve-step or recovery programs. Asserting that portion of one's identity previously denied and narrating one's story are the initial steps to letting go of self-destroying behavior. (Kathryn H. Larson, one of the narrators in this volume, frames her narrative as a move toward recovery and uses explicitly the language of recovery movements.)

How does one assert her lesbian identity, tell her story, further liberate herself from internal and external homophobia while staking her claim to membership in an academic community? There is not, analogous to an old boys' network, an old dykes' network seeking to mentor young dykes and help them establish a place in academia. If such a network were to exist, its likely members would be the narrators in this volume. Batya Hyman in her narrative, "Is 'Out' Now 'In'? A Letter to a First-Year Lesbian Professor," wishes she "might draw upon the wisdom of a lesbian pioneer who has successfully navigated these waters."

Lacking that guide, Hyman writes her own in the form of a letter addressed to, "Dear newly hired assistant professor." She concludes it with the caution:

> Some of my colleagues have suggested I wait until I secure tenure before writing a letter such as this. Others have told me I'm foolishly throwing away my career. After all, they say, investigating the issues of lesbian academics might be a legitimate research activity, but writing a personal statement has no place in academe. (Hyman)

But even writing about lesbian issues has put some of the narrators at risk. Feltey, like Mickey Eliason, another narrator in this volume, was advised ("don't claim it") to remove a publication with lesbian content— her first "good" publication—from her vita. Feltey writes, "I am constantly challenged in a discipline where it is only safe to research, teach, and make public statements about lesbian and gay life when one is clearly and indisputably heterosexual."

The other narrators avoid or address these problems of audience and voice caution in a variety of ways. A few fold their personal stories into a review of the scholarly literature on sexual orientation. Others distance themselves by focusing on their strategies for teaching lesbian and gay subject matter to students. Some, in the manner of Frederick Douglass, use their stories "to plead the cause of their brethren." Like the slave narrators of nineteenth-century America, they seek to establish their own humanity ("Am I Not Your Sister") while exposing the inhumanity of their oppressors. Like Dawn Bennett-Alexander, they seek to change hearts and minds through educating their audience about the gays and lesbians, "The productive, decent, hardworking citizens you know who daily go about their lives quietly, hiding a part of themselves from their families, their friends and their coworkers out of fear of not being accepted for who they are because of the myths and sensationalism surrounding them."

Some narrators write in a confident voice, some in a flat voice, a few almost whoop in their exuberance, but all of them are brave. These stories might help to create "a context where fear in academic institutions is replaced by a collective willingness to challege and change structures that place almost everyone outside the center" (Feltey).

When I told the editors of *Lesbians in Academia*, both of whom are in the social sciences, that I was titling my piece "Degree of Freedom," they asked if I didn't mean "degrees of freedom." In statistics, the degrees of freedom for a distribution is the number of possible outcomes of the experiment minus one. The narratives collected here from graduate students, untenured assistant professors, associate professors, professors, and a professor emerita in a variety of disciplines at institutions, large and small, public and private, across the country render the possible outcomes of being lesbians in academia. The minus one is the story a potential reader will see as she fills in the gaps and omissions from the stories told here. Let her lay her story down beside these.

Works Cited

Aisenberg, Nadya and Mona Harrington, eds. *Women of Academe*. Amherst: University of Massachusetts Press, 1988.

Andrews, William L. "The Novelization of Voice in Early African American Narrative." *PMLA* 105 (1990): 23–34.

Douglass, Frederick. *Narrative of the Life of Frederick Douglass* in *The Classic Slave Narratives*, ed. Henry Louis Gates Jr. New York: New American Library, 1987.

Lorde, Audre. *Sister Outsider*. Trumansburg, NY: The Crossing Press, 1984.

Miner, Valerie. "An Imaginative Collectivity of Writers and Readers." *Lesbian Texts and Contexts*, ed. Karla Jay and Joanne Glasgow. New York: New York University Press, 1990.

The Lesbian Experience
An Analysis

Mary Frances Stuck

Department of Sociology,
State University of New York at Oswego

31

> I have come to believe over and over again that what is most important to me must be spoken, made verbal and shared, even at the risk of having it bruised and misunderstood. That the speaking profits me, beyond any other effect. . . . My silences [will not] protect me. Your silences will not protect you.
>
> (Lorde, *Sister Outsider*, 40–41)

Preface

Writing this essay has been a true challenge, not so much from an intellectual standpoint as from a personal one. For, as a lesbian academic, I could see myself in many of these narratives, but not in others; I could share in the frustrations and the exhilarations; I ached with compassion for the trials of these women, and basked in their reflected accomplishments.

I also experience frustration with the world at large, for its continuing bigotry and silencing; with academia—the proverbial and mythical arena of knowledge sharing and acceptance of people—for its hypocrisy and closed-mindedness. While at the same time I understand her position, I experience frustration and dismay, with my own partner of nineteen years, who chose to remain anonymous in the collection of narratives for this book—she has her reasons, but as I see it, probably "everyone knows" anyway, so why not be out and proud, and a visible acknowledged role model?

"Sample"

The respondents in this volume are from all sections of the United States and many age cohorts, from the thirties through the sixties. Many indicate

The author would like to extend her gratitude to her life partner for reading and commenting on countless drafts of this chapter.

long-term couplehood of which several are in commuting relationships. Nearly all hold Ph.D.'s; one is an M.D.; one is a J.D.; and they represent numerous academic ranks and disciplines. Lesbians, at least in this sample, do *not* flock to stereotypic areas (e.g., physical education, women's studies), and this should lead to an understanding that there is not a singular lesbian "academic community" or type of scholarship in which lesbians specialize and thus may help break down stereotypes.

Foundations of Narrative Analysis

The data, the submitted narratives, were analyzed using standard inductive content analysis procedures (Krippendorf, 1980; Spradley, 1979; Holsti, 1969; Glaser and Strauss, 1967) to identify themes common to contributors (e.g., discomfort with hiding or being forced to hide one's lesbian identity; public stands and/or writing and/or presentations on lesbian/gay themes; institutional support; and so on) and to allow for the possible emergence of other related themes.

In order to determine which data/themes would be included for analysis, I follow Wiseman's (1974:326) lead by asking: Was it (a theme/finding) significant because it illustrates or reveals something of a more general (and significant) nature about human behavior? This allowed for a holistic approach to these data, grounding them in the meanings and contexts of the lives of the women themselves. Direct quotes have been used to illustrate themes.

Themes in the Narratives

The Dominance of "Outness"

Far and away, the major theme emerging from this collection of narratives is "outness," with this issue reflecting both differences and similarities among the lesbian academics, as well as complexities, struggles, and rewards.

Age of Awareness of Self as Lesbian

Awareness of self as a lesbian ranged from age three or four to the thirties. Two women who indicated awareness of lesbian identity later in life (thirties) further elaborated that they felt they had not internalized the homophobia that so many lesbians had because they had not had years of messages about "outgrowing it," and so on. However, sadly, another woman "still struggle[s], sometimes celebrating lesbianism, sometimes wishing for a more acceptable lifestyle . . . entertain[s] a fantasy of returning to a straight life" (Ketrow).

So while it may be that one's "sexual identity" is established by age four or five, these women's lives reveal a whole spectrum of age of awareness of one's self as lesbian. Of course, the heterosexism and heterosexist messages of the world around us probably contribute to the varying ages of coming out to one's self as lesbian, as do the various definitions of "lesbian."

General Theme of "Outness"

Preliminary analysis indicates that nearly all of the writers were out, but the degree of, and the paths to, outness varied. Nineteen of the thirty-two writers indicated that they were out, but to varying degrees: one was out to the players on her softball team; one was out, but only to others in the closet; two wrote that they would not deny that they were lesbian if asked directly.

> I would not deny my affectional orientation to anyone, and a wise person reading cartoons on my door, my posters, and pictures on my desk would know. (Anonymous)

I use the term "affectional orientation" rather than "sexual orientation" because of the emphasis on "sexual" which is such a small part of our identity as lesbians, as it is such a small part of the identity of heterosexuals. I use the term "affectional orientation," to deemphasize the sexual identity.

Complexity of Being Out

A more complex examination of the women's discussions about being out reveals that being out is a dynamic, rather than a one-time decision and as the literature about the coming out process suggests, an ongoing process (Stanley and Wolfe, 1980; Eichberg, 1990; Harbeck, 1992; Goff, 1994). We are not surprised, then, that for many of these lesbian academics, there are stages and degrees of being out. For some, being out is relatively new, and is of their own choosing. For one, being out is a result of having been outed as a couple, and seizing that opportunity to claim the identity publicly: "My relationship with my partner had been discovered. . . . Having been outed, we officially announced our relationship [after being offered and accepting a job]" (Dugan).

For most, being out occurred gradually: "Coming out is a process. Once started, the layers peel away and you become genuine and, in my case, I became a happy person again. It was such a relief not to hide" (Fournier); "even though I am out, it has still been and remains, an an evolutionary process of sorts . . . the evolutionary process is, by its nature, not a static one"

(Bennett-Alexander). Sometimes this means selectively revealing one's self to those whom we thought we could trust, someone who would understand. Often this was done only after a number of years or after receiving tenure.

> I slowly came out to the people who were important to me. (Eliason)

> I was not officially out at Saint Michael's until six years ago [1988; having arrived in 1972]. (Kaplan)

> For the most part, until I received tenure, I did not come out in the class-room, even when it was highly relevant or even awkward not to do so. (Ketrow)

One of the women eventually made a decision to be out totally and com-pletely, and very publicly: "When I decided to come out altogether, no holds barred, I did it by way of the newspaper piece below" (Bennett-Alexander).

For one of the academics being out was not an issue: She was out to the committee that hired her (this was also surprising since the institution was a religious one), although she did not know it at the time: "They knew I was a lesbian when they hired me, but I didn't know they knew. I had gone to no lengths to hide it, but neither had I mentioned it" (McDonald).

Complexity of Being Out—Difference between Partners

For some of the women, the issue of outness was complicated by differences in the degree of outness between themselves and their partners. None how-ever, indicated these differences were either insurmountable or endangered their relationship.

> My partner at that time . . . refused to be closeted. . . . I also had decided not to be closeted on my job yet I wasn't prepared to be totally out immediately. (Dugan)

> Being less open has been a major adjustment for her [the partner] and cre-ated much discomfort and internal dissonances. She feels less genuine and integrated in her identities yet the lack of security she feels in her current environment [new position] has interfered with her ability to be herself . . . made more interesting by her current pregnancy. (Reynolds and Pope)

For yet another couple, one of whom is very out, the difference in outness is because of the position of her partner: "My partner is an elementary school associate principal in a town about forty miles from Burlington. She has not had the luxury of being out, given the Christian conservatism of her town" (Kaplan).

Job Issues: Advice Not to Be Out; Passing

Some writers expressed a generalized concern (perhaps representative of many of the writers in this volume) about being out, and this concern is often named fear: Fear of the conservatism of places of residence, of institutions of higher education, of the reactions of individuals—both students and faculty.

> I'm just cautious [when asked whether she was proud of being gay] because I'm not sure what the repercussions might be. (Cress)

> If I identified myself as lesbian openly, I ran the risk (I thought) of not being promoted and tenured. If I did not . . . then I would—and did—suffer the cognitive dissonance of not being open or totally honest. (Ketrow)

> I was very closeted and lonely at the college, petrified of being denied tenure and *not knowing why*. In 1976, I was approaching my tenure decision. I had *done everything* I was supposed to do and I knew it, however the thought that I might be denied tenure for something unknown haunted me. (Anonymous)

While a couple of women voiced speculation that job offers not extended were due to their lesbianism, a number of others were completely out and obtained positions, and a few indicated that they had seen no real impediments to their progress in their institutions (despite their fears and perceptions). Many indicated varying degrees and types of institutional support, from obtaining positions for their partners on their campuses (only two or three) to implicit support for research or encouragement for developing courses with lesbian/gay content or foci. It is important to note that differences in seeing and living with impediments may be related to the field/discipline and/or division of an institution in which one is. For example, academics in the arts and sciences may have far fewer impediments (self and institution imposed) than academics in teacher education or physical education. These are disciplinary areas where, even today, direct and subtle messages are transmitted to students about the dangers (up to and including loss of job) of acknowledgeing one's lesbianism (or gay identity) or talking with students' about their concerns over affectional orientation. These messages seem to be especially strong still in the area of physical education, with its historical legacy of witch hunts.

> The president assured me that my work [political] was not incompatible with hospital policy, and said that I should use my institutional affiliation whenever I spoke with the media. (Gartrell)

However, some of the women indicated that their colleagues—especially, but not only, closeted lesbian colleagues—try to get everyone to live in a kind of "don't ask, don't tell" world, a world of silence about lesbian identity. (One woman, a Mormon lesbian academic in Utah, who is only out very selectively, also describes herself as "the watchdog of equal rights, of liberation politics, of minority advocacy" and because of these activities additionally describes herself as "a closeted lesbian's greatest fear" [Reagan].)

Vitae—What to Include: Research/Writing

A majority of the lesbian academics conduct research and write on lesbian/gay topics; many of these women voiced apprehension about including on their vitae references to these scholarly, public service, or community activities that dealt with lesbian or gay issues. Many also shared how well-meaning colleagues also suggested that such information be left off vitae. Of course, for some this was particularly problematic as gay/lesbian issues were the focus of either their research or community service or both—each of which is a major criterion for hiring, retention, tenure, promotion. Thus, a major dilemma: Risk the rewards of academia, or risk loss of identity.

> I cried the whole way home when the chair of my retention committee told me to remove that article [on lesbian motherhood] from my vita. . . . I long for a context where fearing academic institutions is replaced by a collective willingness to challenge and change structures that place almost everyone outside the center. (Feltey)

> I ask my new advisor about my future in academia. Is it time to consider going back into the closet, where I haven't been since my late teens? "No," she says, "Just don't put the word "lesbian" in the *title* of your dissertation." (Goldstein)

For some of the lesbian academics, "editing" of the vitae still occurs, after years of being a lesbian academic, and being out in some contexts. One individual who, throughout her narrative, expressed all types of reservations related to being lesbian, however, states: "When this manuscript is published, I will not exclude it from my vita" (Ketrow). For others, the cost to self to "edit" is too great, and the vitae are not purged of references to work on lesbian/gay issues. Obviously, the chapter of the anonymous contributor to this volume will not lengthen her publication list.

Teaching and Classroom Interactions

For many, if not most, of these authors, teaching and classroom interactions, while difficult at times, are also some of the most rewarding of their experiences and often provide the most suitable contexts for coming out.

Dilemmas

Several women comment on one of their dilemmas about coming out in class, but also the rewards:

> [W]hat are the straight students thinking about me? Is there a perceived bias in favor of the queer students? . . . I have also received praise from queer students for being there and being out and vocal. (Monifa)

> I revealed very little about myself and my politics. I felt guilty when students chose to come out to me, often as one of the first "authority" figures they risked telling, and I supported their story without offering any of mine back in return. I talked about being a mother, using examples for lectures on gender socialization and role overload. But, the rest of my life remained *privatized* and privileged information. (Feltey)

Other lesbian academics spoke of the benefits to students of being out, especially in their locations:

> At the University of South Florida, . . . my being out affects more aspects of campus life [than at UCSC]. . . . If I can be a role model . . . in the classroom or outside at their athletic and cultural events, helping to strengthen their sense of self, I will do this. (Ponticelli)

> There have been many times since I made Salt Lake City my home that I have wondered, "What am I doing here?" and, "Will I survive?" But for me, as for many lesbian feminists, making a difference is what gives meaning to

my life. It may be the very silencing by this environment that compels me to speak out. (Morrow)

For many, it is in the classroom that some of the biggest challenges to their existence—to their very being—manifest themselves, either in the specifics of dealing with homophobic writing, or worries about perceived bias, or in the more global and abstract sense of responsibility felt by these women to be honest, to be complete human beings.

Related Themes

Other themes, while appearing in only a few of the narratives, are important nonetheless, for they attest to the diversity (as well as similarity) in our lives as lesbian academics, perhaps shared, but not articulated, by others.

An important theme for some addresses work done around the interconnectedness of oppressions of marginalized peoples, not simply lesbian/gay issues (see Lorde, Smith, Tinney in Stuck, 1994). Related to this, for several of the lesbian academics, was the fact that gender issues, specifically feminist issues, seemed to be identified as of at least equal, if not greater, concern than specifically lesbian issues.

Issues of the need for privacy (see Barale, 1989) and the need to be a role model, for example, are important to a few of the authors. Concerns about lack of a lesbian/gay community (see McDaniel, 1985), or the very closeted nature of any community that exists are very real, and cause much consternation for others.

Benefits of Being Out, Costs of Not Being Out

Some of these explanations about the reasons for, and benefits of, being out, are eloquently passionate, and reflect in lived experiences what psychological findings reveal. For many of the writers, the related themes of claiming one's own voice, of not hiding any more, of ending hypocrisy (i.e., not engaging in passing behaviors which deny essence of self), of not expending energy (Griffin, 1991) to hide and/or to pass (see McNaron, 1982); of honesty and freedom and wholeness and pride through being out, were expressed in rich and detailed fashion.

Costs of Not Being Out

Today, I understand the high price I paid to be in the closet during that period of my life. I hope that no young person will ever hold inside them the beliefs that were so depressing and hurtful to me as a young woman. (Fournier)

I could not—and would not—lie any longer about who I was, even by omission . . . my coming out . . . was motivated, I believe, by a deep-seated and strong desire for integrity; integrity not simply in the ethical sense of telling the truth, but truly in the sense of being whole. I have come to believe that a lesbian cannot achieve a sense of wholeness until she embraces herself completely. Every step out of the closet is a step into self-integration, toward wholeness. (Goedsche)

In contrast with the explanations of the hurtful costs of not being out, are the very positive benefits of being who one is, and the direct connection between being out and being productive in one's work.

Benefits—Relief, Freedom, Pride, Wholeness:

For several years I had been uncomfortable with my hypocrisy when gay and lesbian issues would come up and I heard myself saying, "Lesbian friends tell me. . .". . . . . I wanted to be out, I wanted it to be possible for others more vulnerable within the institution [Roman Catholic] to be out . . . [being out] permits me the luxury of doing what I do best—teaching and writing. (Kaplan)

My brief experience as an out lesbian academic has been nerve-racking at times, exhilarating at times, but mostly, has been personally satisfying. I feel more integrated as a person when my sexual identity is not a secret, and more fulfilled as a researcher when my work feels ethically responsible—like I am giving something back to the community that sustains me in life. (Eliason)

Being out has given momentum and purpose to my work. . . . I have achieved as much or more as my straight colleagues, and am proud to have maintained my integrity as a lesbian in the work that I have done. (Gartrell)

Continuings

This group of lesbian academics may be a group of "academic over-achievers." Successful survivors and ground-breakers might be a more appropriate description, given: The current political climate where non-discrimination statutes and policies taking stands against discrimination on the basis of affectional orientation are being rescinded—rather rapidly and vigorously in some locales (and given past climates where such statements did not even exist); a world where "identity politics" often translates as "high-risk activism" for lesbians and gays (Taylor and Raeburn, 1995); a country in which the two "Contracts" being talked about (and one voted on) in Congress are smokescreens for rescinding the civil rights of all types of "marginalized" people; a nation where "family values" means defining family exclusively as a heterosexual mother and father married to each other; a world where physical violence against lesbians and gays seems to be on the increase.

Despite these facts of our world, the lives of these lesbian academics provide evidence of survival and pride, and attest to the diversities which cross-cut our similarities, which give lie to the stereotype of a monolithic "lesbian culture/community." But we must also not forget that our similarities *do* identify us as an under-represented, marginalized people, sharing similar lived experiences with differing particulars.

The themes described above as found in the narratives of these lesbian academics do seem to provide more evidence of apparent inclusion than of systematic exclusion; much evidence of personal and academic happiness, "wholeness," freedom, finding one's voice—as well as evidence of challenges and some pain; leadership in many areas of human diversity, but especially related to lesbian, gay, bisexual issues; indications of growth—personal, academic, political; and examples of struggles with integration of the many parts of one's self (e.g., degrees of outness; teacher, counselor, mentor, private person, and so on).

The narratives of these lesbian academics' lives are indeed "existing and missing documents [which link] with the social conditions of the time" (Reinharz, 1992:163), and do contribute to our knowledge base about a group of human beings, to borrow from Haggis in Reinharz (1992:162), whose "experiences have not, as yet, been described, identified or included" in our knowledge base as a "result of a series of exclusionary practices operating at various levels within Western academic knowledge," whose inclusion is "of considerable contemporary relevance."

Epilogue

I hope that someday, none of us have to fight for our jobs, or benefits, or the basic freedoms that heterosexuals enjoy. (Fournier)

Bibliography

Barale, M.A. 1989. "The Lesbian Academic" Negotiating New Boundaries," 183–194 in *Loving Boldly: Issues Facing Lesbians*. E.D. Rothblum and E. Cole. New York: Harrington Park Press

Eichberg, R. 1990. *Coming Out: An Act of Love*. New York: Dutton

Glaser, B. G., and A. S. Strauss. 1967. *The Discovery of Grounded Theory*. Chicago: Aldine

Goff, M. (ed.) 1994. *Out in America: A Portrait of Gay and Lesbian Life*. New York: Viking Studio Books

Griffin, P. 1991. "From Hiding Out to Coming Out: Empowering Lesbian and Gay Educators." *Journal of Homosexuality* 22 (3/4): 167–196

Harbeck, K. M (ed.) 1992. *Coming Out of the Classroom Closet*. Binghamton, NY: Harrington Park Press

Holsti, O. P. 1969. *Content Analysis for the Social Sciences and Humanities*. Reading, MA: Addison-Wesley

Krippendorff, K. 1980. *Content Analysis: An Introduction to Its Methodology*. Beverly Hills: Sage

Lorde, Audre. 1981. *Sister Outsider*, Freedom, CA: Crossing Press

McDaniel, J. 1985. "My Life as the Only Lesbian Professor," 160–165 in *The Lesbian Path*. M. Cruikshank, Editor, San Francisco, CA: Grey Fox Press

McNaron, T. A. H. 1982. "'Out' at the University: Myth and Reality," 12–15 in *Lesbian Studies: Present and Future*. M. Cruikshank, Editor, Old Westbury, NY: The Feminist Press

Reinharz, S. 1992. *Feminist Methods in Social Research*. New York: Oxford University Press

Spradley, J. 1979. *The Ethnographic Interview*. New York: Holt, Rinehart and Winston

Stanley, J. P. and S. J. Wolfe (eds.) 1980. *The Coming Out Stories*. Watertown, MA: Persephone Press

Stuck, M. F. (ed.) 1994. *Structures and Processes of Inequality*, Acton, MA: Copley Publishing

Taylor, V. and N. C. Raeburn. 1995. "Identity Politics as High-Risk Activism: Career Consequences for Lesbian, Gay, and Bisexual Sociologists." *Social Problems*, May 1995, 42(2): 252–273

Wiseman, J. 1974. "The research web." *Urban Life and Culture* 3(3): 317–328

Race, Class, Age

The Question of Identity Politics

Lesbians, Class, and Academia

Some Thoughts about Class-Based Identity and Difference

Michelle Tokarczyk

Department of English, Goucher College

Suzanne Sowinska

Independent Scholar, Seattle, Washington

32

Academics are always asking the two of us about class—what working-class texts we use, where to find class-based research. Or, as the editors of this anthology asked: How do the experiences of lesbians in academia compare with those of working-class women in academia? In framing this article, we've arranged our discussion into four topics. Michelle Tokarczyk writes about "Separation from Background" and "Place in the Academic World"; while Suzanne Sowinska discusses "What Coming Out as Poor or Working-Class in Academia Might Mean" and "Mentoring Students from Poor or Working-Class Backgrounds." These topics correspond to recurring issues and concerns raised by the lesbian contributors to this anthology; we expand on these recurring issues to include faculty, researchers, and students from poor or working-class backgrounds.

Before beginning our discussion, however, we want to propose that the first point of praxis be that we never ask a question like: "How do the experiences of lesbians compare with those of working-class women?" Such questions only emphasize the artificiality of the distinct categories "academic," "lesbian," and "working class," suggesting that they don't overlap—as indeed they often do. The problems with attempting such a separation are immediately apparent for the two of us: We are both scholars from working-class backgrounds, but we have different sexual orientations. Or, as Helen Elaine Lee, an African American lesbian, so eloquently states in her contribution to *Out of the Class Closet*: "It only makes sense to examine and discuss my identity as multiple and dynamic, and the challenge, then, is to integrate the coexisting and often warring aspects of myself, and in doing so, to open the way toward building coalitions with people of disparate experience and common values" (Lee 127). Using Lee's words as a kind of blueprint, we begin by describing some potential differences in how women from poor and working-class backgrounds experience academia and then discuss strategies for change.

Separation from Background: Sense of Home and Community

In their writings working-class women academics express alienation from both their working-class backgrounds and their academic institutions (Dews and Leste, 1995; Tokarczyk and Fay, 1993; Ryan and Sackray, 1984). These women were raised in homes where manual labor was valued and intellectual work was often not viewed as work. While some working-class parents are proud of their academic offsprings' accomplishments, many have difficulty perceiving writing and teaching as work. Such attitudes as well as differences between working-class experience and that of those they meet inside academia often cause working-class academics to feel estranged from their work. Unlike many of my colleagues, I was not socialized for professional work and culture. Other working-class academics with whom I've spoken share that as children they often did not have many books around them, did not go to the opera or travel extensively, and in general lacked cultural capital (Bourdieu, 1984; Willis and Corrigan, 1983; 1980). Working-class parents may have idealized notions of upward mobility, not realizing that "crossing class" often involves acquiring new tastes and values, a figurative and literal moving away (Sennett and Cobb, 1973). Males may especially waver between jealousy and pride toward working-class women academics. While families of origin may not understand academia, other academics usually do not understand working-class issues. Otherwise sensitive and politically conscious professors may mock working-class occupations and pastimes, causing anger, shame, and alienation in working-class students, researchers, and faculty.

As titles of many literary texts by working-class women writers suggest—Sandra Cisneros, *The House on Mango Street*; Janet Zandy *Calling Home*; Michelle Tokarczyk, *The House I'm Running From*—home has become a powerful metaphor in working-class literature. Essays and academic texts also examine the importance of community and class-based culture (Dittmar, 1995; Zandy, 1995; Dimock and Gilmore, 1994; Fox, 1994; Aronowitz, 1992; Gardner et al., 1989; Harstock et al., 1989; Steedman, 1987; Roberts, 1984; McRobbie, 1978; Bunch and Myron, 1974). Home is often taken for granted by the privileged, yearned for by those on the margins.

Lesbians, too, often are estranged from families. In coming out many lesbians so strain family ties to the point that they cannot depend on families of origin for emotional support. Instead, the lesbian and gay community becomes family and for some lesbians provides a sense of home. Lesbians inside academia mention a desire for home similar to that expressed by women writers from working-class backgrounds. For example, Kathryn Feltey evokes a need for home; while many of the other contributors bring up issues of safety, ranging from professional safety to economic security to physical safety. Furthermore, most lesbians in this collection imply if not actually state that they want the same opportunities as heterosexuals have to build families, to have these families recognized, and to protect them with medical insurance and other benefits their colleagues take for granted.

Paradoxically, Penelope Dugan's article recounting how she and her partner were treated as a family reveals how biases in construing heterosexual relationships can be transferred to lesbians. Dugan, a tenured professor who moved to join her partner hundreds of miles away, had to fight for a tenure-track position. Once on the faculty, she was treated as a junior member who was hired grudgingly because her partner was a senior member of the administration, a familiar scenario for many married academic women. This experience reminds us that when we set up oppositions we privilege one thing over another. If unchallenged, heterosexual practices will be simply transferred to lesbian relationships.

While many working-class women feel distant from their families of origin, few seem to see academia as a community. Some may associate with other marginalized academics, or as I do, socialize with freelance writers, artists, and others who are socially and economically marginalized. As articles by Christy Ponticelli and Mickey Eliason illustrate, the degree to which a woman affiliates herself with a community depends on the geographical locale of her institution, as well as the institution itself. In most cities a lesbian will find it hard to remain isolated from the local lesbian community, unless she stays totally within the institutional Ivory Tower. Many small colleges also promote a sense of community. If these institutions were less homophobic and more conscious of class relations, more women could feel at home there.

Place in Academic World

Many contributors to this anthology stated that they were drawn to academic careers because they saw academia as a liberal and tolerant environment. As a working-class woman, I too had these perceptions—at least until graduate school. While Carol Moeller expresses disappointment with faculty and administration similar to what I felt, other contributors are pleased that their work is supported and that their sexual orientation is accepted. Generally, contributors to *Working-Class Women in the Academy* and *This Fine Place So Far from Home* express greater difficulty establishing themselves in the academy.

Most of the narratives in this anthology do not appear to be written by working-class women. (In fact, while Bonnie Strickland identifies as working class and Kathryn Larsan reports an economically secure childhood most contributors do not specifically address class). The contributors do not feel estranged by the class-based operating within most academic institutions. Homophobia exists in many workplaces. Academics from the working class seem far more likely than their colleagues to have lost years of academic work struggling to support themselves. Though divorce and the increasing need for two paychecks to support families have made the heterosexual privilege of marriage (and support from a spouse) more perceived than real, it is likely that lesbians are more attuned to the need to be self-sufficient their heterosexual counterparts.

Some contributors to this anthology identified their institutions as working class but did not situate their own class background in relation to their students'—which is interesting because most grappled with whether and how to be out to students as lesbians. Their silence on class is not unusual. The absence of controversy around discussing class background indicates how unconscious Americans on the whole still are about class.

Since the advent of the gay rights movement, gays and lesbians have become more visible on campus and queer theory has been well received in many places. (We remind readers that we are not necessarily looking at lesbians and working-class women as two distinct groups. Someone struggling to come to terms with lesbianism and being from a working-class background may find more ways to represent and understand her sexual orientation than her class background.) Class, in contrast, is examined in many sociology courses, but otherwise remains in academia's closet. Today some commentators deny that the concept of class is applicable in the United States, despite the widening disparity between the very rich and very poor. There are no working-class pride days, no buttons to wear, no working-class groups except for ever-shrinking labor unions. Furthermore, class issues are not categorized as such; the collection of essays I edited with Elizabeth Fay, for example, is only listed under women's studies and sociology. Without easily locatable resources, it is hard for working-class academics to affiliate.

The difficulty in affiliating extends to a difficulty in research, especially in the humanities where there are many more nationally recognized scholars in queer theory than in class-based theory. The women in this collection, especially those in service positions, were generally able to get money for research. In the humanities, however, class-based research is still only provisionally accepted and funding is very hard to obtain.

Of course, some would argue that a woman with a graduate education ceases to be working class. Rather, she may be seen as embodying the American dream that class-based work would critique: upward mobility through education. A woman academic from the working class does indeed have privileges that her family of origin does not. Yet working-class academics do not enjoy the same privileges as many of their counterparts. Working-class academics' status is based on job position and (often low) salary, not inherited wealth. Even fairly successful working-class academics may have huge debts from graduate school, and lack a family safety net.

Those who do work on class issues, as Suzanne points out, may be identified as class scholars, but often the label does not communicate the psychic toll years of struggle and shame have taken on these women. Likewise, queer theory has been fashionable in many academic circles, but many do not understand the psychic toll of being a lesbian and the psychic investment lesbians have in queer theory.

What Coming Out as Poor or Working Class in Academia Might Mean

Although they don't always acknowledge its structural base, a discursive/historical shift in the gay community toward its current powerful emphasis on coming out as a political tool for progressive social change has affected most of the contributors to this anthology in one way or another. The general consensus is that passing as a heterosexual is not good. To be out of the closet as a lesbian in your personal, community, and professional life helps to combat public and internalized homophobia. The essays here carefully examine the myriad possibilities and concerns that surround the question of lesbian visibility in academia. What does it mean to come out as poor or working class in academia? What meanings do the metaphors of passing, internalized oppression, belonging to a specific cultural community, outing someone, or acting out—all familiar to members of the lesbian and gay community— take when counterposed with class-based identities?

I have said before that coming out as a lesbian was what prepared me for the much more difficult ordeal of coming out as working class (Sowinska, 1993). Although I was able to be out as a lesbian during my undergraduate years in the late seventies (even though none of my instructors were), I tried hard to hide my class background. I was deeply ashamed of what I then perceived to be the forms of ethnic and/or redneck behavior that were a familiar part of the cultural landscape of the small rural place where I grew up as a member of my town's only Polish American family. In order to survive at all in academia, I—like many of the students from poor or working-class backgrounds that I now teach and mentor—needed to believe in the myth that academic institutions are sites of equal opportunity. I needed to believe that my education at a state university would equal that of the Ivy League schools my high school classmates from "better" families were attending, and that it would give me a chance for success in America that had not been given prior generations of my family. Not all members of the academic community who come from poor or working-class backgrounds feel as strong a need to pass as I did, but struggling with or against some form of passing is part of the psychology of almost everyone I know who comes from a working-class background. There were very few novels, essays, or theoretical texts available then that examined the experiences of working-class lesbians. Fortunately, more writing on this subject has appeared in recent years (Boyd, 1995; Allison, 1994; Davis and Kennedy, 1994; Penelope, 1994; Anzaldúa et al., 1993; Cardea, 1991/92; Cruikshank, 1982).

Gay, lesbian, bisexual, and transgendered members of the academic community are all too familiar with those whose sexual orientation is not "straight" but who pass as heterosexuals or allow others to assume that they are. Passing takes different forms when class background is what one seeks to make invisible. Among other reasons, members of the academic community from poor and workingclass backgrounds pass to hide family history, accent, ethnicity, religious belief, poverty, poor academic training, hunger, violence, financial concerns, public assistance, and stereotypes of region, neighborhood, or community. The questions regarding class-based passing are the same as for those who pass for other reasons: Is the emotional and psychic toll that the deception, shame, and hiding is taking worth it? Is it safe to come out? Is there a community to come out to? Will you inadvertently out others who associate with you? Will coming out about your class background help others? Will you be tokenized or stereotyped? Does an understanding of and participation in class-based communities offer a unique perspective that can be used in your research?

Combating some form of internalized class-based oppression is also frequently an issue for members of the academic community who were raised poor or working-class and are questioning whether or when they should come out about their class background. Ironically, more than one colleague has confessed to me that when they received student grants given because of economic circumstance, they would distance themselves from the other "scholarship kids,"—the very students with whom they might find commonalities. Another told me that during her first academic appointment she refused to eat at her campus dining hall because one of her relatives worked there and she didn't want anyone to know. In my own teaching experience I find that occasionally I feel very uncomfortable when teaching a story that includes a class perspective. Once teaching Tillie Olsen's, "I Stand Here Ironing," I was so shamed by a student's negative response to the choices made by the working-class mother in the text, that I personalized it, and then stumbled through the rest of the class.

As Michelle describes in an earlier section of this essay, whether they currently associate with them, most members of academia who were raised poor or working class come from specific cultural communities that at least at one time provided them with a vocabulary, set of ethics, an aesthetic sensibility, and a sense of "home." This knowledge can be very much at odds with that of the Ivory Tower. The sense of living more than one life, one inside academia, and one very much outside it, is as common with members of the academic community from poor or working-class backgrounds as it is with members of the lesbian and gay community. Whether riding my motorcycle with the Dykes on Bikes in the local gay pride parade, or giving a talk at the annual meeting of the Modern Language Association, I find I am constantly engaged in often rocky negotiations through the various communities in which I claim membership. How does my being out in the community as a working-class lesbian reflect on my department, my university, and on my chances for advancement in academia? How does my education and profession distance me from those I care most about? When am I acting out? What am I currently being out about?

The most challenging but also most rewarding aspect of being out as working class in academia has come in my research and teaching. It took me quite a while to realize that the best thing for me to do was to take the years of rigorous training in academia that I put myself through and use them to investigate class-based experience. This work is the main way that I'm currently out about class issues in academia. Almost all my writing is concerned with some form of discussion about class-based difference. The texts that I choose to teach and the way that I teach them often raise questions about class relations. When I teach a literary text that contains class-based representations, I'm frequently able to help my students to think about how a writer can use metaphor or symbolism to promote a sense of class-based identity and difference. I know there are class-based signifiers in texts that my colleagues don't read in the same way I do, or events that writers describe whose cultural significance is lost to those without knowledge of working-class life and history.

Mentoring Students from Poor or Working Class Backgrounds

Many of the contributors to this anthology discuss the importance of providing positive mentoring for lesbian and gay students. Examples of positive mentoring by lesbian academics include: being a visible role model, creating a safe, validating classroom environment, challenging homophobia on campus, and working on committees to provide medical benefits for other lesbians and gays on campus. All of these forms of mentoring are equally valuable to students from poor or working-class backgrounds even though student concerns and means of addressing them will often be quite different.

For someone who comes from a poor or working-class background, being a role model might mean just being yourself in the classroom, refusing to pass, and at times teaching from your class-based experiences. For all academics, it means providing reading lists and classroom discussion that includes representations of poor or working-class experience. It also means knowing which texts to recommend for reading and research projects and validating student explorations in making class-based arguments or in using class-based analysis. If your current methodology is one that uses identity politics to give students positions from which to critique the status quo, do you allow ample time for discussion of class-based identity? If your approach is more theoretical, can you point students toward texts that problematize class as well as race, ethnic, and gender relations? If you use a structural analysis, will your poor or working-class students find themselves represented in the arguments you bring to class? In some cases, being a visible role model for poor or working-class students might also mean helping students who have no previous experience with higher education negotiate their way in academic institutions or suggesting how students who are poorly prepared academically might improve their academic standing.

A more difficult question regarding class-based identity in academia is: When and in what context should you encourage a student to come out to others about their class background? In circumstances involving access to financial aid, scholarships, fellowships, or other grants that might be available to students based on financial need, it is almost always good to advise students to reveal details about their financial situation. It might mean making a student aware that such opportunities exist. In some cases you may be the only person who can help a student complete the application and interpret personal or family history to fit the requirements.

In other situations involving advising students to come out about class background or in outing students to colleagues, the decision frequently parallels that made when working with lesbian, gay, or bisexual students: How safe is it for the student? Is there a community for them to come out to? Is class-based research valued at your institutions or at those you are advising a student to apply to? If you decide to out a student as poor or working-class to a colleague or committee, have you considered your reasons and any potential consequences for the student? When should you regard your knowledge of a student's class background or identity as private and/or confidential?

For those who wish to pursue a more activist agenda within the academic community, are there ways that lesbian academics can act out about the often disparaging class discourses all too prevalent in academia? If role models are important should lesbian academics be challenging our peers to examine their own current class positions and/or personal histories in relation to class? Can we aid students from poor or working-class backgrounds in finding ways to act out about class in the context of their intellectual work? Are there activist or community groups we can contact that would help students understand class-based resistance? If we are mentoring lesbian or gay students who also come from poor or working-class backgrounds can we find resources for them within the lesbian and gay community?

Promoting Change

Ideally, academics who have concerns about sexual orientation and class-based identity should use their marginalized status to critique institutional practices and assumptions. As bell hooks argues, marginalized status gives one insight that is unavailable from the standpoint of the privileged (hooks, 1984). Academics who are concerned about sexual orientation and class-based identity must continue to make their presence felt on campus. Some of the contributors here mention that they received service credit for mentoring gay and lesbian students. Such practices could be extended to include volunteering in literacy campaigns or other volunteer programs outside the university.

Within the classroom, one of the best resources is team teaching. One article described a course taught by two women who use the differences in their sexual orientations as part of their pedagogy. A course based on this model could easily include discussions of class difference. Even courses taught by one faculty member might invite speakers who would broaden the perspectives offered. Whenever possible, lesbians and working-class women should include histories of labor and gay rights movements in their lectures and discussion.

Finally, concerned academics could consider conducting collaborative research. A sociological study of impoverished lesbian mothers might be a possibility, as would a study of lesbian working-class aesthetics in film, literature, or art. Also, academics who publish articles might expand their audience by sometimes using a more popular style and occasionally submitting to publications that circulate both inside and outside of academia. For academics investigating class and those studying sexual orientation, the experience of being silenced has been crucial. Until recently most lesbians often felt a need to use ambiguous pronouns in referring to their partners. Working-class women felt they should not relate their family experiences. This silence only reinforces a sense of internalized oppression and shame. The harmful effects of silencing can be combated by those who understand the similarities and important differences of their status in the academy.

Bibliography

Allison, Dorothy. *Skin: Talking About Sex, Class and Literature*. Ithaca, NY: Firebrand Books. 1994.

Anzaldúa, Gloria, Lourdes Arguelles, Kennedy, and Toni A.H. McNaron, eds. "Theorizing Lesbian Experience." *Signs* 18 No. 4, 1993.

Aronowitz, Stanley. *The Politics of Identity: Class, Culture, Social Movements*. New York: Routledge, 1992.

Bourdieu, Pierre. *Distinctions: A Social Critique of the Judgment of Taste*, trans. By Richard Nice Cambridge: Harvard University Press, 1984.

Boyd, Blanche McCrary. *The Redneck Way of Knowledge*. New York: Vintage, 1995.

Bunch, Charlotte, and Nancy Myron. *Class and Feminism*. Baltimore: Diana Press, 1974.

Cardea, Caryatis, ed. "Lesbians and Class." *Sinister Wisdom* 45, Winter 1991/92.

Cisneros, Sandra. *The House on Mango Street*. New York: Alfred Knopf, 1994.

Cruikshank, Margaret. *Lesbian Studies: Present and Future*. Old Westbury, NY: The Feminist Press, 1982.

Davis, Madeline, and Elizabeth Lapovsky Kennedy. *Boots of Leather, Slippers of Gold*. New York: Routledge, 1994.

Dews, C. L. Barney and Carolyn Leste, eds. *This Fine Place So Far from Home: Voices of Academics from the Working Class*. Philadelphia: Temple University Press, 1995.

Dimock, Wai Chee and Michael T. Gilmore, *Rethinking Class*. New York: Columbia University Press, 1994.

Dittmar, Linda. "All That Hollywood Allows: Film and the Working Class." *Radical Teacher* 46:38–45, 1995.

Fox, Pamela. *Class Fictions*. Durham: Duke University Press, 1994.

Gardner, Saundra, Cynthia Dean, and Deo McKaig. "Responding to Differences in the Classroom: The Politics of Knowledge, Class and Sexuality," *Sociology of Education* 62 (1989): 64–74.

Harstock, Nancy, Sonia Alvarez, Patricia Willians, Elaine Zimmerman and Cheryl Schaeffer, "Work, Race and Class: Making the Links in Theory and Practice." NWSA National Conference 1989. Tape #17.

hooks, bell. *Feminist Theory: From Margin to Center*. Boston: South End, 1984.

Lee, Helen Elaine. "Goodbye to the House." *Out of the Class Closet: Lesbians Speak*. Julia Penelope, ed. Freedom, CA: The Crossing Press, 1994:125–148.

McRobbie, Angela. "Working-Class Girls and the Culture of Femininity." *Women Take Issue*. Ed. by the Women's Studies Group, Centre for Contemporary Cultural Studies. Boston and London: Routledge, 1978:96–108.

Olsen, Tillie. *Tell Me A Riddle*. New York: Delacorte Press, 1956.

Penelope, Julia, ed. *Out of the Class Closet: Lesbians and Class*. Freedom, CA: The Crossing Press, 1994.

Roberts, Elizabeth. *A Woman's Place: An Oral History of Working-Class Women, 1890–1940*. Oxford: Blackwell, 1984.

Ryan, Jake and Charles Sackray, eds. *Strangers in Paradise: Academics from the Working Class*. Boston: South End Press 1984.

Sennett, Richard and Jonathan Cobb. *The Hidden Injuries of Class*. New York: Vintage-Random. 1973.

Sowinska, Suzanne. "Yer Own Motha Wouldna Reckanized Ya: Surviving an Apprenticeship in the Knowledge Factory." *Working-Class Women in the Academy*, eds. Michelle M. Tokarczyk and Elizabeth A. Fay. Amherst: University of Mass Press, 1993: 148–161.

Steedman, Carolyn Kay. *Landscape for a Good Woman*. New Jersey: Rutgers University Press, 1987.

Tokarczyk, Michelle M. *The House I'm Running From*. Albuquerque: West End Press. 1989.

Tokarczyk, Michelle M. and Elizabeth A. Fay, eds. *Working-Class Women in the Academy*. Amherst: University of Massachussetts Press, 1993.

Willis, Paul and Phillip Corrigan. "Orders of Experience: The Differences of Working-Class Cultural Forms," *Social Text* 7 (Spring and Summer 1983): 85–103.

Willis, Paul and Phillip Corrigan. "Cultural Forms and Class Mediations." *Media, Culture, and Society* 2 (1980): 297–312.

Zandy, Janet. *Calling Home: Working-Class Women's Writings*. New Brunswick, Rutgers University Press, 1990.

Zandy, Janet. *Liberating Memory: Our Work and Our Working-Class Consciousness*. New Brunswick, Rutgers University Press, 1995.

Women of Color, Sexuality, and the Academy

A Few Thoughts

Maria C. Gonzalez

Department of English,
University of Houston

33

In studying the intersections between sexuality, gender, and ethnicity, I can underscore similarities in issues while acknowledging some of the differences represented by individual experiences. To suggest strategies for more cooperation between women who experience racism and/or heterosexism is to find keys to working together in the future academy. What I offer is an understanding of lesbianism and ethnicity as a social act, with similarities organized around the issue of coming out.

As an academic, my first priority is to the curriculum that I teach and develop. As a woman of color in a heterosexist and racist institution, I have always found that the development of curriculum acts as the best vehicle for creating community and subverting the negative status quo. In creating a curriculum that is rigorous and expansive and no longer tied to the traditional "great books" formula, one can find colleagues and build the links that create community and acceptance for those who are sexually and culturally different. For lesbians specifically—European American lesbians and lesbians of color—an important commonality is represented by the dilemma of whether to come out, although the details of this process differ in important ways. For lesbians and straight women of color, curricula issues provide the strongest base for common ground.

Sexual orientation and race in academia are certainly diffuse subject areas, so much so that one ends up studying the anecdotal more than anything else. Some of the superficial similarities between lesbians—be they European American or women of color—and straight women of color are rooted in the shared status of "other" as opposed to the straight, white, male professoriat. This is of course very obvious, but one of the very first issues one can contemplate continues to be the assumption that one is not the original stereotyped professor.

To be defined in the negative is the starting point for much of the reanalysis of the academy by lesbians and women of color. We can and do recognize the narrowly defined stereotype and its reflection in a straight, white, male-dominated curriculum, but the full panorama of experience escapes our vision of the academy and, hence, the curriculum. The academy is now the domain of the "other," which can include class, sexuality, culture, and any number of "differences." And hence, at first glance, the stereotype is challenged. *Or is it?* There is some very strong evidence within this collection of writings that lesbians are being coopted into the academy. Their work in queer theory and gay and lesbian studies is not filtering broadly into the curriculum but ghettoized and tokenized into marginal spaces.

For those who challenge this description, I respond with the question, "Is lesbianism discussed in the introductory classes of English, history, or biology?" Simply becoming the professoriat with a "minor" difference, as the work of Andrew Sullivan (1995) would have it, does not deconstruct the traditional academy or its curriculum. Yet, I do not believe that a different sexual orientation is a minor difference: It is quite "significant," as was the entrance of people of color into the academy. And while some lesbians in the academy will be coopted as they refuse to address sexuality in their curriculum, the academy will never be the same because of a new and out population of lesbians.

As the academy continues to become as complex an arena as U.S. society in general, the assumption that a professor is a white straight male continues to be eroded and other experiences become the "norm." Hence, we are finally beginning to see a space where the lesbian academic can become a full member of the academy. Women of color, too, are becoming a recognizable group *within* the curriculum and the academic community. Even if our numbers are still small (lesbians and nonlesbian women of color taken together), these individuals represent populations that are coalescing into groups recognized within the academy. Previously, there were so few "others" that such issues raised by their presence could be neglected. Clearly, from the experiences represented in these works, the presence of lesbians in the academy can no longer be neglected.

Yet, the essays collected here suggest that the feeling of "otherness" is one fundamental characteristic and striking experience that lesbians in the academy have in common. It is also the one fundamental experience which women of color and lesbians in the academy have in common, as well.

Beyond that sense of being "other," though, individual experiences quickly diverge into the multitude of differences that make up the complexity of social relations.

One of the first striking differences between women of color and lesbians is the decision to come out. This preoccupation cannot be shared by straight women of color. Ethnicity—very often, at least—is a public designation and not one that can be hidden. Consistently, however, whether to come out preoccupies many lesbians in the academy. Obviously, this is the overwhelming first decision for white lesbians. A woman of color who is lesbian faces a different dilemma. She will probably appear in the academy as a woman of color first. She, too, must decide whether to come out, and in many instances it is easier for her not to do so. The pressures of being a representative of a racial or ethnic community can pull the woman of color in many different directions. Adding the issue of sexuality complicates an already convoluted relationship with the academy. The woman of color has the option of not coming out but not necessarily of forefronting her race or ethnicity. More than likely the university will force this forefronting for her. To show what great strides the university has made, a woman of color is often invited to join many committees. And whether she is interested or not, she will be expected to articulate the issues for the community she has been designated to represent. Very few academicians of color are allowed to opt out of this process, an option lesbians do have by not coming out.

The key issue here is visibility. Women of color often have no choice in their visibility and hence are expected both to represent their group and attempt to include it in the curriculum. Lesbians can choose not to be representative. The pull to represent specific populations on a campus requires making choices about what does not get represented. One of the fundamental challenges facing a lesbian of color in the academy is where to put her energies. She must decide which community she is willing to represent, be an activist for, and attempt to get the curriculum to include those issues. That choice may depend upon the atmosphere at the institution. If the college or university needs more representation in terms of issues of simple diversity, then such committees should become the priority. In my own experience, when I was at a very large midwestern university, diversity in terms of ethnicity was a priority. Right now I am at a large urban university and diversity *in terms* of sexual orientation is my priority. As a lesbian of color, my leadership role has been informed by my sense that women's issues and issues of sexuality are not represented on this campus adequately and that the curriculum is silent about sexual orientation. Hence, a priority can be defined for individuals well before they become members of that academic community. Moreover, there are so few lesbians of color in the academy that one ends up building coalitions with other lesbians and straight women of color.

One of the most important survival tools is to work together with others to fight institutional racism and heterosexism. That the representation of issues concerning lesbians and women of color are not necessarily issues the university is willing to take up invites the concept of coalition building. How do white lesbians, lesbians of color, and straight women of color work together? If the fundamental issues are shared, they can work successfully. What brings diverse communities together is the sense of an outside threat, or the demand of an internal project. Curriculum development is a natural issue for academics and one that can unify women around issues of race and sexual orientation. The need to get lesbians and women of color adequately represented in the curriculum is a challenge to any university. While much of the experience of lesbians and women of color in coalition building has felt like tokenism, attempting to change curriculums has brought diverse communities together in the past and continues to be a strong force for change on campuses.

One problem in dealing with sexual orientation is the preoccupation with coming out. Clearly our world is unsafe, but this forces lesbians to obsess about whether to come out to a class instead of issues like teaching the class about homosexuality or difference. It is very clear from the essay selections that we see here that the academy continues to control the response to lesbianism; it follows that institutional heterosexism is the driving force behind our discussion of sexual orientation. Those institutional forces that reinforce heterosexism in the academy are best challenged in the curriculum.

As part of a faculty group involved in Mexican American studies and in a unit that has a very strong and student centered ethnic studies program, I have had the opportunity to see that there is some safety when there are strong nontraditional institutional programs already a part of the university. As a graduate student at a large midwestern university with a very strong women's studies program but no equivalent in Mexican American studies, I found my priorities to be curriculum recognition for issues of ethnic diversity. This forced a discipline upon the community by making us focus on getting institutional recognition. It is the opposite at my present institution. Ethnic Studies has a strong and legitimized presence on the campus. Instead the women's studies program is still weak and consistently threatened, so weak that now I am preoccupied with getting gender and sexuality into the curriculum. We are in the process of developing a much stronger and broadly based women's studies program. My hope is that someday a program in lesbian and gay studies or queer studies will be established.

I can predict what will happen as sexuality continues to become a legitimized field of study in the academy. Queer studies and lesbian studies will probably come much closer together than in the past. There will be a struggle between the queer theorist and the lesbian studies scholar on campuses throughout the country. At those universities already strong in theoretical fields, queer studies will dominate the discussion. On campuses with strong pragmatic women's studies programs, lesbian and gay studies will be the dominant institutionalized form of study. And like women's studies and ethnic studies, they will represent communities and become institutionalized but will have changed the atmosphere of the campus. The institutionalized homophobia that is a part of the academy will loosen but probably not disappear. Lesbians will be able to be out and able to teach the subjects of sexuality.

This brings me to the fundamental problem of sexual difference becoming a part of the academy. For me, the legitimization of sexuality is paramount to challenging homophobia. Lesbian studies has a very strong chance of becoming the next ethnic study program. It will be given token recognition and ghettoized in the academy. Our challenge is to not allow this to happen. Women's studies as a program has succeeded on some universities. Most fields of study must now acknowledge issues of gender. And while women's studies and feminism has succeeded in the humanities and social sciences, its influence is still minimal in the sciences. Ethnic studies, on the other hand, has not been as successful in forcing issues of difference into the academy. Much of its work is still not integral to the curriculum. However, strides continue to be made and curricula continue to be challenged. Hence, the backlash to multiculturalism, but here is yet another point where issues of sexuality can become part of the discussion.

Unfortunately at too many places multiculturalism is seen as adding an African American to a committee, or a book by a woman to a reading list, or adding the gender variable to a case study. True multiculturalism challenges the very foundation and assumptions upon which a curriculum is defined. The recognition that difference is far more complicated than previously understood or believed is the most challenging implication to the academy. By bringing in issues of difference represented in ethnicity, gender, culture, and sexuality, a simple reading list can become a quagmire of unrelenting challenges and questions as to the criteria by which the reading list was set up. Hence, the backlash to multiculturalism, but here is yet another point where issues of sexuality can become part of the discussion. As multicultural curriculums that challenged the responses can be inclusive of sexuality.

Why do I continue to return to issues of the curriculum? Because it is there that legitimacy is assigned in the academy. When it is a field of study and a part of the community represented in the academy, lesbians will not become another colonized text to study, but a legitimate field of study and members of the community will be included. The question I began with was how do straight women of color, white lesbians, and lesbians of color work together in the academy? My focus is to gain recognition and legitimacy in the academy for women of color and lesbians. How does one gain legitimacy in the academy? By simple demographics and more visibility and by gaining acceptance in the curriculum.

It is difficult to argue and discuss issues of lesbianism, women of color, and the academy without looking at concrete examples, and the experiences recorded in this collection illustrate these issues. I want to address how these issues gain legitimacy in the academy, how we will gain the opportunity to teach these issues in our classes. My analysis takes me to my own experiences in the classroom, and represents an example of how sexuality and culture become a part of the curriculum.

I teach at a large urban university with a significant diverse population in terms of culture. One course I teach is on ethnic literature in the United States, and this course allows me to draw from as many conceptions of diversity as possible in a sixteen-week class. I bring the issues of cultural and ethnic difference, as well as issues of religious difference, class difference, and sexuality. As part of the course I include works that represent homosexuality. I am trying to introduce the concept of sexual difference as a legitimate field of study to a somewhat conservative campus. But it is not just sexual difference that I am interested in. I am more interested in the question of how sexual difference interacts with diverse cultural signals and norms. Homosexuality as it is conceived and is assigned meaning in diverse communities drives the course, and how I examine the issue of sexuality.

One of the fundamental texts I use is Gloria Anzaldúa's *Borderlands/La Frontera*. This text is by a Chicana writer and poet who is also an out lesbian. Her work is a collection of loosely connected essays and poems discussing both theoretical and pragmatic understandings of identity. This book is a work by a radical lesbian feminist who challenges the assumptions of patriarchy and cultural hegemony. Along with this text, I usually have the students read Richard Rodriguez' *Hunger of Memory*. This text is also a loosely connected collection of essays by a Latino who aspires to "assimilation" in the United States. He is, in many ways, the direct opposite of Anzaldua. He has more recently disclosed his homosexuality in his second book, *Days of Obligation*. These two writers deal with the specifics of their communities and cultures and together present a very complex understanding of the Mexican American community.

I take these two works in order to give students an understanding of how culture has an impact on how we address issues of sexuality. Using the familiar tool in women's studies of the coming out paper, I ask students to write a coming out letter for Anzaldúa and one for Rodriguez. They are to put themselves in each authors' shoes and write brief letters to "their" parents explaining their sexual orientation. I usually give them fifteen minutes for each letter with very little instruction on how to construct and word the letters. I then have them get into small groups of five or six and read each other's ones with the goal of choosing the most appropriate letters. The students hand me ten or twelve that I take to copy and discuss at the next class session.

Though I have only had the opportunity to do this twice I am able to draw some preliminary conclusions from these exercises. The students have said that the letter to Anzaldúa's parents is easier to write because there seems to be a tradition of challenging assumptions within her experience. And, the students say, in many ways, her parents are probably not surprised by her challenge to heterosexism—that if it was not homosexuality, Anzaldúa would probably challenge something else sacred to the family. She had already challenged her traditional gendered role, why not her sexual role as well?

The real challenge, as my students explained to me, was writing a coming out letter for Richard Rodriguez. Here was a man who had always been a "good" traditional boy. A fellow who probably went to Catholic Mass on Sundays. Who knew his parents believed in being well behaved and following the rules. My students consistently said it was hard to explain to Rodriguez' parents, who valued tradition very much, that their son was a gay man. The most striking quality about these letters was the desperate need to beg for continued parental love. My students claimed that the world Rodriguez came from offered love only on a contingent basis. If you were willing to follow the rules, if you were willing to accept the norms, if you were willing to be like everyone else, then you could and would be accepted in the family.

This exercise, in my opinion, provides the basis from which we can begin the discussion of sexuality and difference by diverse groups in the academy. I am a firm believer that homosexuality is as diversely experienced in the world as anything else and as intimately involved with the issues of class, race, culture, gender, and environment. And to try and separate out just one of those issues is difficult and somewhat narrow. Books like Anzaldúa's and Rodriguez' works can be used in the social sciences as well as the humanities. The depiction of lesbians in Gloria Naylor's *The Women of Brewster Place* allows for another culture to explore the impact race has on sexuality. I continue to return to the curriculum as a place for further exploration and a place where women of color and lesbians in the academy have a vested interest. Here they can work together and here the issues become clear. While the differences can tear us apart, there is the realization that issues of gender, sexuality, and culture will not be part of the curriculum if we continue the same route where traditional conceptions are not challenged and where lesbians and women of color do not come together to explore their common interest and their diverse needs.

There seem to be some things that women of color and lesbians have in common: the goal of seeing themselves reflected in the curriculum and legitimized in the academy. And while there is still much tokenism and a great deal more lip service, what is clear is that we have come forward into the academy, that we continue to make the academy even more complicated than it was previously. Speaking to a colleague who has been in the academy for over twenty years, he said the biggest change has been the emergence of women. The emergence of people of color has not been as dramatic, but that will have to change due to simple demographics. As evident in all census records, the twenty-first-century workforce will be women and people of color—they will also be the academy's workforce, as well.

Lesbians are becoming a more visible and vocal force on campuses. Issues of sexuality can no longer be heterosexually assumed. But within those parameters, homosexuality can no longer be assumed to be Eurocentric. And while lesbians are challenging the gay white urban experience, there remain cultural and racial as well as class differences. Clearly, the issue of lesbians in the academy is as complex as women in the academy and people of color in the academy. And while this is an excellent collection of such work, it is only the beginning of the continually developing world of the academy.

References

Anzaldúa, Gloria. (1987). *Borderlands/La Frontera: The New Mestiza*. San Francisco: Spinsters/Aunt Lute.

Naylor, Gloria. (1982). *The Women of Brewster Place*. New York: Penguin.

Rodriguez, Richard. (1982). *Hunger of Memory: The Education of Richard Rodriguez*. New York: Bantam.

———. (1992). *Days of Obligation An Argument with My Mexican Father*. New York: Viking.

Sullivan, Andrew. (1995). *Virtually Normal: An Argument About Homosexuality*. New York: Knopf.

Steppin' Into and Out of Academia

Roxanne Lin

Department of English,
University of Vermont

34

In "Feminist Encounters: Locating the Politics of Experience," Chandra Talpade Mohanty claims that, unlike the 1970s when feminists in the U.S. academy had to "contend . . . with phallocentric denials of the legitimacy of gender as a category of analysis," the "crucial questions in the 1990s concern the construction, examination and, most significantly, the institutionalization of difference within feminist discourses."[1] Mohanty's essay stages an encounter between two recent feminist texts, foregrounding how one "uses the notion of sisterhood to construct a cross-cultural unity of women" while the other "uses coalition as the basis to talk about the cross-cultural commonality of struggles, identifying survival, rather than shared oppression, as the ground for coalition" (p. 84). By displaying how a notion of universal sisterhood limits oppositional agency and how a shift to survival as "the ground for coalition" historicizes experience crucial for social change, Mohanty's essay advocates a "politics of location" that would aid in making feminist discourse "self-conscious in its production of notions of experience and difference" (p. 87).[2]

Deploying my rendition of what Mohanty terms the "politics of location," I will argue that this anthology, on one level, participates in an "institutionalization of difference" that, instead of opening up possibilities for identities and identification, circumscribes them and paradoxically restabilizes "academia."[3] On another level though, by detecting the anthology's location of the primary sites of professionalization, and how "academia" materially and symbolically locates its subjects/objects, I remap the landscape, exploring and probing the visible routes and crossings within "academia" to invisible but perhaps *insitu*ational possibilities that encourage cross-cultivation of differences.

This way of responding to the narratives may appear at once appropriate and contrary, given that my mission is to "address some of the overlapping interests between lesbians and women of color" and to envision "how sexual orientation and race are dimensions from which a common agenda could (or perhaps could not) develop."[4] While the editors' request is predicated upon a hope that a coalition could be forged between "lesbians and women of color," it assumes that there is already at work the presence of a "common" ground within "lesbians" or "women of color"; therefore, coalition between these groups occurs by a recogniton of shared or overlapping interests. Underlying the editors' request and reenacted in most of the anthology's narratives is the premise that sexual orientation serves as the common and therefore unifying force among lesbians; and in accordance with this logic, race would be the common and unifying force among women of color.

When I was asked to contribute to this anthology, I knew that a salient part of the request resided in the editors' identification of me as a woman of color, an identification made possible by the fact that I am a female of Chinese descent working at a university in Vermont.[5] This initial identification occurs, in most if not all cases, without my participation, for I bear the external markings that have been culturally and socially designated as Asian, and these markings, within this sociohistorical context, designate me as a woman/person of color. Therefore, without confirming or affirming this identification, I have been identified, and the working assumption is, at this moment and in this professional/institutional context, that this identity presumably will inform my content. Yet my attempt to operate within this assumption led me to consider how these narratives and the editors' guidelines for response regulate the possible forms and contents a woman of color's perspective could take, one that would converge with rather than diverge from them.

I raise this point not to rail against this process but rather to indicate that discursive configurations embed within them the conditions for what can and cannot be produced. Pause for one moment to consider the implications and effects of the current discourses that mark one as a person of color. Although some may consider this discursive marking as a way of acknowledging rather than denying or obscuring an arena within and from which one's identity potentially arises, it nevertheless has the effect of racializing some bodies and leaving others supposedly devoid of racial inscriptions and subscriptions. In what ways does the term "person of color" disrupt the implicit point of orientation, namely the person of "no color?" How does the use of the designation posit a central or determining frame for the subject/object that others are not contained or defined by?

Asked to speak not only as a woman of color but on some level for women of color, I am uncertain what this designation entails. In large part, my difficulty results from an uncertainty about what "color" signifies. Is it understood and used as the originating point, or an effect of my descent or of my consent, or a dynamic between descent and consent? In other words, is my position as a woman of color dependent primarily upon my external form, regardless of the degree to which my ways of perceiving and conceiving the world may or may not be consciously or unconsciously color coded? How does the word-label "color" affect or construct the noun/subject "woman"? How do categories—women of color, white straight women, working-class women, and/or women with disabilities in academia—install the adjectives as the active and differentiating forces while the noun "women" remains stable and unproblematic? In what ways does the appearance of an adjective operate or circulate as the synecdoche for woman? In other words, is color the determining attribute for particular women and one feature among many possible others or perhaps nonexistent for those who are not marked in this manner? More importantly though, what happens to the adjective, "color" for instance, when it is localized? In other words, how does the location "in academia" form, transform, and/or deform the adjective, whatever it may be?

While some of the narratives express how others presumed the author was a lesbian before she re-marked herself, all of the narratives contain some trace of a coming-out story, a disclosure of this identity to self and others. According to these narratives and I suspect the culture at large, the only possibility of a coming-out story for a woman of color resides exclusively within the field of sexual identity/orientation and not in the field of color or race. For, in the case of a woman of color, within the context of late-twentieth-century United States, a story is always or already literally out. What kind of possibilities would emerge for and to bodies if coming-out stories were not primarily read or understood as inscriptions of sexuality? Furthermore, given that coming-out stories occur not just once but under varied conditions and from different locations, what stories are possible within academia and how can these stories reshape academia so as to produce a locale, a landscape that cultivates diverse professionals rather than one that professionalizes diversity?

What I wish to highlight here is that a logic of essence, which underwrites many of the narratives and the editors' request, can eclipse or obscure how the making of a collective identity comes from and becomes one's identity. In other words, the materials for a notion of collective identity come from those who, in some way, already conceive of themselves with that identity, and thus collective identity proceeds from and precedes its membership. Attending to the circulatory process entailed in the making and remaking of collective and individual identities creates cracks from and within which improvisation can occur. Moreover, the governing or starting premise of an essence, while having strategic appeal for its role in group formation and definition, suffers and loses sociopolitical efficacy when the essence appears divorced from time and space, severed from the conditions of its making and enacting. Although the anthology's title, *Lesbians in Academia*, suggests that this potential for dislocation is unlikely, the narratives do not actively re-vision what academia would become with the presences of currently marginalized bodies, for the prevailing tendency of the narratives is to treat in academia as a stable, though not necessarily secure, ground.

The possibilities offered by the anthology for lesbians in academia are almost always represented as having preceded the location in academia, and therefore, academia appears as a particular stage upon which to act up but not as a stage from which one emerges. While I can understand and value why the majority of the narratives constitute a lesbian identity that comes before one's embodiment in academia, I want to consider how this emphasis on the preceding identity and the scant attention upon the proceeding identity sustains rather than disdains the academic apparatus. This sidelong glance at the various bodies produced by, in, and from the anthology should prompt a more critical engagement with the politics of location and identification so that "in academia" can be outed.

If the genre that prevails in this anthology is that of the personal narrative, how are the generic conventions employed and deployed to construct bodies? In general, the personal narrative gives rise to a subject whose doings in a world, when reflected and refracted through a particular sociocultural medium, are rendered productive. While there are multiple ways in which the narratives in this anthology enable hope to those who desire to be in academia by representing how success can be attained within this realm, the path to and the understanding of success are strikingly in harmony with the dominant melody. Although some notes appear that could be the basis of other progressions, many of these narratives display their submission to and acceptance of an institutional score that preserves teaching, scholarship, and service as the bars in and from which a familiar composition emanates. If this sounds as a rendition of a closed figuration, then I wonder what would be made possible if these pieces were jazzed up?

William Blake, in *The Marriage of Heaven and Hell*, tells us that "she who desires but acts not breeds pestilence." Playing throughout the anthology's narratives is, as I've noted, the common refrain of teaching, scholarship, and service that operates as the standard measure by which academia moves and removes the bodies within its domain. While there may be multiple incentives for both parts of this dance—the professional institution and the body that wants in—to continue the beat, maintain the groove, I wonder if the only way to survive in academia is for one to take up this rhythm in the dominant manner. Without diminishing the potential material consequences of not subscribing to what academia designates as the signs and acts of belonging, I suggest that a pointed consideration of what a location (in this case academia) legitimizes and enables a sense of what subjects it desires and produces by its discursive configurations. While this consideration does not require that one discard the conventions and rules that govern reappointment, tenure, and/or promotion, it does focus on how the conventions and rules refashion whatever other identities are presumably active. To a significant degree, regardless of what identities precede one's location in academia, the identity that is most intensely fashioned by academia and proceeding from this location is that of the professional.

If it is accepted that the desideratum of academia is the professional subject, then an inquiry into what consitutes and affirms this subject discloses what room there may or may not be constructed for professionals that are not moldable to the dominant image. Returning to my earlier claim that this collection encodes a logic of essence, I suggest that academia deploys its own version of the logic in order to generate the collective identity of academic professional. Moreover, this collective identity, while potentially formed and reformed by the bodies that enter into the fold, assumes a fixity because of the institutional mechanisms and processes that prescribe what the incoming bodies are to perform. For example, although many of the narratives in this collection express that what constitutes legitimate research and scholarship may prompt one to consider whether to note on one's list of activities and accomplishments research on gay and lesbian issues—an acknowledgment that has the potential of being used against rather than for one—the general tactic for dealing with this quandary is to display signs of other scholarly interests, those already deemed acceptable by the institution or profession, to offset the repercussions. If these narratives suggest that in order to survive within academia one's intellectual commitments must keep the prevailing beat rather than shift the accent to hear another combination, then what purpose is served by supposedly different embodiments? Furthermore, the practice of displaying and highlighting *legitimate* work in order to bring in *illegitimate* work does not inevitably broaden the parameters of academic *legitimacy*, for the practice maintains the professional construction of center and margin. In other words, if the work used to gain a place within academia needs to be already acknowledged and valued by academia, then what enables the hope that work which entered through the back door will make a difference, and if it does, what kind of difference?

In reading and rereading the narratives here, I am struck by and grateful for the impassioned discourse given to pedagogy in its broadest sense. There appears to be considerably less anxiety and fear in revealing one's lesbian identity, either explicitly or implicitly, within spaces in which one is a teacher. This ease or willingness to embody and embrace an identity that, because of its subversive potential, renders one a remarkable teacher fascinates me, for the assurance that seems so present in pedagogical settings is considerably muted in the "area of research and scholarship." Maybe this difference is understandable, given that pedagogy, the star attraction in promotional discourses, is a bit player in the issue of retention—which seemingly has a liberating effect upon the classroom situation. Although the academic apparatus slights teaching—due perhaps to its fluidity, mutability, and indeterminacy—and generally privileges research and scholarship as the grounds for keeping a body—due perhaps to its seeming concreteness and quantifiability—this institutionalized tendency could be challenged. If the narratives suggest that it is within the classroom that one can be and become most fully oneself, then why not work to make this location, in which diverse bodies come together, a critical site of professionalization? Even though it could be argued that the classroom emphasis is to foster "talking heads," this situation does not and cannot entail the disembodiment that is a likely and desired effect of the institutional emphasis on research and scholarship. Perhaps what I envision is an academic landscape in which presences are as full as possible rather than drained in order to appear as professional absences.[6]

Notes

1. Chandra Talpade Mohanty, "Feminist Encounters: Locating the Politics of Experience," *Destabilizing Theory: Contemporary Feminist Debates,* Michele Barrett and Anne Phillips eds. (Stanford: Stanford University Press, 1992) 74.
2. For Mohanty, the "politics of location" refers "to the historical, geographical, cultural, psychic and imaginative boundaries which provide the ground for political definition and self-definition for contemporary U.S. feminists" (74).
3. I use "academia" to signify what I view as the dominant sensibility and its attendant practices within higher education institutions in the United States. This sensibility makes reproduction, perhaps masked as production, its means and end. See Daniel T. O'Hara's entry in *Critical Terms for Literary Study,* eds.

Frank Lentricchia and Thomas McLaughlin eds. (Chicago: University of Chicago Press, 1995) for a pointed representation of the American academy as the site of class analysis which has been instructive in my thinking about institutionalization.

4. Quotations are from Beth Mintz's letter describing this book and my task. Since I was asked to refer to "overall themes" rather than specific authors/texts, for the drafts I read may change, I found myself lost in space with no particles to prove my points. Evidently the effects of my disciplinary training were coming out and finding no place to go.

5. While I find the formulation "woman/person of color" problematic because the implication is that those whose skin is white is not colored, thereby repeating and reinforcing the various privileges endowed to whites, I use it throughout my musings as a matter of convenience.

6. Although my response in this essay toward the "profession" is less than enthusiastic, I want to convey that my experiences have been marked by significant presences. I want to thank the presences of Anne Clark, Karin Coddon, Mary Jane Dickerson, Robin Fawcett, Beth Mintz, Karen Stewart, and Robyn Warhol for helping me to work through and out of this piece.

Older Women
in Academia

Phyllis Bronstein

Department of Psychology,
University of Vermont

35

When I was invited to write a chapter comparing the experiences of lesbians to those of older nonlesbian women in academia, I found myself with more questions than facts or opinions. What should be the definition of "older women"—at what age do women cross that boundary? Are the issues they face the same ones any woman might encounter in her academic career, or are there additional ones particular to women in this group? Finally, have their experiences been similar to, or very different from, other female subgroups within academia—in this case, lesbians?

Because I could find no published information on older academic women as a group, I conducted informal interviews of my own with fourteen women faculty, ranging in age from fifty to seventy-two. They represent a variety of disciplines, and like most older academic women (including myself), they are white, and most are married—only one is an out lesbian. Then I read the narratives in the present volume, keeping in mind the older women's stories. Among the major themes that emerged from the lesbian narratives, there were three that seemed particularly important for older women as well: discrimination, sense of identity, and political commitment. Here I will compare the career experiences of lesbian and older women academics in terms of those themes, and will also examine the relationships between the themes as factors in shaping personal and professional lives.

Patterns of Career Development

Although some women are members of both groups, there are general differences between the groups in life histories and present circumstances that have had important consequences for career development. Older women faculty entered academia in two main waves. The first included those who came in the 1940s, '50s, and '60s, early in their own adult lives, at a time when cultural dictates were keeping most women in the home, with very few finding their way into any kind of professional position. These women had frequently married men they had met in graduate school, and like most women of that period, had had children fairly early on. While their husbands moved easily into tenure-track positions, the women, if they finished graduate school, usually became research associates or temporary faculty— positions they dutifully relinquished if childcare responsibilities became more pressing, or if their husbands chose to relocate. A small number of women of this first wave eventually achieved prominence in their fields, but most have remained on the periphery, as faculty at low-prestige institutions that allot no time for scholarly pursuits, as part-time lecturers at their husbands' institutions, or as research associates on other people's grants.

The second wave of older women in academia included women who entered graduate school in the 1970s and '80s, after an educational hiatus of ten years or more. For these women, who had generally been homemakers, the women's movement and the burgeoning "divorce movement" of the 1970s and '80s gave them the opportunity to reexamine their life choices— and Affirmative Action mandates made an academic career a choice to be considered. Yet because the academic job market in most fields was shrinking, many of the women in this second wave found themselves facing limitations similar to those faced by their first-wave counterparts. Their husbands' careers, well established by this time, were often not very portable, and relocating might jeopardize family finances, or affect children's educational opportunities. Thus, unlike young, single female Ph.D.'s and single and married male Ph.D.'s, they generally did not feel free to accept jobs in out-of-the-way college towns, or take one-year positions to build their credentials while continuing to search for tenure-track appointments. As a result, many women of this second wave never got on the tenure track, and have spent their academic years in temporary and often part time positions. (Aisenberg and Harrington's *Women of Academe: Outsiders in the Sacred Grove*) provides an insightful analysis of the career difficulties and disappointments of women scholars whose lives unfolded in this way.)

For lesbians in academia, on the other hand, career paths have usually been more straightforward. Most entered academia as young adults, between the late 1970s and the present, as the doors were opening more widely for women. Like many professional women of their age group (and unlike most of the women described above), lesbian scholars have generally expected to earn their own status, and provide their own financial support. Unfettered by husbands' expectations or children's needs, most of the contributors to this volume describe careers that followed an unbroken line from college to graduate school to full-time academic position. Of the eight women who are (or are about to be) mothers, five have only one child, in most cases born after their careers were established, and another appears to have started working toward an academic career after losing custody of her children when she came out. Thus, contrary to what happened for many older non-lesbian women of both waves, parenting did not divert these lesbian mothers from pursuing their career aspirations. Similarly, whereas it was typical for older nonlesbian academics to put their husband's career ahead of their own, only two of the lesbian authors in this volume report having given up a position in order to be with their partner.

Experiences of Discrimination

It is clear from the accounts in this book and in my interviews that both lesbians and older women have experienced discrimination in academia related to their group membership. Sometimes this involved being rejected for a position they had applied for. For example, among the older women I interviewed, a fifty-year-old lesbian, with a strong scholarly record acquired over many years in academia, told of having been turned down for a tenure-track position in gay and lesbian studies within an interdisciplinary program. She had been a finalist, and willing to accept the appointment at the entry level; but although her qualifications were very strong and appropriate for the position, they hired a young ABD who didn't even fit the job description. She currently has an age-discrimination complaint filed with the state's Department of Fair Employment. Another example is a poet who, when she was sixty-one and teaching part-time at a local college, was not informed by her department that a full-time tenure-track position had become available. She applied anyway, and was told that her application was marvelous—but did not get an interview. She is certain that her age was a factor, because she had an excellent teaching record and more publications and recognition for her work than anyone on the faculty.

Similarly, three of the contributors in this volume described rejections that were based on their sexual orientation. Sandra Ketrow, following an interview during which she spoke openly about her partner for the first time, was told verbally that she would be receiving an offer, only to receive a letter informing her that they had selected a male candidate. Penelope Dugan, who was the top-rated applicant for a position at her partner's institution, found herself being treated as a faculty wife rather than a viable candidate during her interview, because her relationship with her partner had been discovered. Under pressure from the administration, she finally was offered the position, but continued to be discounted and isolated the entire time she remained in that department. Nanette Gartrell, who was out in her applications for psychiatric residencies, was rejected at Columbia because she refused to collude with the program's psychopathologizing of lesbianism.

Another form of discrimination that lesbian and older women academics have encountered is in their institutions' disregard for diverse life circumstances. The governance and traditions of academic institutions presume a faculty made up of married males, with full-time homemaker wives. In regard to older women with children, there has been little awareness that because of their parental commitments, they might need to be on a slower track, at least for a while. In reality, although they may be superb teachers, and do high quality scholarly work, they are often not able—or willing—to work twelve-hour days, six or seven days a week. Yet the tenure clock moves at the same speed as it does for everyone else. Younger academic women who become mothers often suffer similar time conflicts, but because of a primary commitment to career, have usually postponed childbearing until after tenure, and are more savvy about negotiating for stopping the tenure clock and taking leave. Further, they are more likely to have help with child care from husbands or partners than are older women, whose husbands are likely to be more traditional, or who may be divorced.

In addition, the older women I spoke with who have had to deal with the illness or disability of a child, or family emotional and financial struggles following a divorce, found that there was no institutional consideration of their circumstance when their performance was evaluated for tenure, promotion, or merit raise. Thus, even if older women make it through tenure, they may take longer to be promoted to the next level, and end up with lower salaries than their male and younger female counterparts. Of course, evaluations have a way of extending beyond the formal processes, so that these women are likely to feel overall that they are less valued by their colleagues for their contributions to the field.

The strongest evidence of institutional disregard can be seen in the treatment of temporary and part-time faculty, whose ranks include many older women from both the first and second wave. Most are lecturers, working for very low pay, with no benefits, no job security, and often no voice in deciding teaching schedules, curricular issues, or departmental policy. Usually hired on a year-to-year basis, they are the first to be let go when financial belt-tightening occurs, or curricular changes are made. Some of the older part-timers I interviewed spoke of small indignities, which on a daily basis, reminded them of their "place"—such as not being given an office or a space to meet with students, or even to leave their coat and briefcase.

Many of these older nonpermanent faculty are admired and beloved teachers. Some manage to get grants to fund their research, and many produce important books and articles. Yet, when tenure-track positions come available in the institution that is employing them on a temporary basis, they are seldom considered. Some of the factors related to ageism and stereotyping, which are discussed below, come into play here. But the institutions also know these women are not going to leave, and so can continue to exploit them, while expanding their ranks with new young faculty.

For lesbians, institutional disregard is evident in the refusal to recognize the validity of lesbian families. It is still the case that partners and partners' children are, in most institutions across the country, denied the benefits automatically granted to spouses and children in heterosexual married families. A number of contributors to the present volume have discussed the lack of domestic partner health benefits as a financial hardship in their lives, and a clear form of salary discrimination, in violation of their institution's nondiscrimination policies. Maggie Fournier describes her leadership in challenging her campus's refusal to provide domestic partner benefits. But there can be risks in taking on this fight; Sue Morrow wonders whether letting herself be used as a test case at her university might cause problems with the administration, when she comes up for tenure.

A particularly insidious aspect of discrimination that older women and lesbians encounter in academia is the stereotyped perceptions of who they are, as people. Older women experience it in several different ways. Rothblum (1992) has talked of "first generation women"—women who were part of either the first or the second wave described above, who became targets of institutional and individual sexism because they were the first women in their departments; it was as if their very presence represented an affront to the patriarchy. Shunned by colleagues and students, these women were seen as being inappropriate and "difficult," sometimes to the extent that their mental stability was questioned. Many were denied tenure, or left because of the indignities they suffered; those who survived have tended to remain isolated and discounted in their departments. On the other hand, firstcomers who somehow made a niche for themselves despite the prevailing power structure are likely to have been labeled as "queen bees." Their focus on their own advancement, rather than on the expected nurture and support of others, has evoked resentment and dislike from colleagues and students, with little understanding of the necessities that might be motivating their behavior.

Older women with children have also been stereotyped as homemakers, whose scholarly interest and abilities are presumed not to meet professional standards. Interestingly, this does not tend to happen to younger women who wait until after tenure to have their children; it is as if, in the eyes of the patriarchy, they have their priorities in order. Some of the women I interviewed encountered this kind of stereotyping beginning in graduate school. A biologist related that in her first year, three labs turned her down, and the fourth let her in only on probation. Because she was a twice-divorced, thirty-two-year-old single mother and sole support of four children, their attitude was, how could she possibly be serious about being a scientist?

A more subtle kind of stereotyping described by a number of the women was a kind of "momism." There was a way that they were interrupted or ignored at meetings, and that their ideas and work were discounted, which reminded them of the ways that mothers have often been regarded in this society. They saw this as more than sexism, noting that their younger female colleagues were often treated as if they were more dynamic, interesting, and influential. Sometimes this lack of respect reached the magnitude of verbal abusiveness. A psychologist described blow-ups by women students, who saw her as a substitute mother, and were very rude. A woman who had been chair of a department of romance languages described how the male dean of the college used to call her up on the phone, yell at her, and then hang up. A sociologist noted that the male chair of her department sometimes yelled at the older women faculty, but at no one else.

On the other hand, when lesbians are denigrated or attacked in academia, it is often very overt and very specifically related to their sexual orientation. The stereotypes, which range from the simply ignorant to the vitriolic, focus on imagined extremes of behavior. Several of the contributors mention students' and colleagues' concerns about "flaunting," and Jan McDonald tells how her prospective employers checked to see whether she had ever done anything to "embarrass" her previous institution. Lynn Walkiewicz describes a female nonlesbian coworker assuming her simple compliment was a come-on. "Man-hating" is another term mentioned in a number of the narratives—although Nanette Gartrell's psychoanalytic interviewer at Columbia had the opposite stereotype—that being a lesbian really meant wanting to be a man. Several contributors who work at religious institutions, or in Christian conservative parts of the country, have had to deal with accusations from students and members of the local community that they are sinners, perverts, and recruiters of innocent youth into a forbidden lifestyle. The media have also played a role in this process; Dawn Bennett-Alexander points out the many ways they have sensationalized and perpetuated lesbian and gay stereotypes.

These different patterns of stereotyping of older women and lesbian academics have different effects. Because for older women the stereotyping is usually covert, they may not recognize it as underlying the demeaning treatment they receive, and are therefore more likely to attribute that treatment to flaws within themselves. For lesbians, the attempts to label them as undesirable "others" can be very marginalizing, leading to a sense of isolation within their institution. Sometimes these labels are associated with intimidation. For Sandra Ketrow, it went as far as death threats.

Sense of Identity

The reactions of older women and lesbians in academia to the discrimination they encounter highlight very basic differences in their sense of identity. Many of the older academic women I interviewed had to think hard before acknowledging that age might be a factor in their academic lives. If they felt that some of their experiences had been discriminatory, they were more likely at first to attribute them to sexism alone, than to think that ageism had played a role. It is as if the "older" part of themselves is in the closet; in their thoughts as well as in their behaviors, most seem to be trying to blend in as age-neutral academics. In addition, older women faculty don't generally study or teach about older women; it appears that they have internalized society's perspective, that women's lives beyond their reproductive years are not worth examining (Macdonald, 1989). And although many strive to be mentors and models for female students, none of the women I spoke with mentioned mentoring older women students, or emphasized age as a positive factor to be modeled.

For the contributors to this volume, on the other hand, being a lesbian is a major part of how they view themselves; experiences of discrimination, if anything, seem to have heightened their sense of identity. Charlotte Goedsche, noting the importance of this process of owning one's lesbian identity, writes that every step out of the closet is a step into self-integration, toward wholeness. All but four of the contributors regard themselves as fully out, despite possible risks to career advancement and personal acceptance by colleagues and students. In addition, almost all of them link this identity to their academic role. Many have committed themselves to doing scholarly work on gays and lesbians, to incorporating lesbian issues into their teaching, to making the challenging of heterosexism and homophobia an important aspect of classroom process, and to serving as mentors and models for gay and lesbian students.

Political Commitment

Not surprisingly, there are striking differences between older women and lesbian academics in levels of political activism and commitment to change. Older women generally do not speak out about their own issues, or seek one another out for purposes of support and political advocacy. They are silenced by a number of factors. For a start, institutional commissions and programs related to diversity, equality, and justice usually do not address ageism—which, in effect, says that if it exists at all, it is not worthy of the attention other forms of discrimination receive. In addition, at the very core of ageism is the message that ageing itself is shameful—and women in particular are taught that it must be hidden and denied for as long as possible. Furthermore, as mentioned earlier, the covert nature of the stereotyping older women experience may lead them to make personalized rather than politicized interpretations of any ageist and sexist treatment they receive. Thus they are unlikely to call attention to this problem, or even to see it as a problem that goes beyond themselves.

For lesbian academics, on the other hand, homophobia is often a clear and present danger—professionally, psychologically, and sometimes phys-ically. Whereas a few of the contributors to the present volume have attempted to protect themselves by remaining closeted in their work envi-ronment, most have opted for political activism as a way to empower them-selves and to bring about change. The activism takes place in the classroom, in the research they do, and in the campus organizations they have helped to form, to provide support for gays and lesbians, promote institutional nondiscrimination policies, educate the campus community, combat homophobia, and gain domestic partner benefits. Some are lone voices in their departments or institutions. A number have reached beyond the campus, to their local communities, to the media, and to state and national networks.

Forging Alliances

Both lesbians and older women in academia have much to gain from con-sidering the commonalities of their experiences. It is important to under-stand how members of both groups can be made to feel isolated and marginalized and thus disempowered from effecting change. In addition, it is important to understand the ways that institutional disregard of their needs results in economic disadvantage for both groups, and for older women, often impedes their career advancement.

There are also lessons of value to be learned from these two groups' differences. Younger women, both lesbian and straight, need to recognize the courage and determination that older women have shown. Older women are the ones who pushed open the doors, often getting bruised and beaten down in the process, which allowed the next generation of women to pass through more easily. Despite disregard and disrespect, many have stayed on and held those doors open, making valuable contributions to scholarship, and touching the lives of students year after year. The younger generation of women needs to appreciate them for the changes they helped bring about.

For their part, older women in academia can learn from the models lesbians have provided. In particular, they can take note of lesbians' pride in their identity, their determination to be fully out and visible, their connections with gays and allies for purposes of education and advocacy, and their individual acts of courage in the face of ignorance and homophobia.

The accumulated wisdom and experience of older women can be a valuable resource in creating an equitable and humane academic environment. They need to join with one another to explore the meaning of their identity as older women and to amplify their voices as they provide education and advocacy about ageism in academia. At the same time, they need to become visible allies to colleagues combatting other forms of oppression, such as racism, classism, heterosexism, and homophobia, and enlist those colleagues as allies in their own cause.

For older women to forge alliances with lesbians, it will mean learning to recognize and stand up against the homophobia that permeates the male-dominated structures in their lives, and moving beyond their own heterosexist assumptions about women's lives and needs. For lesbians, it will mean acknowledging that women who in an earlier time may have traded their own ambitions and independence for the financial support, reflected status, and societal acceptance that marriage offered, can also be feminists who recognize the oppressiveness of the patriarchy and are fighting to bring about change. It will mean incorporating ageism into the feminist agenda that lesbians have always taken leadership in promoting, both inside and outside of academia. One route to political connection is through personal information: reading and hearing one another's stories. For example, older nonlesbian academic women, reading the narratives in this book, will have a much deeper understanding of their lesbian colleagues' courage and accomplishments, and the challenges they face. Similarly, writings such as this chapter may provide insight into the life choices, struggles, and accomplishments of older academic women.

In terms of our common educational mission, the sharing of such stories, through readings, guest speakers, and panels, can provide rich classroom material to broaden students' perspectives on the shaping of women's lives, and the multidimensional nature of feminism. Barbara Macdonald (1989) writes that although ageism is a central feminist issue, both older women and ageism have been ignored in women's studies. It is time to include older women's stories and a feminist analysis of women's ageing as part of women's studies curricula. And it is time for younger academic women, lesbian and straight, to meet the women they will soon become.

References

Aisenberg, N. and Harrington, M. (1988). *Women of Academe: Outsiders in the Sacred Grove*. Amherst, MA: University of Massachusetts Press.

Macdonald, B. (1989). "Outside the Sisterhood: Ageism in Women's Studies." *Women's Studies Quarterly*, 17 (1 and 2), 6–11.

Rothblum, E. D. (1992). "Mentoring the Next Generation of Women Students: Survival in the Patriarchy or Feminist Revolution?" University scholar address, University of Vermont.

Lesbian Studies, Queer Studies

Theorizing the Lesbian Experience

Queer Theory

The Monster That is
Destroying Lesbianville

Lynda Goldstein

Departments of English and Women's Studies Program,
Pennsylvania State University

36

> I beheld the wretch—the miserable monster
> whom I had created. . . . I escaped.
>
> —Mary Wollstonecraft Shelley, *Frankenstein*

Dateline: Lesbianville

While I'll admit to watching entirely too many Godzilla movies on Saturday afternoons as a kid, the title of this chapter reflects the considerable anxiety some lesbians experience when faced with queer theory's incursions upon and dismantling of notions of lesbian identity and community. Indeed, many view queer theory with the same unmitigated horror as did Victor Frankenstein his imprudent animation: it moves as the latest epistemological mutation in postmodernity to stomp lesbian subjectivity into oblivion. As one of many players in the contemporary crisis over binary paradigms, queer theory shakes up either/or and hetero/homo notions of identity. In so doing, the inhabitants of Lesbianville have discovered much to their displeasure that, as Colleen Lamos writes, "it is no longer theoretically feasible nor politically practical to demarcate lesbianism as a unique identity." "The widely feared loss of lesbianism as an identity presents queer theorists with the opportunity to challenge the constitution of sexuality in general,"[1] but it presents "lesbians" with their worst nightmare. "Real lesbians" aren't happy about queer theory chewing up Lesbianville in the name of liberation from fractious and stifling sexual identity politics. For them, clearing the ground for retheorizing the cultural categories of sexuality, identity, and community will be accomplished over the real bodies of lesbians.

Now, facetious as the Frankenstein and Godzilla tropes may be, I don't mean to dismiss the very real concern that yet another theoretical monstrosity leaping and bounding through North American academies could damage other paradigms (such as feminist theory) that have been generally supportive of lesbians as scholars, teachers, students, and objects of study. Surely, queer theory's teeth and claws, sharpened by poststructuralist critiques of narrative, experience, and the unified authenticity of the subject, slash at efforts to self-determine, and thereby value within traditional liberal thought, what the reality of an authentic lesbian subject might mean. Those of us who have fought hard and long for the liberal rights to claim and signify (by wearing lambda necklaces, sporting leather jackets and combat boots, or gaining domestic partner benefits) look on queer theory as a generational brat with little care or knowledge of what it has taken to stake out the politically necessary claims to authenticity in a world quick to write us off as unreal, unnatural, and undeserving of rights. Used to our often precarious perches being shaken by both overt and subtle forms of homophobia, we may now tremble in the wake of queer theory's thudding steps to denaturalize sexuality *as* identity. Threatened by our own, we fear.

Indeed, few of us possess a star stature that privileges (rather than simply tolerates) being visibly and politically out in discursive and institutional regimes, not to mention our very neighborhoods. All too often we lesbian academics must negotiate the strains of quietly closeted lives with families and friends while teaching class-loads full of conservative students at small liberal arts colleges, battling colleagues and deans for tenure (provided we have tenure-track jobs in the first place), performing research on government grants dispensed by a queer-baiting Congress, enticing homophobic alumna/ae to give money to campuses with vocal LGBSAs or visible queer faculty, justifying the purchase of gender studies books and journals in our libraries, and hitting the glass ceiling at the assistant dean level.[2] Playful, performative, irreverent queer theory seems only to make a mockery of the very real and difficult conditions of our academic and home lives within a variety of communities. By holding the electrifying promise of "mess[ing] up the desexualized spaces of the academy,"[3] queer theory seems to some lesbians to mean a monstrously abstract theorization of sexuality they fought hard right in front of the lectern to establish in its embodied form. Thus, warns Sagri Dhairyam, "the body yields to intellect, and a spectrum of sexualities denies the lesbian center stage"[4] as an embodied academic and object of legitimate scholarly inquiry.

I realize, too, that queer theory, like other theories with a stake in critiquing and changing the conditions under which subjects are constructed, can be coopted as a methodology and bled dry of the street activist edge that holds a promise of dismantling the paradigms of "normal" sexuality or of building politicized coalitions with feminism, postcolonial studies, or ethnic/race studies—to name a few. We all know academics who "do feminist theory" or "do ethnic/race studies" with as much political investment as they apply to their Sunday battle with the *New York Times* crossword. Too, the recent proliferation of queer theory publications, buzzing with legitimation from best-selling publishers, privileges textual analyses of canonical and popular culture texts (work in which I engage), which can mean the devaluation and erasure of lesbian academics whose research and teaching—especially in the social sciences, utilizes traditional methodologies and focuses on people rather than texts.[5] Further, queer theory's acceptance by review boards in colleges and journals can mean that lesbian (and gay) academics are expected to live their subjectivity through their work, not through the reality of their lives in/out of the classroom: a perversion of "don't ask, don't tell": "just write, don't be—especially in front of the kids of taxpayers."

But for all this, the question remains: What are the quaking citizens of Lesbianville to do in the face of queerolous theory? Its monstrous form puts Lesbianville on notice that the "lesbian" might not be a useful category for subject identity or community in the global queer village of posteverything politics. It rages against the ways in which a lesbian's personal politics follow from the discovery of a "true identity."[6] It holds a mirror to the experientially constructed lesbian—the transparent self of "I am what I am"—only to reveal itself. If queer theory problematizes (or eradicates) "real lesbians" in the academy, does it necessarily decenter, dehumanize, or "de-dyke" the lesbian academics in this volume and on our campuses? And if queer theory challenges our "realness" by emphasizing the ways in which we are *institutional* and discursive constructs, how is that such a truly awful thing?

The Realities of Visibility

Visible to whom? And as what? As most of us (including those of us who can impeccably apply Lancome's Rouge Absolu one-handed while driving) clearly understood during the popular media's one year affair with the "lipstick lesbian" in 1994, visibility is a matter of circulation and readability outside the real. Whether that visibility is constituted by positive or negative images is not the point; visibility is an effect of being figured outside of our realities, at least as we define them. Thus, as Annamarie Jagose argues, following Teresa de Lauretis, the lesbian is not so much visible everywhere as *elsewhere*—working as a kind of liberatory, utopic space distinct from real, embodied lesbians.[7] In narrating our own lives, we seek not only to construct our identities discursively but to insist that the lesbian *is* an identity. But such an impulse to construct the self is illusory and, idealized as it often is, utopic, in Jagose's terms. That is, to the extent that the lesbian polis, were there such a thing, constructs lesbian, it also polices its borders, maintaining what is/isn't subsumed under the category. It sets up defenses. It seethes with righteous indignation when straight folks, bisexual babes, or gay male theorists seem to ignore or erase it.

But real life is messier than the utopic lesbian spaces, theories, and identities we've established for ourselves in struggling for recognition and rights. It is "real life" that queer theory attempts to address by allowing us to construct knowledges of sexualities and identities that account for this messiness. It allows us a way to negotiate the divisiveness of identity politics.

Queer is a Verb

We all know that identity politics is [are?] rooted in historical and necessary strategies for building and protecting communities of affinity. But identity politics can also be barriers to realities and perspectives different from those of a community. The politics of identity often help us ward off the monsters of oppression and assimilation at our gates. For theorists such as Jacqueline Zita, queer theory is just such a monster posing as a friendly ally to the feminist inhabitants of Lesbianville. Warning that queer theory privileges sexuality above all other categories of analysis, queer then supplants and homogenizes different and valuable identities, histories, and structures of oppression belonging to each affinity group. Lesbians, especially, get lost in the gay muscleboy shuffle of queer theory.

Zita worries that queer theory "reduces gender to an extended concept of sexual aesthetics, style, and individual expression"—a move away from the *structural* and historical dynamics of oppression that gender analyses have continually targeted (263). Zita is dead-on in taking aim at queer theory's excesses, but not because it privileges style or performativity. Because the queer theorists she targets do not do their homework. Queer theory need not valorize the performative over the political or style over history. At its best, queer theory uncovers the necessary inextricability of politics, performativity, history, and style.

Indeed, queer is not so much an umbrella for identity, however unstable and contingent, as it is a verb. Used as an adjective, we are prone to stabilization. We tend to attach it to some knowable quantity or category: queer identity, queer nation, queer theory. Yes, we say, used thusly "queer" seems to indicate some messing with the usual meanings of those concepts, as well as the usual dyke/queen dichotomy, but queer is ever more slippery than this. For it wants to be a verb; to queer. It doesn't simply want to indicate but wants to cut across all the nonsense of identities as valuable (and reliable) conveyors of whatever sexual practices, affectional relations, or living arrangements we might make with others. To queer identity, nation, or theory is to subvert expectations, open up possibilities for multiplicity, erase lines of division by repositioning the debate. No more ownership of identities or discourses. No borders. No ethnic models of identity as a basis for formulating a coherent politics. No coherence. No utopics. Bi? Trans? Straight? Gay? Lesbian? Whatever, queer theory responds. Get over categories.

Of course, liberatory discourses easily lead to smugness. There are no promises here, so let's not get sucked into some "oh, if only we could achieve true queerness, everything would be wonderful" mentality. Godzilla kicks butt in Lesbianville only to build multiculti, intergenerational, pansexual condo units? I don't think so. That's the real challenge, of course. To queer theory, to queer identity is to move away from a model of equity politics, in which each category has equal status and access to the same meager pile of goodies the dominant categories have always had. To queer theory is to propose liberation *from* categories. I am loathe to draw analogies to other movements, especially those attached to race or ethnicity. Facile comparisons between gay/lesbian liberation and African American movements, for example, have been damaging to all, not the least of which are African American gays and lesbians. But like their queer theorist colleagues, there are some bi- and multiracial folks who refuse the either/or pull of categories. While some might want a proliferation of identity boxes (making the U.S. Census bureau's job a nightmare), still others practice a kind of color liberation theory that does away with racial and ethnic categories all together. Fears of whitewashing abound, as you might guess, but if we were less concerned with what group we belonged to we might actually get what we need.

Consider the example of queer activists of whatever gender and sexuality who started work with AIDS projects. We soon learned the real issue isn't a matter of a syndrome that was targeting one of "our" categories, then crossing into other identity categories. The real issue is the fragmentation of medical research funding and projects and the inequities of access to its promises. We discovered that anyone with a so-called preexisting condition (such as coronary disease) is routinely shut out by insurance companies. That breast and cervical cancers have been low priorities for the NIH. That symptoms manifested by women don't count as AIDS-related, lowering the numbers of the afflicted and denying those women access to specialized medical care and services. Queer theory and queer activism gave us ways of understanding that health care in America should be a right for all. It remains to be seen whether there will be a movement to radically reconstruct the present system. Whether the fight for marital rights in Hawaii will problematize marriage as a privileged category. Whether the struggle for domestic partner benefits will become a movement to define domestic affiliation outside the couple. But these are the promises, if promises they be, that queer theory holds. But it can hold no promises alone. While it can move us beyond the straightlaced categories of sexuality to which we all are held, it can not contribute to a truly progressive politics unless it is conjoined with theories of race and class and gender.

Some lesbians may look on queer theory with considerable fear and loathing. There is a history to that skepticism. But we owe it to ourselves, our communities, and our allies to move, as Zita does, from skepticism to a watchful optimism. As the guardians of Lesbianville perhaps we can do no more. But it is my hope that we will. Let us reveal inadequate scholarship for what it is, but let us not mistake fierce and playful queer theory as monstrous. Its practioners will honor lesbian lives and work if we show them we are not afraid.

Notes

1. Colleen Lamos, "The Postmodern Lesbian Position: On Our Backs," in *The Lesbian Postmodern*, Laura Doan, ed. New York: Columbia Press, 1994, 99–100.

2. Michael Warner's introduction to the anthology, *Fear of a Queer Planet: Queer Politics and Social Theory* (Minneapolis: University of Minnesota Press, 1993), vii–xxxi outlines these difficulties more globally.

3. Warner, xxvi.

4. Sagri Dhairyam, "Racing the Lesbian, Dodging White Critics," in *The Lesbian Postmodern*, ed. Laura Doan, New York: Columbia Press, 1994, 30.

5. Lisa Duggan outlines this in "The Discipline Problem: Queer Theory Meets Lesbian and Gay History," *GLQ* 2.3 (1995): 179–91.

6. Diana Fuss, *Essentially Speaking: Feminism, Nature, and Difference* (New York: Routledge, 1989), 99–101.

7. Annamarie Jagose, *Lesbian Utopics* (New York: Routledge, 1994), 2.

8. Jacquelyn N. Zita's "Gay and Lesbian Studies: Yet Another Unhappy Marriage?" in *Tilting the Tower*, Linda Garber, ed., (New York: Routledge, 1994): 258–76 narratives a lesbian fear of erasure in the "marriage" of gay/lesbian studies (why this het metaphor?) as seduction of lesbians (away from their true love of feminism) by gay men masquerading as "queer" theorists.

The Queer Disappearance of Lesbians

Sheila Jeffreys

Department of Political Science,
University of Melbourne

37

It should be cause for rejoicing that lesbian academics can now be out in some universities and colleges. This collection demonstrates the growing self-confidence of lesbians in the academy. That some of these women are now able to teach material relevant to lesbians, lesbian literature, history, politics, should be cause for satisfaction. But, as I suggest here, the teaching of lesbian studies has not flourished with the self-confidence that we might expect: Lesbian studies, and some of those who teach it, seem to be entering still another closet within the new lesbian and gay or queer studies. There may now be less urgent need for academic lesbians to conceal their love for women, but that very love is now under threat of becoming invisible within this new discipline.

The appearance of queer theory and queer studies threatens to mean the disappearance of lesbians; the developing field of lesbian and gay studies, dominated by the queer impulse, finds lesbian feminism conspicuous in its absence. Lesbian feminism starts with the understanding that the interests of lesbians and gay men are different in many respects because lesbians are members of the political class of women. Lesbian liberation requires, according to this, the destruction of men's power over women. In queer theory and queer studies, on the other hand, lesbians seem to appear only where they can assimilate seamlessly into gay male culture and politics. No difference in interests, culture, or history, between men and women is generally recognized. The new field of the study of sexuality seems similarly to

An earlier version of this paper appeared in *Women's Studies International Forum*, 1994, 17: 459–72.

be dominated by gay male sexual politics and interests; both areas are remarkably free of feminist influence. Seldom, for example, is there any mention in queer theorizing of sexuality of issues which are of concern to feminists such as sexual violence and pornography, or any analysis of the politics of sexual desire or practice.

Within traditional women's studies, lesbian students and teachers have long been angry at the "lesbian-free" nature of courses and textbooks. While many readers include pieces by lesbians, lesbian feminism as a variety of feminist thought is typically absent. Lesbians might have expected the new lesbian and gay studies to be more sympathetic to their interests, but this is true only if they see themselves as a variety of gay men, rather than as women: The emerging field is "feminism-free." It was precisely this absence of women's interests and experience in the "malestream" academic world that produced women's studies in the first place. It cannot, therefore, be an unalloyed cause for celebration in the '90s that lesbian and gay studies are becoming sufficiently recognized to have generated a new journal, *GLQ*, and a prestigious anthology, *The Lesbian and Gay Studies Reader* (Abelove et al., 1993). Both are American in origin and content; and even a casual glance at these publications suggests that lesbians and feminists have considerable cause for concern.

The editorial of the first issue of *GLQ* celebrates its commitment to "queer" politics, but the queer perspective is not a gender-neutral one. Many lesbians, especially lesbian feminists, see queer politics as very specifically masculine. The editorial tells us that the journal will view all topics through a queer lens. "We seek to publish a journal that will bring a queer perspective to bear on any and all topics touching on sex and sexuality" (Dinshaw and Halperin, 1993, p. iii). Moreover, the "Q" in the title of the journal has two meanings, quarterly and also: "The fractious, the disruptive, the irritable, the impatient, the unapologetic, the bitchy, the camp, the queer." This definition should alert readers to its masculine focus. The adjectives above refer to male gay culture and are rooted in traditional notions of what is camp. Camp, as we shall see, lies at the foundation of queer theory and politics and is inimical to both women's and lesbian interests.

While there remains controversy over the exact meaning of camp and its centrality to the notion of queer, some queer studies writers have sought to establish camp as a fundamental part of queerness. Some have considered camp to be the "total body of performative practices and strategies used to enact a queer identity" (Meyer, 1994, p. 5). Note, however, that camp appears on examination to be based largely on a male gay notion of the feminine. For example, Moe Meyer (1994) illustrates camp political tactics with the black drag queen, Joan Jett Blakk, who ran as the Queer Nation mayoral candidate in Chicago in 1991. For women and lesbians who have rejected femininity, the celebration of it by a gay man is more likely to be seen as insulting than as a symbol of "queer" solidarity.

Lesbian feminists, then, are likely to see gay men's use of femininity as an anachronism. Gay men's identification with effeminacy, before the 1970s, was an understandable effect of a system of oppression in which same-sex love was identified with not being real men and, thus, the adoption of an effeminate identity as an identification with the values of the oppressor. One would expect, however, that with gay liberation, gay men would reject the old culture of oppression and develop a new vision of what it might mean to love men. But it seems that traditional gay male culture has triumphed over the revolutionary possibilities of the 1970s. In the '80s, drag and camp were rehabilitated from even the little criticism which some gay theorists were prepared to launch. The celebration of camp and the queer culture which seems to derive from it, is finding a new respectability even in the academy amongst gay theorists who we might have expected to see its problems.

But many of the lesbian theorists of the new queer studies are also failing to see why camp is a problem. Women are included in anthologies and journals devoted to lesbian and gay studies and queer theory—although women as *subject*, are not. The editors of the *GLQ* write that they strive for the widest possible historical, geographical and cultural scope, seeking resources before the twentieth century, on "nonanglophone cultures, and into the experiences of those whose race, ethnicity, age, social class, or sexual practice has detached them from dominant cultures." Women are not mentioned here, not even the anodyne term "gender" which is frequently employed to remove the question of agency from consideration of women's oppression; this despite an editorial team comprised of a majority of women. And while the inaugural issue of the journal begins with two pieces by women, if we look closely at the content we can see why attention to issues that particularly interest women do not seem to be part of the queer studies agenda.

The two important theorists of the new lesbian and gay studies whose work begins this journal are Eve Kosofsky Sedgwick and Judith Butler. They are stars of lesbian and gay studies perhaps because they do not challenge the gay male agenda that dominates the field. Sedgwick writes on issues of interest to gay men such as gay male anal eroticism. In writing about Henry James in *GLQ*, she shows an ability to see the male model as representing homosexuality and what it is to be queer.

The thing I *least* want to be heard as offering here is a "theory of homosexuality." . . . When I attempt to do some justice to the specificity, the richness, above all the explicitness of James's particular erotics, it is not with an eye to making him an exemplar of "homosexuality" or even of one "kind" of "homosexuality," though I certainly don't want, either, to make him sound as if he *isn't* gay. Nonetheless I do mean to nominate the James of the Prefaces as a kind of prototype of—not "homosexuality"—but *queerness*, or queer performativity. In this usage, "queer performativity" is the name of a strategy for the production of meaning and being, in relation to the affect shame and to the later and related fact of stigma. (Sedgwick, 1993, p. 11)

Here a woman is using the example of a man to define that which is queer. It is not surprising that lesbian feminists might feel a little excluded from this discussion. Sedgwick's work is stimulating, so long as the reader is not looking for *feminist* stimulation. What is striking about the contributions by men and women to this new field is that they are so "feminism-free"; no distinctions between the political interests of women and men are made and there is no mention of lesbian specificity.

The adherence of the female stars of lesbian and gay studies to a gay male agenda is even clearer in the second piece by Judith Butler who explains that her approach is critically "queer." She celebrates "performativity" which turns out to mean traditional gay male cultural forms with lesbian role-playing added in for balance. This performativity is politically progressive because it serves to demonstrate the socially constructed nature of gender. Performativity as resistance and hyperbolic display comprises: "cross-dressing, drag balls, streetwalking, butch-femme spectacles, die-ins by ACT-UP, kiss-ins by Queer Nation, drag performance benefits for AIDS, e.g., Liza Minelli does Judy" (Butler, 1993, p. 23). It should be clear from this list that the practices that are to be celebrated as political ways are largely those of gay men. Butler does not simply fail to recognize that lesbians might have different interests, a culture and traditions of their own, but she selects, as the way forward, precisely those aspects of gay male culture that have been subjected to fairly rigorous criticism by lesbian feminists and by some gay male theorists, too.

Moreover, Butler represents the enthusiasm for postmodern male masters in lesbian and gay studies. It is puzzling that the variety of postmodern thought deriving directly from the practices and pleasures of certain French male gay icons and lauding traditional practices of camp and drag is what is adopted by some lesbians, as if this could easily be suited to their experience. Suzanne Moore (1988) has characterized the obsession of male postmodernists with genderbending as "gender tourism," "whereby male theorists are able to take package trips into the world of femininity." These male theorists essentialize a notion of the "feminine" as a place of otherness and transformation which does, they admit, have little to do with real women. Women merely simulate the feminine and men can do it too to their advantage.

This idea "disappears" women who end up as nothing but a simulation while preserving the notion of the masculine. And just as women end up with nowhere to go as postmodern men appropriate the feminine, so lesbians find themselves with nowhere very comfortable to go as gay men make their own appropriation of the feminine the very touchstone of both lesbian and gay culture.

A good example of how lesbians are disappeared in practice was found in the 1994 gay Mardi Gras in Sydney. Drag, gay appropriation of the feminine, was the central motif of the parade. This left lesbians in a difficult position. What were they to wear? Interestingly they did not seek to appropriate the masculine. Many tried to be feminine too. Men and women dressed as Playboy bunnies, for instance. For the men this might have seemed a transgressive incursion into the otherness of the sex industry, but for the lesbian, it could not be transgressive. The sexual objectification that Playboy bunnies represent so well is still the routine condition of women and is precisely what twenty-five years of feminist campaigning has sought to eliminate. Thus, despite the desperate contortions by which some lesbian postmodernists try to tell women that they too are being subversive by being "feminine" and that they are really engaged in "parody," this somehow does not ring true.

The manufacture of femininity by gay men provides the same benefits that it provides to heterosexual men, which is the opportunity to take pleasure from good old-fashioned masculinity. Heterosexual men are able to experience all the sexual and other delights of being "real" men by projecting femininity onto women. Without the feminine, which women are supposed to act out, men could not be men. The sexual excitements of masculinity, of aggression and objectification, of dominance, cannot exist in a vacuum. They require their opposite if they are to be experienced. Thus femininity must be constructed, if masculinity is to be found exciting by both its players and its admirers.

Catharine MacKinnon, a feminist theorist of sexuality, who, not surprisingly, is very unpopular in the field of lesbian and gay studies offers an analysis linking dominance/submission sexuality with the construction of gender that helps us understand this eroticizing of fetishized gender-difference in gay male culture. By gender fetishism here I mean sexual excitement produced by the trappings of exaggerated gender stereotypes. MacKinnon argues that "[m]ale and female are created through the erotization of dominance and submission. The man/woman difference and the dominance/submission dynamic define each other" (MacKinnon, 1989, p. 114).

Thus, gay male cross-dressers and those who delight in this type of play can be seen as constructing femininity for their own erotic purposes while fueling and maintaining a sexuality of inequality. Feminists such as MacKinnon and myself see the construction of sexuality under male supremacy as arising from the eroticized subordination of women and the project of those feminists who wish to eliminate male violence is the dismantling of the sexuality of inequality. If this project were successful then the excitements which presently fuel the fascination with gender would evaporate.

These points are not lost on all lesbians writing in the new gay and lesbian studies tradition. *The Politics and Poetics of Camp*, for example, includes some contributions from lesbians who are critical of camp. Kate Davy points out the purely masculine nature of drag:

> [F]emale impersonation, while it certainly says something about women, is primarily about men, addressed to men, and for men. . . . Both female and male impersonation foreground the male voice and, either way, women are erased. (Davy, 1994, p. 133)

Davy explains, with reference to the theater, that lesbians cannot simply be fitted into camp by performing in gender roles. In a very interesting article she compares the way that female impersonation, as in the plays of Charles Ludlum, can move into malestream culture in a way that male impersonation cannot. She suggests that there is "something magical and compelling about a cross-dressed male" but not a cross-dressed female, positing, in an analysis consistent with Marjorie Garber's, that what matters about male cross-dressers is that there is a male underneath. But the acceptability of male cross-dressing, from performances by army theater troupes in the Second World War, to drag performances now, to malestream audiences, must depend upon the investment of men in general, heterosexual and gay, in female vestments. Drag is an established form in malestream culture; male impersonation is not.

Interestingly, Davy, like the other lesbian theorists who seek to remain within the pale of queer studies, is not critical of camp itself. Instead he is critical of the idea that lesbians can fit into it and sees the theatrical portrayal of butch/femme role-playing as subversive, but not any part of camp.

Postmodern theory has legitimized the 1980s revival of lesbian role-playing which provided mild sadomasochistic satisfactions to fashionable lesbians who found that the pursuit of equality damaged their orgasmic potential (Jeffreys, 1989). This sexual practice has been represented in the academy as the lesbian version of drag and the way that lesbians can fit into camp. It appears above in Butler's list of forms of performativity. Any serious examination of the politics of female and male impersonation, however, shows such differences between this and butch/femme role playing that these practices cannot be neatly rolled together as varieties of queer performativity.

Feminist analysis of gender suggests that masculinity and femininity are not just harmless variations in human behavior that can be swapped at will. This gender-swapping ideal contains the same faulty analysis that underlies the androgynous ideal. Well-meaning antisexist men tend to say that they are developing the feminine sides of themselves and expect approval from feminists for this odd project. But, as the French feminist theorist Christine Delphy has pointed out (1993), masculinity and femininity do not represent timeless universal human values that simply need to be in balance in individuals. They represent, in fact, the values of a male supremacist hierarchy. Emerging from hierarchy, they cannot be expected to survive the creation of a nonhierarchical society. That which is seen as archetypal feminine behavior, much of what is reproduced in drag and camp, is in fact the learned behavior of the oppressed, learned to avoid punishment. It is behavior which shows awareness of one's low status and suitable respect for the powerful male class. "Feminine" body language, use of space, of eyes, touch, and voice, represent lack of power (Henley, 1977). Examples include keeping knees together, eyes down, qualities of attention which are the opposite of the behaviors allowed to those with power; in a post-hierarchical world it is hard to imagine that these certainly nonuniversal qualities would survive. It is the task of feminism for women and for the men who support the feminist project to imagine and create ways of behaving which represent the nonhierarchical values to which we aspire.

Feminist analysis does not just see gender as something which can be subversively swapped and played with but as emerging from the real material oppression of women. "Playing" with gender is a problem precisely because it keeps gender "in play" and contributes to maintaining the political classes of male supremacy in place. Indeed, feminists who are conscientious objectors to the idea of gender, who refuse to take sides, refuse to empower the whole system by their participation, who have lived and continue to live beyond gender, are derided as utopian and essentialist by those committed to the supposedly revolutionary or simply pleasurable possibilities of playing with it. Though the theorists of genderbending defend it by emphasizing its socially transformative potential, the ideology which underlies it is deeply pessimistic, one in which only accommodation to male supremacist duality is seen as possible or desirable.

Another aspect of the new lesbian and gay studies that does not bode well for lesbians and feminists is the study of sexuality as a field of inquiry quite separate from and impervious to feminist theory. This approach serves to afford intellectual protection to a broad spectrum of sexual interests of men, in general, and gay men, most particularly. The 1993 reader in lesbian and gay studies makes this clear. As the first collection of its kind it is and will be important in affecting the shape lesbian and gay studies is to take. This gives weight to the editors' choice to place first, in the opening section on philosophy, Gayle Rubin's piece titled "Thinking Sex," which was originally a paper contributed to the Barnard conference in 1982 and anthologized in *Pleasure and Danger* (Vance, 1984).

Rubin seeks to put feminism in its place and establish the illegitimacy of feminist analysis for many areas of sexual behavior. Her project suits the male interests represented in the new queer studies very well. In the early '70s gay liberation theorists, both lesbian and gay, explained and criticized many aspects of male gay behavior from a feminist perspective, showing the way goal-orientated phallic sexuality supported male supremacy. In the '80s, however, we find an analysis ignoring the relationship between sexual practice and the oppression of women. Rubin's article has been crucial to this process.

In "Thinking Sex" she explains that she has rejected her earlier ground-breaking analysis (1982) which showed how sex and gender were interlinked, recognizing now that there are only some areas of sexuality that are appropriate objects for feminist analysis. While not specifying exactly what feminists are allowed to look at here, she makes clear that there is a great deal they are required politely to avoid, such as sexual minorities including transvestites, transsexuals, sadomasochists, and those interested in what Rubin calls "cross-generational sex." These, she suggests, are oppressed in a separate system from that of gender and hence not relevant to a feminist analysis.

Yet, Rubin's sexual freedom analysis is very old fashioned. Feminist theory threw this view of sexual liberalism into disrepute by showing how it protected men's privileges and prevented women from protecting themselves from sexual violence and exploitation. Feminist analyses of rape, sexual abuse of children, prostitution, sexual harassment, and of sexuality and its role in the social control of women in general depended upon vigorously deracinating the whole male philosophy of sexual liberalism. While not mentioning sexual violence in "Thinking Sex," Rubin defends traditional sexual liberalism against the impertinence of feminism and its creation a theory of sexuality that enables gay men to view their practices, history, and experience as somehow immune from feminist analysis. At the same time, of course, it does make it difficult for lesbians to recognize that their interests, in the areas of sexuality, as women, are different from those of men.

Note that the 1993 reader in lesbian and gay studies did not completely ignore feminism, but placed it as a minor theme within the discipline. Four strong feminist pieces are included by Monique Wittig, Adrienne Rich, Audre Lorde, and Marilyn Frye. But the place of feminism is asserted in the foundation piece by Rubin. The feminist pieces here float in a vacuum, as examples of an interesting but slightly quirky minority perspective.

Equally discomforting, the celebration of gay male culture by both women and men in the academy is paralleled by similar developments in popular lesbian culture which threaten the existence of both lesbian pride and the specific culture that a generation of lesbians has been dedicated to constructing over the last twenty-five years. I have written elsewhere (Jeffreys, 1993) of the pressures upon lesbians outside the academy to assimilate into traditional gay male culture.

This makes it particularly important that feminists do not just ignore lesbian and gay studies. In the academy, it has the potential to give strength and confidence to lesbian students as women's studies has for women students, in general. The ideas will influence the way that lesbianism is thought and practiced in the larger community as well, and, thus, it is too important to ignore. It should be shaped to recognize the experience of women. This will entail a serious challenge to the use of the term "queer" which disappears lesbians by subsuming them, at best, into a variety of gay men, and to the dominant politics of queer theory and practice. The very considerable pressure exerted within lesbian and gay studies for lesbians to suppress any difference, either in bodies or in interests from gay men needs to be resisted if the new lesbian and gay studies is not to prove to be a new and oppressive closet in which lesbians must hide their bodies, their interest, their specificity.

References

Abelove, Henry, Michele Aina Barale and David Halperin, eds., (1993), *The Lesbian and Gay Studies Reader*. New York: Routledge.

Butler, Judith, (1993). "Critically Queer," *GLQ* 1 (1) pps. 17–32.

Davy, Kate, (1994). "Fe/male Impersonation. The discourse of camp." in Meyer, Moe ed., *The Politics and Poetics of Camp*. London: Routledge.

Delphy, Christine, (1993). "Rethinking Sex and Gender," *Women's Studies International Forum*. 16 (1) pps. 1–9.

Dinshaw, Carolyn and David M. Halperin, (1993). "From the Editors," *GLQ* 1 (1) pps. iii–iv.

Garber, Marjorie, (1993). "Spare Parts: The Surgical Construction of Gender." In Abelove et al, ed., *The Lesbian and Gay Studies Reader*. New York: Routledge.

Henley, Nancy M., (1977). *Body Politics. Power, Sex, and Nonverbal Communication*. New Jersey: Prentice-Hall.

Jeffreys, Sheila, (1989). "Butch and Femme: Now and Then." In Lesbian History Group ed., *Not a Passing Phase*. London: The Women's Press.

Jeffreys, Sheila, (1993). *The Lesbian Heresy. A Feminist Perspective on the Lesbian Sexual Revolution*. Melbourne: Spinifex. (1994), London: The Women's Press.

MacKinnon, Catharine, (1989). *Toward a Feminist Theory of the State*. Cambridge, MA: Harvard University Press.

Meyer, Moe, (1994). "Introduction. Reclaiming the Discourse of Camp." in Meyer, Moe, ed., *The Politics and Poetics of Camp*. London: Routledge.

Moore, Suzanne, (1988). "Getting a Bit of the Other—the Pimps of Postmodernism." In *Male Order: Unwrapping Masculinity*. Chapman, Rowena and Jonathan Rutherford, eds., London:Lawrence and Wishart.

Rubin, Gayle S., (1993). "Thinking Sex: Notes for a Radical Theory of the Politics of Sexuality." In Abelove et al eds., *The Lesbian and Gay Studies Reader*. New York: Routledge.

Sedgwick, Eve Kosofsky, (1993). "Queer Performativity. Henry James's The Art of the Novel." *GLQ* 1 (1) pps. 1–16.

Vance, Carol ed., (1984). *Pleasure and Danger: Exploring Women's Sexuality*. London: Routledge Kegan Paul.

Contributors

Anonymous. The author of this segment is a full professor of education at an upstate New York public college. She has served on her local school board for the past six years. She and her partner enjoy their home in a historic village in New York, playing lots of tennis and traveling, as well as working together and separately on scholarly activities. Although she was born in the South (and never got rid of her accent), she has now lived half her life (the first half) as a "proper" southern young lady and half (the latter half) as a northern academic lesbian.

Dawn D. Bennett-Alexander, Esq., is an African American associate professor of employment law and legal studies at the University of Georgia's Terry College of Business, a lawyer, a founding partner in BJD Consulting-Diversity Consultants, and a mother of three daughters, ages eighteen, sixteen, and nine. For the very public work of trying to make the world aware of the profound importance of valuing diversity on all bases—including race, gender, and affinity orientation—she grounds herself by gardening, quilting, knitting, needlework, reading, writing, and being a prize-winning bread baker. She is the author of two ground-breaking textbooks, *Employment Law for Business* (Irwin, 1995, second edition being released in 1997) and *The Legal, Ethical, and Regulatory Environment of Business* (South-Western, 1996), as well as a book on Valuing Diversity (South-Western, due out in 1997), and several personal pieces in journals and books, including *Common Lives/Lesbian Lives, SAGE: A Scholarly Journal on Black Women* and *Life Notes: Personal Writings of Contemporary Black Women* (Norton, 1994).

Phyllis Bronstein is a professor of clinical psychology at the University of Vermont. She is the coeditor of two books, *Teaching a Psychology of People: Resources For Gender and Sociocultural Awareness*, and of *Fatherhood Today: Men's Changing Role in the Family*. She has published numerous articles on families and parenting, and on women and ethnic minorities in academia. She is currently writing two books, one about the career histories of feminist and ethnic minority faculty scholars, and another about women in their fifties.

Christine Cress is a counselor in the Career Services Center at Western Washington University. She has a master's degree in higher education and works with issues related to career decision-making and identity formation. When she's not negotiating with the university administration to implement domestic partner benefits, she can usually be found hiking in the Grand Canyon or in the North Cascades Mountains.

Mildred Dickemann, A.B., University of Michigan 1950; Ph.D. University of California, Berkeley, 1958. Has taught at Oakland (Merritt) City College, University of Kansas and Sonoma State University, retiring in 1990. Published in educational anthropology, ethnic studies, human behavioral ecology, and homosexuality. Current research is in gender. Cofounder, U.C. Lesbian and Gay Alumni Association, member of a number of gay, transgender, environmental, and civil liberties organizations.

Jill Dolan is the author of *The Feminist Spectator as Critic* (1988) and *Presence and Desire: Essays on Gender, Sexuality, Performance* (1993), as well as other articles on feminism, lesbian studies, and theatre studies. She is the executive officer of the theatre program at the Graduate Center of the City University of New York, and is the executive director of the Center for Lesbian and Gay Studies, also at CUNY.

Penelope Dugan lives in Willsboro, N.Y., and teaches at Richard Stockton College. She has published articles on early American literature, curriculum transformation, feminist pedagogy, and composition, as well as personal essays and short fiction. She serves on the editorial boards of *Radical Teacher* and *Journal of Lesbian Studies* and is a contributing editor to *Puerto del Sol*.

Michele J. Eliason has a Ph.D. in educational psychology and is currently an associate professor of nursing at the University of Iowa. Her primary research interests are in attitudes toward lesbian, gay, and bisexual people, and sexual identity formation. She is author of *Who Cares? Institutional Barriers to Health Care for Lesbian, Gay, and Bisexual People* (National League of Nursing Press, 1996).

Kathryn M. Feltey is an associate professor of sociology at the University of Akron, Director of Undergraduate Studies, and editor of *Network News* (the newsletter of Sociologists for Women in Society). She is also the single mother of a eleven-year-old-son, and is known at his Waldorf elementary school as the "hot lunch mom" since she ran the lunch program there for the last two school years. She is co-founder of MotherWit, a support and information group for lesbian mothers, their partners, and children.

Maggie Fournier is a tenured, associate professor of nursing at the University of Southern Maine. A forty-six-year-old lesbian, Maggie is in her twentieth year of service at the university. Her research agenda centers around issues of lesbian parenting. A campus activist, Maggie has been working diligently to secure domestic partner benefits for lesbians and gay men at the University of Maine System. Maggie is a member of the Board of Directors of Gay and Lesbian Advocates and Defenders in Boston. She serves on the Professional Advisory Committee to the Lesbian Health Project of Southern Maine and on the President's Task Force on Lesbian/Gay/Bisexual Issues at USM. Other community service entails volunteering her time with Maine Won't Discriminate and Freedom to Marry Roundtable. Maggie and her partner of twenty-five years, Cheryl Ciechomski, are the happy parents of eight-year-old daughter Emily Rose Ciechomski Fournier. Maggie gave birth to Emily in 1986. Their family also includes a quarter horse, sheltie, black lab, and an aging, deaf cat. They enjoy spending time together traveling, cooking, and cross-country skiing.

Nanette K. Gartrell, M.D., was the first out lesbian on the Harvard Medical School faculty. She is currently associate clinical professor of psychiatry at the University of California, San Francisco, where she teaches ethics and feminist psychotherapy theory. She has been documenting sexual abuse by physicians since 1982 and conducting a national longitudinal lesbian family study since 1986. She is the editor of *Bringing Ethics Alive: Feminist Ethics for Psychotherapy Practice* (Haworth Press, 1994). She has a private psychotherapy practice in San Francisco.

Barbara W. Gerber, Ed.D., is distinguished service professor, chair of the Department of Counseling and Psychological Services and President of the

National Women's Studies Association, 1997–1998. She is licensed as a psychologist in New York State and does some private practice work. She and her partner of twenty-five years share two daughters, a son, and three grandsons.

Charlotte L. Goedsche grew up in Evanston, Illinois. She attended Wellesley College, and received her B.A. and Ph.D. from Northwestern University. Goedsche lived and worked in the Federal Republic of Germany for eight years. Her spouse, Cynthia L. Janes, Ph.D., also grew up in Evanston. They now reside in Asheville, North Carolina, where Goedsche is an associate professor of German at the University of North Carolina at Asheville. Goedsche and Janes have been active in the gay community in Asheville, and in 1996 they received the Dr. Marketta Laurila Free Speech Award for "their courageous struggle to preserve the right of free speech."

Lynda Goldstein teaches in the English department and women's studies program at the Penn State University, Wilkes-Barre campus. She writes on issues of representational politics in contemporary culture.

Nancy Goldstein currently directs tutorials and senior theses for the program in Women's Studies at Harvard University. In the summer of 1995 she cochaired the first National Women's Studies Association Conference panel to critique current research methodologies on women and AIDS. Her article on lesbians, HIV, and the medical profession appears in her coedited anthology on women and AIDS, *The Gender Politics of HIV/AIDS in Women: Perspectives on the Pandemic in the United States*, published by New York University Press in June 1997. She is currently working on turning her dissertation, on the construction of heterosexual female subjects in the nineteenth-century English novel, into a book for New York University Press, due out in 1998.

Maria C. Gonzalez is an assistant professor of English at the University of Houston where she teaches Mexican American literature, American literature, women writers, and feminist theory and criticism. Her present interests include research on Chicana queer theory. Her publications include a monograph, *Contemporary Mexican American Women Novelists: Toward a Feminist Identity* (Peter Lang, 1996), and essays on Chicana literature and sexuality.

Batya Hyman left her position at an eastern university and is now an assistant professor at Arizona State University West in Phoenix. Her new colleagues are committed to a process of addressing diversity. During the past fifteen years, she has worked in several public and private nonprofit social service agencies as both a clinician and administrator. Batya is currently researching the long-term consequences of childhood victimization, investigating both adverse and resilient outcomes. Her other interests include the intersection of violence and work roles in our society and the development of strategies for teaching about privilege and oppression. Batya received her Ph.D. from the Heller School for Advanced Studies in Social Welfare at Brandeis University and completed an NIMH (National Institute of Mental Health) post-doctoral fellowship at the Family Research Laboratory of the University of New Hampshire.

Julie Inness is associate professor of philosophy at Mount Holyoke College. Her past research has focused on privacy, including her book *Privacy, Intimacy, and Isolation.* She is currently working on questions about coming out and passing.

Sherrie Inness is assistant professor of English at Miami University. Her research interests include nineteenth- and twentieth-century American literature, lesbian studies, popular culture, children's literature, and gender studies. She has published articles on these topics in a number of journals, including *American Literary Realism, Edith Wharton Review, Journal of American Culture, Journal of Popular Culture, NWSA Journal, Studies in Scottish Literature, Studies in Short Fiction, and Women's Studies: An Interdisciplinary Journal.* She is the author of *Intimate Communities: Representation and Social Transformation in Women's College fiction, 1895–1910* (Bowling Green Popular Press, 1995) and *The Lesbian Menace: Ideology, Identity, and the Representation of Lesbian Life* (University of Massachusetts Press, 1997). She is also the editor of *Nancy Drew and Company: Culture, Gender, and Girls' Series* (Bowling Green Popular Press, 1997) and the co-editor of *Breaking Boundaries: New Perspectives on Regional and Fiction* (University of Iowa Press, 1997).

Sheila Jeffreys is a senior lecturer in political science at the University of Melbourne. She is author of three books on the history and politics of sexuality, *The Spinster and Her Enemies* (1985), *Anticlimax* (1991), and *The Lesbian Heresy* (1993). She was active in feminist and lesbian feminist politics in the U.K. for nearly twenty years, particularly in campaigns against male violence, before migrating to Australia in 1991.

Carey Kaplan is professor of English at Saint Michael's College in Colchester, Vermont. Carey has published books on the Modern British writer, Doris Lessing. Her most recent book, written with Ellen Cronan Rose, is

The Canon and the Common Reader, a feminist analysis of the current curriculum debates.

Sandra M. Ketrow is an associate professor of communication studies at the University of Rhode Island. She has held other academic posts, as well as positions in marketing, advertising, publishing, and public television. Her research interests lie in nonverbal messages and groups/organizations, leadership and communication, argumentation and interaction processes in group decisionmaking, and gender issues.

Kathryn H. Larson is currently completing work on her Ph.D. in economics from Iowa State University following an eight-year period of teaching economics at Elon College in North Carolina, where she formally "came out" in 1993. She holds a B.Sc. from the University of Wisconsin-Madison and an M.A. from Columbia University. She spent three years in the Peace Corps in West Africa, discovering the importance of economics, and four years working with a U.S./Zambia project, including two winters in Zambia. Her approach to the study of economic development is broad-based and interdisciplinary, with current work focusing on small farm households in Zambia, and the economic status of lesbian households in the U.S. She and her partner of fifteen years live in Boalsburg, PA with their three cats.

Roxanne Lin is currently stepping out of academia by relocating to New York City where diverse and unkown possibilities reside.

Jan McDonald was born in upstate New York, the middle of three sisters. Her academic life started as a high school mathematics teacher. She later taught at the University at Albany-State University of New York, preparing mathematics and science teachers. After living in the closet for over twenty-six years, at the age of forty-two, she came out to her husband of twenty-two years, her five year old son, and the rest of her family. At the same time, she left her academic position at Union College in Schenectady, New York and moved to Stillwater, Oklahoma to live with her lesbian partner, Judy Kaufman. Jan and Judy have recently relocated to New York, and Jan is currently Professor of Education and dean of the School of Education at Pace University.

Beth Mintz is professor of sociology at the University of Vermont. Her fields of specialization include political sociology, health care and women's studies. She is the author of *The Power Structure of American Business* (with M. Schwartz), University of Chicago Press, 1985 (Japanese edition: 1994); editor of *Corporate Control, Capital Formation, and Organizational Networks* (with T. Takuyoshi and M. Schwartz), Chuo University Press, 1996; and has numerous articles including contributions to the *American Sociological Review, Social Problems, Theory and Society, Sociological Methodology*, and *Social Science History*.

Carol J. Moeller is a feminist philosopher, theorist, and cultural critic, living in Pittsburgh with her fabulous girlfriend and their three sweet cats. She works with Clean Needles, Pittsburgh, a direct action AIDS prevention group which collects used needles in exchange for clean ones, and hands out safer sex supplies on the street. She received her B.A. in philosophy and women's studies at Oberlin College, and is now a Ph.D. candidate in philosophy, and a Ph.D. certificate candidate in the program for the study of culture, University of Pittsburgh. She is writing her dissertation on feminist critiques of dominant philosophical accounts of ethics, arguing for a conception of ethics which is more responsive to ethical problems of our everyday world, and to questions of power and difference among people. Beginning in the fall of 1997, she will be an assistant professor of philosophy at Moravian College in Bethlehem, Pennsylvania.

Akilah Monifa is a writer and professor of law at New College of California, the oldest public interest law school in the country, where she has taught since 1991. She has taught torts, sexual orientation and the law, criminal law, legal methods, and legal research and writing. Additionally, she sits on the following committees: personnel, admissions, faculty advisor to the women's forum, queer caucus, and third world law student caucus. She is on the Committee on Sexual Orientation Discrimination (CSOD) for the State Bar of California. She was born in Manhattan, Kansas, reared in the space-and-rocket capital of the world, Huntsville, Alabama. A graduate of SUNY (State University of New York) at Binghamton with a B.A. in history she received her J.D. from the University of Santa Clara, School of Law. After graduation her legal career continued as a Reginald Heber Smith Community Lawyer Fellow (Reggie) at the Legal Aid Society of Alameda County in her beloved Oakland where she still resides. She would gladly give up academia to be a full-time lecturer and writer.

Sue Morrow relocated to Salt Lake City after twenty years in Tempe, Arizona. During those twenty years, she came out as a lesbian, lost custody of her two children, and embarked on a relationship with her life partner, Donna Hawxhurst. Sue and Donna have been activists, feminist therapists, and authors together for over twenty years. Sue defended her doctoral dissertation on her fiftieth birthday and is currently completing her fourth year as assistant professor of counseling psychology in the Educational Psychology Department at the University of Utah.

Sally O'Driscoll is a comparatist working on women's novels in France and England in the late seventeenth and early eighteenth centuries. Since completing her Ph.D., her work has been in transition from a feminist to a specifically lesbian theoretical approach. She is now associate professor at Fairfield University.

Christy M. Ponticelli is an assistant professor of sociology at the University of South Florida where she teaches classical and contemporary theory, qualitative methods, gender and sexuality, and religion. She holds degrees from Smith College, Harvard Divinity School, and the University of California at Santa Cruz. She is the review editor for the *Journal of Contemporary Ethnography*, and guest edited a special issue (in press), "Opening Doors: Gateways to Improving Lesbian Health and Health Care" for the *Journal of Lesbian Studies*. Her research focuses on the construction of homosexuality as a "social problem" in traditional institutions, like religion and medicine.

Raechele L. Pope is an assistant professor of higher education at Teachers College, Columbia University, which is a private graduate school of education in New York City. Her areas of scholarly research and interest include: multicultural issues in higher education, multicultural competencies of student affairs professionals, and psychosocial development of students of color.

Patty Reagan has been an associate professor of health education and women's studies at the University of Utah for eighteen years. She is a recipient of the U of U Distinguished Teaching Award and the President's Teaching Scholar Award. Publications include *Community Health in the 21st Century* and *Intimate Issues—A Sexuality Workbook*. She was the director of the women's studies program for five years.

Amy L. Reynolds is an assistant professor of counseling psychology in the Graduate School of Education at Fordham University which is a Catholic university in New York City. Prior to her current academic position, she was a psychologist at a university counseling center. Her areas of scholarly research and interest include: multicultural counseling, training, and supervision; lesbian, gay, and bisexual issues; and feminist psychology.

Esther Rothblum is professor in the department of psychology, University of Vermont, and editor of the *Journal of Lesbian Studies*. Her research and writing have focused on lesbian mental health, and she is former chair of the Committee on Lesbian and Gay Concerns of the American Psychological Association. Esther has edited twenty-one books including *Lesbian Friendships* (New York University Press), *Preventing Heterosexism and Homophobia* (Sage Publications), Loving Boldly: Issues Facing Lesbians (Haworth Press, 1989) and *Boston Marriages: Romantic But Asexual Relationships Among Contemporary Lesbians* (University of Massachusetts Press, 1993).

Jennifer Rycenga is assistant professor of comparative religious studies at San José State University. Her area of specialization is religious experience in relation to sexuality and the arts. She is also a composer, and contributed an article on lesbians and music in the volume *Queering the Pitch* (ed. Philip Brett, Elizabeth Wood, and Gary Thomas, New York: Routledge 1994). She works as an activist in lesbian, feminist, antiracist, revolutionary, and other life-loving causes.

Suzanne Sowinska is an independent scholar who lives in Seattle, Washington. She has published essays in *Working Class Women in the Academy* (University of Massachusetts, 1993), *Radical Revisions: ReReading 1930s Culture* (University of Illinois Press, 1996) and wrote the "Introduction" to the reissue of Grace Lumpkin's, *To Make My Bread* (University of Illinois Press, 1995), as part of the Radical Novel Reconsidered series.

Bonnie Ruth Strickland received her Ph.D. in clinical psychology from the Ohio State University in 1962. She has been on the faculties of Emory University and the University of Massachusetts at Amherst as teacher, researcher, administrator, clinician, and consultant. A diplomate in clinical psychology, she has been in practice for over thirty years. Dr. Strickland has served as presidents of the American Psychological Association, the Division of Clinical Psychology, and the American Association of Applied and Preventive Psychology. She was founder and on the board of the American Psychological Society. She has been a long-time advocate for women and minorities, testifying before the United States Congress, and serving on numerous boards and committees. She has over a hundred scholarly publications, including two citation classics. She lives in a lake front home in Belchertown, Massachusetts with her Chocolate Labrador, Murphy Brown and three cats, Callie, Daisy, and Dexter.

Mary Frances Stuck, Ph.D., is a professor of sociology, and assistant dean of arts and sciences, at the State University of New York, College at Oswego and is a recipient of the SUNY Chancellor's Award for Excellence in Teaching (1991). She has authored *Adolescent Worlds: Drug Use and Athletic Activity* (1992, Greenwood Press) and edited *Issues in Diversity: Voices of the Silenced (1990)* and *Structures and Processes of Inequality* (1994), both Copley Publishing, and is a frequent reviewer for *The Annals of The American Academy of Political and Social Science* as well as other journals. She is a lesbian academic who has devoted most of her career to broadening the definition of human diversity to include lesbians and gays, as well as other traditionally underrepresented people, and to curriculum transformation work and teaching which is inclusive of all of our lives. She and her partner of nineteen years are tennis aficionadas, and enjoy traveling and writing together.

Michelle M. Tokarczyk was born and raised in New York City. Her father was a toll collector, her mother a homemaker. Both her undergraduate and graduate degrees are from public institutions. With Elizabeth Fay she edited *Working-Class Women in the Academy: Laborers in the Knowledge Factory*, an anthology by and about women from the working-class who have become academics. Additionally, she has published criticism on contemporary American literature and a book of poetry, *The House I'm Running From*. An associate professor of English at Goucher College, she specializes in contemporary American literature and culture, women's studies, and writing.

Lynn A. Walkiewicz received her Ph.D. in applied philosophy from Bowling Green State University in Ohio. She is an assistant professor of interdisciplinary studies at Cazenovia College in central New York, where she teaches philosophy and ethics while inserting feminist theory and multicultural awareness into her classrooms whenever possible.

Stacy Wolf is an assistant professor in the departments of theatre/dance and English at George Washington University. She has published articles in *Modern Drama, New Theatre Quarterly, Journal of Dramatic Theory and Criticism* and other publications. She is at work on a manuscript about lesbians and musical theatre.

Index